For Robert Trager,

with gratitude and admiration

Contents

Preface

Books are about particular subject areas, but they also provide insight into their authors. Years in the academy have taught me that research reflects the background, beliefs, priorities, and temperament of those who engage in it. *Burning Crosses and Activist Journalism: Hazel Brannon Smith and the Mississippi Civil Rights Movement* is no exception.

This book is the culmination of a body of research, to be certain, but it is also the result of events I have lived and from which I have learned. I believe readers deserve full disclosure, and I would like to introduce the study of Hazel Brannon Smith by discussing my personal interest in Mississippi and in the literature and culture of the American South, my belief in the evolution of the human spirit, and my attitudes about the impact of race and ethnicity in the twenty-first century.

First, much of my research is drawn from the literary renaissances of the American South. For many years, I studied and believed in the approach to literature advocated by 12 unreconstructed Southern agrarians called the "New Criticism." Some of the poets, essayists, and critics featured in *I'll Take My Stand: The South and the Agrarian Tradition* (1930) believed in the supremacy of the text and argued that it could and should stand on its own. Although they didn't argue that the text should be divorced entirely from its historical context or from its religious, ethical, and social underpinnings, they believed that we should come to each piece of poetry and prose without preconceptions and unburdened by expectations. The New Criticism determines much of my analysis even today because it makes the text itself the most important part of the interpretive process, demanding that readers separate themselves imaginatively from their own preconceptions, assumptions, and prejudices. I consider this a worthy goal.

The influence of *I'll Take My Stand* and the New Criticism is difficult to discount. As Richard Gray writes of *I'll Take My Stand,* "Is it a literary work or polemic? Does it offer an invitation to thought or incitement to action? Could it best be described as a meditation upon principle, an elegy for many, departed, lovely things, or a provocative call for a change of economic policy?" (133). Whatever its primary focus, the collection most definitely exemplifies what Gray calls the "mythic potential of the Old South" (134). The allure of the American South is at the heart of *Burning Crosses and Activist Journalism,* which focuses upon the life and work of Hazel Brannon Smith while relying heavily upon portrayals of a region often depicted in film, journalism, and literature.

Certainly, as I developed as a critic, I became more and more interested in the rich contextual possibilities of each individual work of Southern literature. I was fascinated by how my students could interpret a short story such as "A Good Man Is Hard to Find" and discover that it was a different text for each of them, depending upon whether they knew that Flannery O'Connor was a Catholic living in the Protestant South; whether they knew that she collected peacocks (never mind whether they knew that peacocks are a medieval symbol for Christ); whether they knew that she had lived most of her life in Milledgeville, Georgia, rather than in a metropolitan area of the Deep South; or whether they knew she suffered from lupus, was unmarried, or wrote copious letters. The interpretations of the story the students submitted were rich and thoughtful, whether they understood the story as a secular tale about finding the essential meaning in each of our lives; whether they understood it as an allegory about finding salvation in a moment of violence; or whether they considered the characters bizarre, disconnected from their individual realities, and caricatured.

What I understand now is that Hazel Brannon Smith is what we know of Hazel Brannon Smith. This would be true even if she were still alive and willing to submit to years of personal interviews. It would be true even if she had collected her letters and papers to be perused by scholars after her death. My goal in writing a book about her is to distort her as little as possible, to contribute to a mounting collection of work about her, and to present her work and her philosophies as purely as possible.

But I also understand that I am drawn to her story for particular reasons, and it is this self-disclosure that is appropriate for a preface. I know that I see the experiences of Hazel Brannon Smith and the work that resulted from those experiences through my own lens. I know that I might have selected any number of subject areas, any number of regional studies, any number of newspaper editors, and any number of time periods. Instead, I chose to write about her and about those who both supported and opposed her.

Hazel Brannon Smith is compelling for several reasons: She is part of a cultural and literary tradition that includes authors such as William Faulkner, Walker Percy, William Styron, and Eudora Welty and editors such as Hodding Carter Jr., P.D. East, and Mark Ethridge. She was a newspaper-woman in a male-dominated profession, a topic I've addressed in books such as *Women in Journalism: A New History* (2008) and *Settling the Borderland: Other Voices in Literary Journalism* (2008). She is described as having been attractive, energetic, determined, and interested in those around her. She lived during a time and in a place that would have challenged the best among us: The 1950s and 1960s in the Deep South are as terrifying as they are compelling. But what draws me most powerfully to Hazel Brannon Smith's story is her humanity, her vulnerability, and her willingness to be wrong. She admitted her errors publicly. Her attitudes about social mores evolved and eventually cost her both her livelihood and her health.

In addition to her significance in the history of the American South, I was drawn to Hazel Brannon Smith because of her flawed humanity and her heroic determination to overcome both the obstacles of her own humanity and the formidable obstacles put in her path by those who despised her. Her heroic qualities are real, and she is not alone. Many of us long to live our beliefs. We want our time on earth to matter. We want to contribute to the lives of others, yes, but we also want to be considered people of integrity. Not insignificantly, we want to be loved.

Drawn to her story because of the work of the late Professor Arthur J. Kaul of the University of Southern Mississippi, I became interested in learning more about Hazel Brannon Smith because I needed her to be heroic, to be a role model, to show me how to be strong in the face of ignorance, racism, and personal loss. And she was heroic, but she was heroic because of her ability to change her mind, to enlarge her circle, to argue for equality—first in small steps and later in great strides. She was too busy challenging the status quo, unsettling the comfortable, and writing history on the run to worry about being perceived as heroic, about leaving a legacy, about gaining the adoration of those around her.

Hazel Brannon Smith was an inadvertent champion of civil rights for African Americans. She was conflicted about desegregation and other social and political issues. Her notoriety surprised her. She would not have considered herself a hero; instead, she considered herself to be a moderate, even though her stand in the middle of the road ultimately cost her financial solvency in the newspaper business.

Yet her story is not lost like the stories of so many women in American journalism history. Just as it was male editors who tried to help her survive financially when white supremacist groups attacked her personally and professionally, those who celebrate her contributions are often men. Among them is John A. Whalen, who wrote a meticulous biography entitled *Maverick Among the Magnolias: The Hazel Brannon Smith Story.* Her life would be the focus of journalism historians even if women did not conduct research about her, which sets her apart from some lesser-known women journalists. For complex and diverse reasons, her story resonates with many scholars.

The literature and culture of the American South, the civil rights movement as an especially compelling time period, and the character of Hazel Brannon Smith are still only part of the reason for this book. Perhaps the most important motivation is my commitment to a study of diversity, whether that study is based on gender, on race and ethnicity, on interculturalism, or on sexual orientation. Hazel Brannon Smith appeals to me because like her, I have enjoyed white privilege. Although I have been poor and have been discriminated against because of my gender, I may enter any business establishment I choose, sit in any seat on any bus, drive through any neighborhood without arousing suspicion, and gain employment without wondering how much attention is paid to the color of my skin.

An alumnus of Baylor University, I read with great interest a profile entitled "Trail Blazer: The Story of Baylor's First African-American Professor" in the spring 2008 issue of the university alumni magazine. Stories about the "first" woman or "first" person of color in a particular field have lost their allure for many readers; however, this article describes Vivienne Malone-Mayes, who was born in Waco, Texas, in 1932 and was rejected for admission to the Southern Baptist institution because of its racial segregation policy in 1961. Malone-Mayes kept the rejection letter she received from the Baylor registrar, which said in part: "We have not yet taken down the racial barriers here, although I have been hopeful it would be done eventually. It seems that everyone is waiting on everyone else and no one will take the initiative" (Blount 80).

This brief narrative is central to a study of the civil rights movement for at least two reasons. First, a university founded on Christian principles refused admission to a black woman, although it hired her as a professor after she received a Ph.D. in mathematics from the University of Texas. Second, the registrar articulated the thesis of this study: Much of the turmoil and violence of the 1950s and 1960s resulted—not only from the actions of racists determined to preserve a outdated caste system—but from the fear and passivity of those who knew better, who longed for a different social system, and who waited for others to take the first step.

This study tells the story of a woman who was afraid but who refused to stand aside. Hazel Brannon Smith was for many years the darling of the South. She charmed those around her. She wore large, stylish hats. She drove a convertible. She was a guest in the homes of the upper-echelon in a hierarchical Southern town. She was intelligent and well educated. But her white privilege couldn't save her from seeing the community as it really was, couldn't prevent her from confronting what lay beneath the system of manners and the finely manicured lawns of the white people of Holmes County.

Ultimately, I am drawn to the story of Hazel Brannon Smith because she was privileged and flawed; because she was a Dixiecrat who changed her mind about segregation; because she exhibited tenacity in the face of mounting opposition; because she committed heroic acts, sometimes in spite of herself; and because she deserves to be remembered in the company of Medgar Evers, William Faulkner, Martin Luther King Jr., and others who shattered previous ways of understanding prejudice and its impact on a race of people in Mississippi. Although this admission is perhaps not common in books by journalism and literary historians, I am quite frankly drawn to the story of Hazel Brannon Smith because I long to be like her. The chapters that follow will suggest why.

Finally, for purposes of this study, I should identify myself as a white person who has spent a great deal of time in the American South and who studies the literature and journalism of the region. I have conducted research in Jackson and Oxford, Mississippi, on numerous occasions. The impact of walking to Rowan Oak, Faulkner's home near the University of Mississippi campus, and of visiting the historical exhibits and archives in Jackson has never lessened.

Much of my devotion to the culture of the American South can be explained, I believe, by my own admittedly murky memories of childhood summers spent in Charlotte, North Carolina. One day, however, is particularly vivid. On that day, I was not allowed to play with the African-American children who were animatedly engaged in a baseball game in the street outside the house. They watched me wordlessly as I was led away. Afterwards, I protested what had occurred, and for the first time, I understood that there was something different about those children and that there was, presumably, something wrong with me for wanting to play with them. For the life of me, I could not understand what separated me from the children I wanted to know, and years passed before I understood the significance of that event and before my lost relationship with the children in the neighborhood became a part of my research agenda.

Other similar experiences followed, but only one is worth recounting here. My high school in El Paso, Texas, was predominantly Latino, and most mornings I stared at myself in the mirror and wondered why I had white skin and freckles and did not look like Vera Gonzalez, the most beautiful girl in school, or Martha Eugenia Angulo, my Sunday School teacher, a stunning teenager who was part Chinese and part Hispanic. And then—into a world that was divided into high school students who were white- or brown-skinned walked Roger Bell—a drum major with the brightest smile I had ever seen. He was athletic and handsome and black, and although we were friends in school, our social circles beyond the walls of Irvin High School did not intersect.

As a doctoral student in the English department at the University of Denver and as a faculty member in the School of Journalism and Mass Communication at the University of Colorado, I have continued research on disenfranchised populations in the United States, including Japanese Americans, African Americans, and other racial and ethnic groups, as well as those in the gay, lesbian, bisexual, and transgender community. Whenever possible, I travel to Texas and the Deep South, partly because the climate, vegetation, and accents of the region are familiar to me and partly because I enjoy the diversity of the population.

Although I have resided in Colorado since 1980 and celebrate the Latino culture of my chosen state, I teach at a predominantly white university and live in a predominantly white subdivision outside of Boulder. Visits to Atlanta and other multicultural centers of the South reinforce my love for the region and my interest in its history and literature.

These events and personal reminiscences might be inappropriate and/or irrelevant in a book about white civil rights journalists except for one essential fact: Authors are not accidentally or inadvertently drawn to particular stories about particular persons and events. The threads may be less clear than they are in my case, but they are never absent. Suffice it to say that I am captivated by the lives of heterosexual white people who struggle with racism, sexism, and homophobia and who not only endured—as Faulkner said in his "Nobel Prize Acceptance Speech"—but prevailed.

My master's thesis dealt with Faulkner's panoramic vision in his treatment of *Go Down, Moses; The Hamlet;* and *The Unvanquished.* My dissertation dealt with allegory and the modern Southern novel, focusing on books by Faulkner, Carson McCullers, and Flannery O'Connor. Although I consider Faulkner one of the greatest novelists of the twentieth century, it is his role as the conscience of the South that is of interest to me here. Hodding Carter Jr. in *First Person Rural* captures Faulkner's ability to "prod" the women and men of Mississippi and suggest that they could be more than their flawed and benighted political leaders had encouraged them to be. Carter Jr. writes:

> It is Faulkner as prodder of the Southern conscience—albeit not the only nor even the most persistent one—that concerns me here, though not to the exclusion of Faulkner the legend, Faulkner the citizen of Oxford, and Faulkner the authentic Southerner. As legend he was known to many of us in Mississippi. Vastly fewer among us knew him as friend and citizen, and fewer still comprehended the authenticity of his Southernness. But he pricked the consciences of his widest Southern audience in the last meaningful days; not as an unforgiving castigator, as does the impatient outsider whom he has also warned, but as one of us, feeling more strongly than most the ancient pull between our love and our anger at our region...
>
> And so William Faulkner became for the majority of his Mississippi contemporaries a renegade in his homeland. What was doubted most of all was his Southernness, and this is ironical because William Faulkner was as Southern and as Mississippian as was the late, odious Senator Theodore G. Bilbo. This is so because the South, the white South, is today and has long been at war with itself in a struggle as old as mankind. Faulkner was on the side of today's minority, which is not necessarily the losing side.
>
> By every standard, Faulkner was Southern. The town in which he lived by choice is an epitome of Southernness. So is the faded majesty of the ante-bellum home in which he dwelt there. He was Southern in his pride in the past, in his adoration of the courageous, violent, doomed predecessors who also made legendary the name of Faulkner. He was Southern in his clannishness; in his unposed love of the land, and in the ambivalent love and outrage with which he confronted the South...

But to the Mississippi and Southern majority, because he aligned himself at the last with the soul of the nation rather than with the meaner spirited in his own land, he became Weeping Willie Faulkner, nigger-lover, purveyor of filthy books, a sixth grader who would give lessons in running our schools, a would-be destroyer of the Southern way of life. I suspect that he reacted in several ways to this newer and pitifully uncomplex characterization; angry that his intent and his identification should be challenged; amused at the wryly comic turn of events which made a Mississippi writer, once shrugged off by his Mississippi peers as incomprehensible, now understood too well; and determined that the fight must go on. It is a fight we have been waging in the South a long time, and it is not as one-sided as some would have us believe.

And this regional struggle has a certain cosmic quality, not pessimistic. William Faulkner, in Stockholm, might have been talking to his neighbors and fellow Mississippians when he ended thus one of the grandest messages of man to man:

"I believe that man will not merely endure: he will prevail. He is immortal, not because he alone among creatures has an inexhaustible voice, but because he has a soul, a spirit capable of compassion and sacrifice and endurance. The poet's, the writer's duty is to write about things. It is his privilege to help man endure by lifting his heart, by reminding him of the courage and honor and hope and pride and compassion and pity and sacrifice which have been the glory of his past. The poet's voice need not merely be the record of man, it can be one of the props, the pillars to help him endure and prevail." (73, 83-85)

Hazel Brannon Smith prevailed, and this book is a tribute to her and to Ira B. Harkey Jr. and a group of white male editors who supported her emotionally and financially. That they ultimately failed to save her is of paramount importance and of no importance at all. Admittedly, their compassion and financial assistance might not have made it possible for Smith to publish her newspapers for another decade, but their efforts and their published accounts of those efforts are part of the reason we remember her and mourn her demise. For reasons described briefly here, her life is a symbol for me and for others: Hazel Brannon Smith is a metaphor for life writ large, for a world in which we believe in ourselves, advocate for others, and support journalism that is fair, balanced, socially responsible, and revolutionary.

Certainly, because of this and other contributions that a study of her life makes possible, this is not the first attempt to deal with the life and work of Hazel Brannon Smith. Arthur J. Kaul, Susan Weill, and John A. Whalen have devoted much of their research to understanding white editors during the civil rights era—and Smith in particular. Weill has compared Smith to Allyne Arrington, the only other woman who edited and published more than one newspaper in 1964 in Mississippi, and Mary Cain of the *Summit Sun,* who stridently opposed federal interference during the Mississippi civil rights movement. "Alone among the white women editors and publishers of the Mississippi press," Smith agreed with the 1964 Civil Rights Act, writes Weill. Smith supported the "basic rights" the act made possible:

"equal treatment in voting, equal schooling and use of public facilities" ("Hazel" 553), she adds.

But this book is also an explication of the attitudes held by white Mississippians in the 1950s and 1960s and a disclosure of the essential elements of Southern culture. All communities define themselves, and the American South is a particularly rich cauldron of powerful and often contradictory self-definitions. David Goldfield is especially articulate in his book *Southern Histories: Public, Personal, and Sacred* when he writes:

> Nations acquire symbols, artifacts, and holidays. So did the South, and intertwined them with faith so that their very existence transcended the secular to the sacred. Flags, Bibles, vestments of soldiers; commemorations of battles, memorial days, and heroes' birthdays; erection of monuments and public displays that drew tens of thousands of pilgrims— all became part of the invented "tradition" of southern history, an instant past to salve a troubled present. The creation of collective memory proved essential for the survival of southern society. Rather than a backward-looking creation, the construction of southern history after the Civil War reflected a forward-looking vision, a foundation from which to forge into the future, self-assured and self-righteous. (7)

One cannot separate Hazel Brannon Smith from the rigidly held beliefs of her neighbors or from the internal conflict that defined her as she tried to break free from her own biases and preconceptions. It is this part of her story that makes her an Everywoman and that makes her life significant for those who may not be invested in a history of journalism but who want to understand themselves and the traditions that both sustain and limit them.

Jan Whitt
Boulder, Colorado
July 2009

Acknowledgements

This book is dedicated to Robert Trager, former associate dean of graduate studies in the School of Journalism and Mass Communication at the University of Colorado at Boulder. With a J.D. degree from Stanford Law School (1982) and a Ph.D. from the University of Minnesota (1972), he is a formidable but humble scholar and an intimidating but beloved teacher. Trager's insistence on equality, fairness, and justice—both in his research and in his life—has endeared him to many of us, especially the women and people of color with whom he works.

I am grateful for the opportunity to have served on the thesis committee of David James Wallace. His research for "The Freedom of the Press in a Closed Society: Civil Rights Movement Journalism and Segregationist Pressure" (2006) was thorough and illustrative, and listening to him and reading his work reminded me of how much I enjoy studying this era of American history. I hope he will continue to study media history, especially the press and the civil rights movement.

The proposal for *Burning Crosses and Activist Journalism* won the Joseph McKerns Research Grant ($1,250) from the American Journalism Historians Association (2007) and the Dorothy Martin Woman Faculty Research Award ($3,000) from the Office of the Vice Chancellor for Research and Dean of the Graduate School at the University of Colorado (2007). In 2006, I was awarded a Big 12 Research Fellowship ($1,500) from the Office of Diversity and Equity to conduct research for the book. As a result, I express my deep gratitude to the American Journalism Historians Association and to the University of Colorado.

I also am grateful to Stanley Harrold of South Carolina State University and Randall M. Miller of Saint Joseph's University, professors of history and editors of a book series on "Southern Dissent." In 2000, I traveled to Charleston, South Carolina, for The Citadel Conference on the South. They saw my presentation about white journalists during the civil rights movement on the program and encouraged me to pursue the topic. I will be forever grateful to them for providing the catalyst for this study.

In the same year, I traveled to Phoenix for the Association for Education in Journalism and Mass Communication conference to present a paper about Ira B. Harkey Jr. and Hazel Brannon Smith. Diane L. Borden, director of the School of Journalism and Media Studies at San Diego State University, attended the conference and suggested ways to broaden the study. I very much appreciate her advice and her encouragement.

The members of AJHA and the history division of AEJMC have made the decades I have spent in historical research rich and exciting. Maurine H. Beasley of the University of Maryland, a caring and supportive mentor and colleague, sent me her book *Voices of Change: Southern Pulitzer Winners*, which includes an interview with Hazel Brannon Smith. The book reminded me again that no matter where we journalism historians have traveled, Maurine arrived there first. Caryl A. Cooper of the University of Alabama contributed a chapter to *The Press and Race: Mississippi Journalists Confront the Movement* and has exhibited through her life and her work the values of compassion and equality for all.

I am especially grateful to Janet M. Cramer for joining me at the conference at The Citadel and for talking with me about Southern literature and culture while we walked the beaches of Kiawah Island, South Carolina.

I also thank Michael Danny Whitt, always a "Southern boy," for the years of long conversations about life in the South.

Throughout my research, I relied on several works by well-known scholars in civil rights journalism history. With affection and admiration, I list them here: Gene Roberts and Hank Klibanoff, authors of *The Race Beat: The Press, the Civil Rights Struggle, and the Awakening of a Nation;* John A. Whalen, author of *Maverick Among the Magnolias: The Hazel Brannon Smith Story;* David R. Davies, editor of *The Press and Race: Mississippi Journalists Confront the Movement;* and Susan M. Weill, author of *In a Madhouse's Din: Civil Rights Coverage by Mississippi's Daily Press.*

The photograph on the cover of *Burning Crosses and Activist Journalism* is available to me because of hard work by Mattie Sink, manuscripts librarian at the Mitchell Memorial Library at Mississippi State University, a caring and supportive person who is committed to research projects that highlight Mississippi writers. Use of the photo is courtesy of the Wilson F. "Bill" Minor Papers, Special Collections Department, Mitchell Memorial Library, Mississippi State University Libraries.

Extensive references to *The Smell of Burning Crosses: A White Integrationist Editor in Mississippi* by the late Ira B. Harkey Jr. and to *Maverick Among the Magnolias: The Hazel Brannon Smith Story* by the late John A.

Whalen are possible because of permissions granted by the families and representatives of the authors. I also thank Alfred A. Knopf, a division of Random House, Inc., for permission to cite liberally from *The Race Beat: The Press, the Civil Rights Struggle, and the Awakening of a Nation* by Gene Roberts and Hank Klibanoff.

I thank the editors of Mercer University Press for publishing *Allegory and the Modern Southern Novel* (1994) and the editors of *Southern Studies* for publishing "Burning Crosses and Activist Journalism: The Unlikely Heroism of Two Mississippi Editors," 9 (Summer/Fall 1998): 87-108 and for granting me permission to use material from the book and the article. Their initial publication of my work reinforced my determination to return often to the land of red clay and porch swings.

Last, I express my gratitude to University Press of America, most especially Judith Rothman, vice president and director; Brooke Bascietto, associate editor; and Brian DeRocco editorial administrator. Thank you for the scholarship you make possible.

Introduction.
The American South
In Literature and Popular Culture

Hazel Brannon Smith was a reluctant hero. She never wanted to be considered a reactionary, a revolutionary, a dissident, or a crusading editor. She might have approved of the word "activist" in the title of this book, but even that is not certain. Had she known a book such as *Burning Crosses and Activist Journalism* would be written about her, she would have been surprised and, perhaps, reluctant to read it.

Smith graduated from the University of Alabama with a degree in journalism and a minor in political science. Having loved her job at the *Etowah Observer,* she looked up ads listing newspapers for sale and traveled to Durant, Mississippi, with her boyfriend to look at one such newspaper. After borrowing $3,000, she purchased the *Durant News,* the first of four Mississippi weeklies she would own in her lifetime.

Smith had been popular in college and wanted a wide circle of friends when she moved to Mississippi. Later, when she married Walter D. (Smitty) Smith, she wanted them both to be accepted throughout Mississippi society and wanted to be part of the social activities in Lexington, Mississippi. But it was not to be.

Before Smith died in a Cleveland, Tennessee, nursing home in 1994, she became an icon for progressive thought on racial and ethnic issues in Mississippi and the target of the White Citizens' Council and other segregationists. A cross was burned on her front yard. One of her newspaper offices was firebombed. She endured foreclosure and public humiliation.

She also was considered a reactionary, a revolutionary, a dissident, a crusading editor, and an activist. She was beloved by those who believed in equality across the country. She was featured in national magazines and documentary films. She was the first woman to win a Pulitzer Prize for editorial writing.

And no one would have been more surprised than she. In fact, Hazel Brannon Smith's perception of herself is best illustrated by her response to an accusation that she wasn't following Southern protocol: "Well, I ain't no lady...I'm a newspaper woman" (Harris 122).

It is particularly appropriate in a book that deals with journalism, literature, and popular culture to cite a statement from a 1965 article by T. George Harris in *Look* magazine. "If this lady did not exist," Harris wrote, "some Southern novelist would invent her" (122). I could not agree more. *Burning Crosses and Activist Journalism* is not a biography of Hazel Brannon Smith or a historical study of a region. It is instead a compilation of some of the best research about white editors during the civil rights era and an attempt to illustrate the ways in which the themes and images from film, journalism, and literature about the American South during this turbulent time period converge. The study is both an introduction to Hazel Brannon Smith and the Mississippi civil rights movement and an ancillary collection for those who teach courses in media history and/or women's studies.

The Cost of Passivity

In "The Displaced Person," Georgia writer Flannery O'Connor describes a fictional world in which an immigrant becomes the target of discrimination by those around him. When he is murdered, those responsible stand nearby, passively, and watch. This theme is central to *Burning Crosses and Activist Journalism* and to the lives of Hazel Brannon Smith and the white male editors who supported her personally and financially: Hodding Carter Jr., Mark Ethridge, Ira B. Harkey Jr., John Netherland Heiskell, and Ralph Emerson McGill. Although the fear of personal injury and bankruptcy affected all of them, it was not the white supremacists who attacked them publicly who were the greatest threat. Instead, it was the masses who stood passively by while they and their families were targeted, ridiculed, and threatened.

In O'Connor's story, Guizac, a Polish immigrant, works longer and harder than the other hired help on Mrs. McIntyre's farm. Recommended to Mrs. McIntyre by a local priest, Guizac and members of his family are called names such as "Gobblehook" and "Sledgewig" and are ignored. As is often true in O'Connor's work, a central character's pride and lack of compassion drives the plot, and the title of the story alludes both to the immigrant Guizac and to Christ. Both, according to the Catholic writer, were displaced, mistreated, and murdered by those who should have respected and cared for them.

Unfamiliar with life anywhere else but the Deep South, one of the characters, Mrs. Shortley, expresses the racism prevalent throughout "The Displaced Person": "She began to imagine a war of words, to see the Polish words and the English words coming at each other, stalking forward, not sentences, just words, gabble gabble gabble, flung out high and shrill and stalking forward and then grappling with each other. She saw the Polish words, dirty and all-knowing and unreformed, flinging mud on the clean English words until everything was equally dirty" (216-17).

Telling the priest that she is not responsible for Guizac and did not "create his situation" (239), Mrs. McIntyre begins to plot to rid herself of Guizac, even though he is by far her most industrious worker: "Mr. Guizac...is very efficient. I'll admit that. But he doesn't understand how to get on with my niggers and they don't like him. I can't have my niggers run off. And I don't like his attitude. He's not in the least grateful for being here" (238).

When Mrs. McIntyre tells Father Flynn that Guizac is "extra" and "didn't have to come here in the first place," he tells her that Guizac came to "redeem us" (239-40). This obvious reference to Christ is lost on Mrs. McIntyre, whose anger fuels the plot and makes it possible for Mr. Shortley to kill Guizac. Caring for someone who is lost in a new land would be an act of redemption, but Mrs. McIntyre cannot see the ways in which her prejudices will facilitate murder. Guizac, lying under a tractor while repairing it, never suspects that he will be killed. O'Connor writes:

> Mr. Shortley had got on the large tractor and was backing it out from under the shed. He seemed to be warmed by it as if its heat and strength sent impulses up through him that he obeyed instantly. He had headed it toward the small tractor but he braked it on a slight incline and jumped off and turned back toward the shed. Mrs. McIntyre was looking fixedly at Mr. Guizac's legs lying flat on the ground now. She heard the brake on the large tractor slip and, looking up, she saw it move forward, calculating its own path. Later she remembered that she had seen the Negro jump silently out of the way as if a spring in the earth had released him and that she had seen Mr. Shortly turn his head with incredible slowness and stare silently over his shoulder and that she had started to shout to the Displaced Person but that she had not. She had felt her eyes and Mr. Shortley's eyes and the Negro's eyes come together in one look that froze them in collusion forever, and she had heard the little noise the Pole made as the tractor wheel broke his backbone. (250)

This horrific (and understated) tale of vengeance, cruelty, and passivity lies at the heart of *Burning Crosses and Activist Journalism.* Hazel Brannon Smith was not destroyed simply by those wearing white sheets and articulating hatred. She was destroyed by those who remained silent as the tractor rolled.

Chapter 1, "The Unlikely Heroism of Hazel Brannon Smith," deals with the life and contributions of Hazel Brannon Smith. She befriended the African Americans in her community as well as several civil rights leaders including Medgar Evers and Martin Luther King Jr. The African-American community and a few white civil rights editors returned the favor.

The second chapter, entitled "Hazel Brannon Smith and Editor Ira B. Harkey Jr.," focuses on the connection between Harkey, editor of the *Pascagoula Chronicle,* and Smith. Author of *The Smell of Burning Crosses,* Harkey won the Pulitzer Prize for editorial writing in 1963, the year before Smith won the award. When Harkey was most under threat as an integrationist editor, he believed that only one man in his community stood by him. He and Smith maintained a cordial and supportive professional relationship, and they congratulated each other for their respective awards and accolades.

Chapter 3, "White Hate Groups and Mississippi Newspapers," deals with the source of much of the discord and fear that permeated the lives of both Smith and Harkey, the White Citizens' Council. A group that proudly differentiated itself from the Ku Klux Klan, it nonetheless sponsored hatred and perpetrated violence and economic discrimination throughout the state. In some ways it was more dangerous than the Ku Klux Klan because its members were white professionals and law enforcement officials who described themselves as protectors of African Americans and supporters of order. They helped to found a newspaper designed to drive Smith out of business, and they contributed to her husband's losing his administrative position.

The fourth chapter, "White Civil Rights Editors and Hazel Brannnon Smith," is a tribute to several editors who publicly assisted Hazel Brannon Smith when she faced bankruptcy. The group established a committee to raise money for her, and when the committee ceased to function, they remained her support system. They were all significantly more powerful than she, and at least two of them enjoyed the national spotlight. Although none of them faced the level of financial threat she endured, they empathized with her and appreciated her tenacity and belief in equality. All of them evolved in their support for equality; several of them never advocated integration, but all believed that Mississippi should take seriously the mandates of the Supreme Court that protected all citizens from discrimination and harassment.

Journalists, historians, and filmmakers have told the story of Hazel Brannon Smith as best they can. *Burning Crosses and Activist Journalism* is another attempt to celebrate her life and place it in a meaningful context. To accomplish these goals, it is important to consider the allegorical significance of individual lives such as hers; to analyze several films that portray with varying degrees of historical accuracy the events that shaped her and other editors of her time; and to describe the economic, political, and social climate in Mississippi in the 1950s and 1960s. Finally, the introduction underscores the central themes of the chapters that follow, most importantly the role of average people who sometimes make courageous choices in the face of apathy or fear.

Historical figures such as Hodding Carter Jr., Mark Ethridge, Medgar Evers, Ira B. Harkey Jr., Robert Kennedy, Martin Luther King Jr., Ralph McGill, and Hazel Brannon Smith are heroic and not heroic. The stories we tell about them in newspaper copy, in biographies, in film, and in everyday conversation are both accurate and inaccurate. Our descriptions may or may not have allegorical or symbolic import. *Burning Crosses and Activist Journalism* is the story of Hazel Brannon Smith, but it is also the story of those who knew her and of the simultaneously rich and terrible context of life in the Deep South in the 1950s and 1960s.

Today, much of what transpired during the civil rights movement is available to us through newspapers and other documents in archives and libraries throughout the United States. It is also available to us through film and other texts in popular culture. Several films about the civil rights movement are especially significant to the story of Hazel Brannon Smith and appear in the introduction; another film, "A Long Walk Home," is discussed in "White Hate Groups and Mississippi Newspapers," a chapter that deals with the White Citizens' Councils.

For many American moviegoers, these popular films determine much of what they know—or believe they know—about the history of the South. My objective in including them is not to address the historical reliability or the often unfortunate white male perspective they illustrate but to document how compelling the American South is to moviegoers, readers, and scholars.

The American South in Film

In *Still Fighting the Civil War: The American South and Southern History*, David Goldfield includes chapters entitled "The Past Is" and "God-Haunted." These two phrases are pertinent to a study that focuses upon region and its importance in understanding the world of Hazel Brannon Smith. In a broad-based study of everything from the Civil War to images of masculinity to "religious orthodoxy" (82) to descriptions of representative cities such as Richmond, Virginia, to news events such as the expulsion of Shannon Faulkner from The Citadel in 1996, Goldfield addresses the multi-faceted nature of the American South.

It is his statements about what lies beneath the beauty of the region that complement a discussion of modern films set in the land of magnolias and red clay. "Its sensual climate lures the unsuspecting, and the grace, manners, and civility of its citizens impart a preternatural quietude that belies the storm beneath," Goldfield writes. "Its culture is rich in music, food, conversation, and literature; yet it can be a barren place, a tundra of conformity, a murderer of imagination, inquiry, and innovation" (1).

In *Media-Made Dixie: The South in the American Imagination,* Jack Temple Kirby breaks Southern cinematic and television history into several chapters: "The Embarrassing New South," "The Grand Old South," "The Visceral South," "Dixie Mellow," "The Devilish South," "Dixie Redux and Demise," and "Re-Redux and Reconciliation." The journey begins with "Birth of a Nation" (1914) and ends with "The Color Purple" (1982) and "Places in the Heart" (1985). Temple admirably establishes the interest of Americans in film and television portrayals of everything from "The Beverly Hillbillies" to "The Andy Griffith Show" to "The Waltons." The emphasis on what Earl Hamner, creator of "The Waltons," called "self-reliance, thrift, independence, freedom, love of God, respect for one's fellow man, an affirmation of values" (144) and a commitment to the traditional nuclear family drew 40 million viewers each week two years after "The Waltons" first aired in 1971. Set in Virginia, the television series became so popular that viewers no longer thought about where Walton's Mountain was or where the near-omniscient narrator developed his accent. The stories about family and morality were universal.

Films and television series set in the South have continued to draw viewers. Among the best known are "The Client," "The Color Purple," "Conrack," "Driving Miss Daisy," "The Firm," "Fried Green Tomatoes," "Gone with the Wind," "The Pelican Brief," "Prince of Tides," "Something to Talk About," "Sophie's Choice," "Steel Magnolias," and "To Kill a Mockingbird." Among the less well known are "Bastard Out of Carolina," "Cookie's Fortune," "The Great Santini," "Lone Star," "A Long Walk Home," and "Miss Firecracker." Alex Haley's epic television series "Roots" portrayed well-known actors such as Lorne Green and O.J. Simpson as they reenacted the horrors of slavery and plantation life, and the subsequent miniseries "North and South" took viewers from slavery through the Civil War and into the New South.

More specific to this study, the films that framed mainstream America's understanding of race relations in the Deep South during the 1960s include "Mississippi Burning," "Ghosts of Mississippi," "A Time to Kill," and "The Chamber." The films deal with the bloodbath of racism in the American South. As grisly and terrifying as the events portrayed by the films might be, reality was often more harrowing.

For example, convicted on circumstantial evidence, African Americans were sometimes tortured and killed slowly as part of public spectacles. They were lynched. They were also burned to death. Neil R. McMillen writes in *Dark Journey: Black Mississippians in the Age of Jim Crow* that between 1900 and 1940 at least 15 blacks died in "public burnings," which one newspaper, the *Richland* (La.) *Beacon News* described on Nov. 9, 1901, as "Negro barbeques." Blacks also were tortured and killed using blow torches and hot irons. They were drowned, bludgeoned, and dragged behind automobiles (234).

In "Going to Meet the Man" (1965), James Baldwin writes about a white 42-year-old deputy sheriff who suffers from nightmares and who perpetuates hatred against blacks: "They were animals, they were no better than animals, what could be done with people like that?" the protagonist says. "Here they had been in a civilized country for years and they still lived like animals" (260). As a child, the deputy sheriff had watched a black man hung by his hands, castrated, and burned to death while he, his parents, and other white townspeople watched. Terrified of the black men with whom he engages in his job and tortured by his own demons, he says of the blacks with whom he deals: "They hated him, and this hatred was blacker than their hearts, blacker than their skins, redder than their blood, and harder, by far, than his club" (264).

It is a world characterized by this level of hatred and despair that screenwriters, producers, and directors created in "Mississippi Burning," "Ghosts of Mississippi," "A Time to Kill," and "The Chamber." Alice Walker writes in "To My Young Husband" (2000) about trying to build a relationship with a white man whom she loved—while Mississippi "howled all around us" (311). No phrase better describes the cauldron at the center of these and other films about the civil rights era. Mississippi did, in fact, seem to "howl," and a majority of its white residents opted to protect themselves and a familiar social structure. It was this world in which Hazel Brannon Smith lived and worked. A brief review of the most influential films will provide a context for the introduction of Hazel Brannon Smith in "The Unlikely Heroism of Hazel Brannon Smith."

"Mississippi Burning"

"Mississippi Burning" (1988), although not historically accurate in every detail (including its portrayal of a white Freedom Rider as the one who drove the car while his black colleague cowers in the back seat), contributed to what many American filmgoers understood about the events of Freedom Summer in 1964. The introduction of the film—similar to that of "Frank's Place," a television program starring a black cast and set in New Orleans—depicts water fountains for white and "colored" people and other historical images against a sepia-toned background. Hymns play in the distance. Nominated for seven Oscars, including "Best Picture," "Mississippi Burning" won an Academy Award for best cinematography.

Played by Gene Hackman, one of the agents of the Federal Bureau of Investigation who comes to Mississippi to research the murder of three civil rights workers in "The Magnolia State" asks his colleague, played by Willem Dafoe: "What's got four eyes and can't see?" The answer, appropriately enough, is, "Mississippi." As the film directed by Alan Parker gains momentum, the viewer learns that Jessup County, Mississippi, is separated from the rest of the state and the rest of the nation. Its blindness to progress and social justice is illustrated by Rupert Anderson (Hackman), who was previously a sheriff in a small town called Thornton, Mississippi, and who describes the county by saying that it's "ten miles from Memphis and a million miles from the rest of the world." His opinion is reinforced by the sheriff, who says, "Rest of America don't mean Jack Shit. You're in Mississippi now."

In June 1964 between 600 and 1,000 Freedom Summer civil rights workers came to Mississippi, primarily to encourage black voter registration and to establish schools to provide academic instruction and a place to discuss political processes and cultural awareness. Among them were three volunteers—James Earl Chaney, 21, Andrew Goodman, 20, and Michael Henry Schwerner, 24—who disappeared in Mississippi on June 21, 1964. Goodman and Schwerner were from New York; Chaney, from Meridian, Mississippi. In "Mississippi Burning," carloads of Klan members follow the young men, forcing them off the road and shooting them at close range. When the bodies of the two white and one black man were found buried, shock and sadness drew many more Americans to the civil rights movement.

In "Mississippi Burning," it is clear that the "Hoover Boys" are not welcome in Mississippi as they seek to solve the murders of what the local mayor calls "beatnik college students." Even Anderson questions the purpose of the Freedom Riders: "I think they're being sent down here in their Volkswagens and their sneakers just to get their heads cracked open." The sheriff is even less committed to finding the murderers than Anderson, attributing the alleged disappearance of the three young men to a "publicity stunt cooked up by that Martin Luther King fella."

According to historians, civil rights organizations had come together as the Council of Federated Organizations and sent volunteers to Mississippi to set up voter registration centers, health clinics, legal aid, and schools for blacks. To address the influx of civil rights workers, 200 men met in Brookhaven, Mississippi, to form a group of the White Knights of the Ku Klux Klan. They adopted a 40-page manifesto that "set forth a four-step program for achieving its goals. The fourth stage called for 'extermination'" of those who opposed them *(Race Beat* 354). It did not take long for the White Knights of the Ku Klux Klan to make themselves known: "The Mississippi countryside was hit by a rash of cross-burnings—seven in Vicksburg on one night, twelve in Neshoba County on another, and sixty-four across the state on one weekend. All were preceded by anonymous phone calls to alert reporters. The White Knights also distributed literature claiming a Mississippi membership of 91,003 'sober, intelligent, courageous, Christian, American white men'" *(Race Beat* 354).

In historical summaries of the event, Chaney, Goodman, and Schwerner were driving on back roads in Neshoba County to investigate a fire at Mount Zion Baptist Church in Sandtown, Mississippi. At 3 p.m. they were arrested by Deputy Sheriff Cecil Price for speeding and put in Neshoba County Jail. William Bradford Huie includes a haunting fact about the arrest in his landmark book *Three Lives for Mississippi*. He reveals a community that could sing hymns and celebrate the life of Christ while fostering racism at the same time: "In fact, as they stood in their cells during the hot, steamy Sunday evening, held incommunicado and waiting to be delivered to the mob, Mickey Schwerner, Andy Goodman, and James Chaney could hear the Baptists singing 'Blessed Assurance,' 'My Faith Looks Up to Thee,' and 'What a Friend We Have in Jesus'" (27), Huie writes.

Released about 10:30 p.m., the young men were stopped again by Price 10 miles south of town and were turned over to the carloads of Klansmen who killed and buried them. An "avowed pacifist" (Huie 35) who "believed that every human being can be reached in time by love" (Huie 32), Schwerner and his colleagues were killed before midnight about four miles from where their station wagon had been stopped. They were buried in a trench alongside a dam under two feet of dirt and 18 feet below the top of the dam. According to Huie, heavy rains fell during June and July, and by August, the dam was "massive and grassed over—a permanent tomb for three bodies if nobody ever talked" (120).

However, informants eventually did talk, and 44 days after the murders, the bodies were unearthed in spite of lack of assistance from local law enforcement officials. More than $3 million was spent to find the bodies. Reporters and investigators had been pouring into Mississippi since the young men disappeared, and in the film Sheriff Ray Stuckey asks the FBI agents if they are "down here to help us solve our nigger problems." He suggests that they leave because he and his deputies will "take care of this local problem." Countering Stuckey's fictional film portrayal of the sheriff, a very real Smith "mourned the murders" (Weill, "Hazel" 556) and what the murders represented for the future of the state. On Aug. 6, 1964, she wrote, "The finding of the three bodies in a shallow grave was almost too much to take. Mississippi is now blotted with another crime which we will never live down" (Weill, "Hazel" 556).

In spite of the resistance by local officials and residents, seven men eventually were convicted by an all-white jury for plotting and carrying out the murders. Three years and four months after Chaney, Goodman, and Schwerner disappeared, 18 defendants faced prosecution and seven of them were found guilty. According to Huie, two of the men were sentenced to 10 years; one to six years; and the others to four years (143). Historians who consulted with the writers and producers of the film list different sentences for the seven, although most sources agree that none of those convicted served more than six years. In the film, the sentences include: Frank Bailey (Michael Rooker), 10 years; Lester Cowens (Pruitt Taylor Vince), three years; Floyd Swilley (Marc Clement), seven years; Clinton Pell (Brad Dourif), 10 years; Wesley Cooke (Stephen Wesley Bridgewater), seven years; and Clayton Townley (Stephen Tobolowsky), 10 years. Stuckey (Gailard Sartain) was acquitted. According to Huie, Schwerner's wife Rita and his parents wanted Schwerner buried in Mississippi alongside Chaney. With obvious anger, Huie writes, "There is no way to bury a white man with a Negro in Mississippi—unless you bury them at night in a dam" (143).

But the story would not end here; in fact, one of the defendants would surface again many years later. Because federal statutes against murder did not exist at the time Chaney, Goodman, and Schwerner were killed, the federal government had charged 18 men, including Edgar Ray Killen, for conspiring to violate civil rights. Killen was acquitted of those charges and maintained his innocence in the crime against the civil rights workers.

Ironically, on June 19, 1964, the Civil Rights Act, prohibiting discrimination in employment, public access, and housing, passed 73-27, and many in the judicial system expected the ruling to have a more direct bearing on cases such as Killen's. "It made some changes in voting rights and school desegregation, extended the Civil Rights Commission, created a community relations service to resolve discrimination disputes, and strengthened the federal government's power to enforce the law" *(Race Beat* 359). However, in 1967, the Killen jury was deadlocked 11-1 and would have convicted Killen, but, as CNN reported, the "lone holdout said she could never convict a preacher" ("'Mississippi Burning' Trial Begins" n.p.). (In his youth, Killen had been a preacher, had operated a sawmill, and had been a member of the Ku Klux Klan.)

But prosecutors did not forget those like Killen who had been acquitted. On June 23, 2005, in Philadelphia, Mississippi, Edgar Ray Killen was convicted of manslaughter for his role in the deaths of the three civil rights workers 41 years before. He would later be sentenced to 60 years in prison. At the time, eight of the original defendants were still alive. In the *International Herald Tribune,* Shaila Dewan wrote, "Killen, 80, sat in a wheelchair, the tubes of an oxygen tank under his nose, his expression impassive...Throughout the courtroom, people wept" (n.p.).

A journalist whose tenacity contributed to the verdict indirectly was Jerry Mitchell of the *Jackson Clarion-Ledger,* later owned by Gannett. Mitchell wrote stories that led to the reopening of the Philadelphia murders and the Medgar Evers case. The murder of Medgar Evers is the focus of the next film of importance to this study, "Ghosts of Mississippi."

"Ghosts of Mississippi"

In "Ghosts of Mississippi," director Rob Reiner introduces a mosaic of images from the civil rights movement in the introduction to the film. John F. Kennedy's voice rings out, warning Americans of a "moral crisis": "The fires of frustration and discord are burning in every city...Where legal remedies are not at hand, redress is sought in the streets." "This story is true," the audience is told, and, in fact, Medgar Evers' wife Myrlie Evers and Mississippi author Willie Morris are listed as consultants in the credits.

Taking place in the Mississippi Delta in 1963 and 1964, "Ghosts of Mississippi" depicts the aftermath of the murder of Medgar Evers, a champion of integration, in front of his home on June 12, 1963. Evers never thought of abandoning his beloved state, and his wife quotes him as saying,

"I don't know whether I'm going to heaven or to hell. But I'm going from Jackson."

Evers worked as an influential Mississippi field secretary for the NAACP, and segregationists rightfully considered him a formidable threat to the status quo. Since 1958, the Mississippi Sovereignty Commission and law enforcement had been watching him *(Race Beat* 335). Evers attended a rally at New Jerusalem Baptist Church in Jackson, Mississippi, on Tuesday evening, June 11, 1963. At 12:20 a.m. on Wednesday, June 12, he pulled into the driveway of his Jackson home and got out of his car carrying a bundle of NAACP T-shirts, proclaiming "Jim Crow Must Go." As he neared the door to the kitchen where his wife, Myrlie, and their children were waiting to greet him, a gunman, crouching in the bushes some 120 feet away, shot him in the back with a high-powered rifle, dropped the gun and fled.

Gene Roberts and Hank Klibanoff, authors of *The Race Beat,* tell a similar story but provide compelling details: "Here comes Daddy," said Evers' oldest son Darrell, who had stayed up late with his siblings to watch television. "Evers got out, closed the car door, and was standing with an armful of sweatshirts when a gunshot rang out, sending a bullet from a World War I-era 30.06 Enfield rifle into his back" (340). According to the journalists, Evers "was clinging to life when friends put him on a mattress and into the back of a station wagon and raced him to the University of Mississippi Hospital. He died minutes later. He was thirty-seven" (341).

As depicted in "Ghosts of Mississippi," Byron De La Beckwith is arrested for the murder. At his trial in the Hinds County Courthouse, De La Beckwith (James Woods) is greeted enthusiastically by Ross Barnett, former governor of Mississippi, as Evers' wife Myrlie (Whoopi Goldberg) looks on. Responding to those who are shocked by the display, a reporter says, "What's America got to do with anything? This is Mississippi." The White Citizens' Council set up a legal fund for De La Beckwith. He was tried twice in 1964 and released by all-white juries. The first mistrial ended Feb. 7, 1964; the second, April 17, 1964.

In 1994, De La Beckwith was arrested again for the murder of Evers. Hinds County district attorney Bobby DeLaughter (Alec Baldwin) convinces the jury to convict De La Beckwith of first-degree murder, joining Rupert Anderson of "Mississippi Burning" and Jake Brigance of "A Time to Kill" as another white man who recognizes the plight of his black brothers in the Deep South.

This fact links the FBI agent and the two criminal attorneys with numerous white newspaper editors who also found themselves learning and changing their minds about segregation and other social issues, often at significant cost to themselves. It is worth mentioning, of course, that the white protagonists depicted in these films highlight the tendency of Hollywood writers and producers to employ a white male's point of view to the exclusion of the perspectives of others.

Later, police recovered the rifle and identified fingerprints on it as those of De La Beckwith, a White Citizens' Council member from Greenwood, Mississippi. De La Beckwith was arrested 10 days later and charged with Evers' murder. Two days after the murder, before Beckwith had been apprehended, Hazel Brannon Smith published an editorial denouncing the assassination as "shocking, hate-inspired...a reprehensible crime against the law of God and man...a vicious and dastardly act" (152-53):

> "The criminal...did not kill a civil rights movement, as he may have supposed," [Smith] declared. "He did kill a man who was a living symbol of freedom that Mississippi Negroes are determined to achieve. But far from killing the freedom movement in Mississippi, the perpetrator of the crime only made certain it will be increased tenfold. This murder was committed by an ignorant product of our sick, hate-filled society...
> "It is imperative that each of us examine our own heart and conscience and determine what part we have played, either in things done or left undone, in acts of commission or omission, in creating a society which permits a man to be murdered because of his desire to be free and equal under the law—a man who fought Hitlerism in Germany for all our freedom." (Whalen 153)

Mississippi novelist and short story writer Eudora Welty wrote about blacks such as Phoenix Jackson in "A Worn Path" with obvious affection, but she rarely engaged in political debates about civil rights in her native state. A notable exception is the *New Yorker* piece "Where Is the Voice Coming From?" (1963) in which Welty's protagonist is Evers' fictional assassin. Shocked by Evers' murder in Jackson in 1963, Welty said, "Whoever the murderer is, I know him: not his identity but his coming about in time and place" (Cobb 207). In "Where Is the Voice Coming From?" Welty's central character says: "I'd already brought up my rifle, I'd already taken my sights. And I'd already got him, because it was too late then for him or me to turn by one hair" (215). The story is particularly powerful because it is told in first person and speculates about the motives of the as-yet-unnamed murderer.

The story of Medgar Evers is richly symbolic; he was an Everyman who fought for equality and paid dearly for his struggle. His accomplishments live on. Evers "wanted Negroes hired as police officers and as employees in downtown businesses, and he wanted all schools, playgrounds, parks, libraries, and lunch counters to be open to Negroes," write Roberts and Klibanoff. "Although the NAACP had been marginalized throughout the rest of the South, the thirty-seven-year-old Evers had made it the dominant Negro organization in Mississippi. He had done so by bridging the gap between the old heads, who believed change would come only by persistent knocking on the door, and more aggressive young blacks, who felt the door had to be pushed down and removed" *(Race Beat* 334). Buried in Arlington National Cemetery on June 19, 1963, Evers was celebrated by the 25,000 who walked by his casket where it lay in state at the John Wesley A.M.E. Zion Church in Washington, D.C., for two days.

"The Chamber"

Another film well known to devotees of cinema is "The Chamber" (1996), which begins in April 1967 with the murder of twins and their father in a law office in Indianola, Mississippi. Directed by James Foley, the film portrays the terror after the boys open two windows in the upper story of the building as a bomb explodes; the blast silences them and tears the front off of the red-brick building.

Born two years after the murders, Adam Hall (Chris O'Donnell) travels from Chicago to Indianola to defend his grandfather, Sam Cayhall (Gene Hackman), who was convicted of the crime and is on Death Row. He goes to the home of his aunt, Lee Bowen (Faye Dunaway), who is excited to see him but concerned about his reason for coming to Mississippi. She explains to Hall that she and other family members changed their last name to protect themselves after the murders, and she describes her racist childhood and explains why her brother—and Hall's father—killed himself in 1980.

Calling herself "Hitler's daughter," Bowen says she left home when she was eighteen but later married a wealthy man and tried to put her past behind her. "Done pretty well for poor white trash, don't you think?" she asks her nephew. Later, she warns him: "Be very careful dredging the past, Adam. You might not like what comes up." Terrified by a headline in the local *Clarion-Ledger* ("Racist Killer's Grandson/Arrives To Save the Day"), Bowen tells Hall, "Oh, I know the *Clarion-Ledger* is not the *Chicago Tribune,* but in our small pond, it's everything."

Descended from four generations of Klansmen and incarcerated in the Mississippi State Penitentiary, Cayhall is a caricature of a hateful, racist man. When his 26-year-old grandson proposes to save him from his execution that is 28 days away, Cayhall ridicules the young man's father, who died by his own hand, and snarls: "Save me? This from the son of a man who blew his own brains out?...Save me?...You don't look like you could save a turkey from Thanksgiving."

Described as "the land of secrets" in "The Chamber," Mississippi was once the home of the Sovereignty Commission, an official state agency that was coordinated by the White Citizens' Councils (It is discussed in detail in "White Hate Groups and Mississippi Newspapers"). Bowen tells Hall ominously, "You want to know about the past? I'll tell you about the past." Her allusion is to the death of a local black man whom her father murdered when she was a child, and it is Bowen who is the link to the earlier time and to what she describes as "a long line of hate." She describes her father to Hall by saying: "Problem is, he was raised to be a monster. Trained from birth. We come from a long line of hate, Adam...Blood and death were served with Sunday breakfast...He was raised by his family and by this state to become the man that he became."

The reference to her father as a product of his society makes clear what Smith and other white civil rights editors faced: There were those so consumed by rage and so entrenched in their beliefs that they were irredeemable. In "Advancing Luna—and Ida B. Wells" (1977), Alice Walker recalls what an artist in Cuba said about Walker's inability to believe in the existence of such evil. The words are terrifying because they remind us that there may be people without compassion, without governing principles, and that these people can perpetrate the most heinous of crimes against humanity. "You are unable to conceive of the man without conscience," Walker remembers her saying. "The man who cares nothing about the state of his soul because he's long since sold it. In short...you do not understand that some people are simply evil, a disease on the lives of other people, and that to remove the disease altogether is preferable to trying to interpret, contain, or forgive it" (247).

Cayhall is such a man. His humanity is evident only in his intermittent concern for his grandson, who will deal with his family's legacy for the remainder of his life.

"A Time to Kill"

Another film released in 1996 contributed to the interest in the civil rights era among American moviegoers. "A Time to Kill" was directed by Joel Schumacher, who also directed "The Client," another film drawn from a John Grisham novel and set in the South.

Set in Canton, part of Madison County, Mississippi, "A Time to Kill" deals with the torture and rape of a 10-year-old girl named Tonya Haley. Avenged by her father Carl Lee Haley (Samuel L. Jackson), Haley is defended by Jake Brigance (Matthew McConaughey). He enlists the assistance of Ellen Roark (Sandra Bullock), a capable young law student invested in civil rights issues. Brigance's wife Carla (Ashley Judd) leaves him because of the danger to which she believes he is subjecting his family. Speaking of Haley and of himself, Brigance says, "Ain't nothin' more dangerous in this world than a fool with a cause."

In the county that is 30 percent black, Haley selects Brigance partially because he is white, but Brigance retaliates against Haley's characterization: "You think just like them," Haley says. "That's why I picked you...fact is, you're just like all the rest of them." Brigance replies by saying, "Carl Lee, I am your friend." "We ain't no friends, Jake," Haley says. "I ain't never seen you in my part of town."

In the end, Haley's characterization of his attorney proves correct. In fact, Brigance wins the trial because he asks the jurors to close their eyes and imagine the crime against the child, who was hit with beer cans, urinated upon, raped, and left for dead. "This is a story about a little girl,"

Brigance begins. "Can you see her? Her raped, beaten, broken body, soaked in their urine, soaked in their semen, soaked in her blood. Left to die. Can you see her? I want you to picture that little girl." As the camera pans the faces of the white jurors, he then says: "Now, imagine she's white."

These films and the literature of Mississippi authors such as William Faulkner, Walker Percy, and Eudora Welty fictionally represent the world we will explore in *Burning Crosses and Activist Journalism*. Films based on news stories, "Mississippi Burning," "Ghosts of Mississippi," "The Chamber," and "A Time to Kill" grip the contemporary imagination and challenge viewers to know more about The Magnolia State in all its beauty and in all its tragic past.

The Economic, Political, and Social Climate

It is tempting for those in many disciplines—American studies, history, journalism, literature, media studies, sociology, women's studies, etc.—to write the stories of everyday citizens as if their subjects were somehow more courageous, more spiritual, more committed, or less concerned with the opinions of others than the average person might be. Little appeals more to the American sensibility than a tale about overcoming insurmountable odds in the interest of a higher goal; the phrase "overcoming insurmountable odds" itself suggests the possibility that things that cannot be surmounted might, in fact, be overcome by heroes, and the more Detective Columbo-like the hero, the better the story, the more surprising the heroism.

However, this study is not about fictional characters such as Jake Brigance and Adam Hall, although it relies somewhat on the concept of heroism woven into the cultural sensibility. Telling the stories of Ira B. Harkey Jr., Hazel Brannon Smith, and their contemporaries requires both journalism and history; the telling is both journalistic and historical. This study resists the temptation to build monuments to white Mississippi editors—at the same time that it acknowledges their acts of quiet and not-so-quiet courage. No doubt their stories could be translated into an action-packed screenplay or a nonfiction novel, but that is not the purpose here.

One of the "heroes" in this study left the Deep South emotionally wounded, bitter, and cynical; the other remained as long as she could but was devastated by her husband's death and the loss of her Tara-like home, her friends, and her livelihood. Penniless and suffering memory loss, she was led quietly into retirement by her sister. Editors such as Ira B. Harkey Jr. and Hazel Brannon Smith had feet of clay. They should not be considered more noble simply because they were all too human. They did not overcome insurmountable odds; in fact, their odds were literally insurmountable. Harkey and Smith second-guessed themselves. They embraced journalistic principles, but they sometimes embraced them too little and too late. They worried about the reactions of their neighbors and friends. They suffered and raged against the loss of their financial security and the respect of their communities.

Neither editor saw himself or herself as a champion of civil rights; in fact, one of them did not believe in integration. Both were unlikely heroes, and, ironically, although their life's work was spent telling the stories of others, their own lives proved more dramatic, sensational, and controversial than many of the stories they told. They saw themselves as average people trying to exercise the tenets of good journalism—fairness, balance, and the broad and accurate representation of their communities. Exercising those tenets did not make them heroes; it made them good journalists.

After being driven out of the newspaper industry by their advertisers and readers, Mississippi editors Ira B. Harkey Jr. (1918-2006) and Hazel Brannon Smith (1914-1994) won Pulitzer Prizes. Harkey also won the Sidney Hillman Foundation Award for editorials, a National Sigma Delta Chi award, a Brotherhood Award from the National Conference of Christians and Jews, and a New York City chapter of the American Newspaper Guild award. Harkey also earned a master's degree and a doctorate and published two books, one of which was *The Smell of Burning Crosses: An Autobiography of a Mississippi Newspaperman* (later entitled *The Smell of Burning Crosses: A White Integrationist Editor in Mississippi).*

Smith was featured in a made-for-television movie ("A Passion for Justice") and a documentary ("An Independent Voice"). By the time her career ended, she had been an officer in or a member of numerous professional organizations and had won awards from many of them. The groups include the Mississippi Press Women, the International Society of Weekly Newspaper Editors, the Mississippi Press Association, the National Newspaper Association, the National Editorial Association, the National Federation of Press Women, the Mississippi Council of Human Relations, and the U.S. Civil Rights Commission.

Smith also won the Elijah Parish Lovejoy Award for Courage in Journalism (1960), was named "Mississippi Woman of the Year" (1964), and was named to Who's Who in America (1968-69). In addition, she won the top editorial award from the NFPW in 1948 and 1955 and was named "Woman of Conscience" by the National Council of Women of the U.S. in 1964. The secretary of the Holmes County Democratic executive committee from 1940-48, Smith was a delegate to the Democratic National Convention in 1940 and 1944.

The accolades are only part of Harkey's and Smith's stories. The fact is that during their careers as reform journalists, both were called "pariahs" by local politicians and residents, had crosses burned on their lawns, and had their offices firebombed. They did not leave their profession voluntarily: They were driven out. Harkey acknowledges his honors for his autobiography but writes that he gained them "at the forfeit of a life's work I had loved" (2006, 19). This study traces the careers of editors such as Harkey and Smith and argues that they—even in hindsight—underestimated the impact of what was for them simple human fairness and adherence to quality journalism.

It is important to understand the world in which Harkey and Smith found themselves in the 1950s and 1960s. Citing two historical studies, journalism historian Susan Weill argues that "an agricultural economy, a socially conservative white mentality, and a large black underclass defined Mississippi in the 1950s." She writes:

> The state was largely rural, the capital city of Jackson was the only actual metropolitan area, and the racial composition was unique to the country. · In no other state did blacks constitute such a large percentage of the population as they did in Mississippi, where for more than a century they had, as the descendants of slaves, comprised a majority. In 1954, the lack of education, denial of involvement in the political process, and burden of poverty hung over them in the dark cloud of second class citizenship. ("Conserving" 77-78)

Citing eight studies—several of them theses and dissertations ("Conserving" 94)—Weill argues that "Mississippi press reaction to the civil rights movement has not been studied extensively" ("Conserving" 78).

According to a document from the Mississippi Power and Light Company's economic research department, Jackson, Mississippi, had a population in 1954 that was 44 percent black. Of Jackson, Weill writes, "The city was also the home of the two most widely-circulated daily newspapers in the state, the conservative *Clarion-Ledger* and the equally conservative *Daily News*" ("Conserving" 85). Both newspapers supported segregation in all areas of Southern life. An example of prevalent racial attitudes is evident in one letter to the *Clarion-Ledger* written by state representative Edwin White: "There is only one thing in the whole situation which the white man asks for and that is the privilege of his children, and his children's children, continuing to be white people. It's God's law" ("Conserving" 86).

It was the people of Mississippi whom Weill describes who were to be the readers for the newspapers edited and published by Harkey and Smith. Although both editors were Southerners, neither was prepared for what would happen before their newspaper careers came to a bitter and controversial end.

Ralph McGill, Weill, and David James Wallace make clear that white editors during the civil rights movement were in the impossible position of wanting to relay their opinions on the editorial page but knowing that whatever they wrote could make their readers terminate subscriptions and refuse to advertise in their newspapers. In his thesis entitled "The Freedom of the Press in a Closed Society," Wallace argues that a few Mississippi journalists believed in justice for all and lived it, although they did so at great risk to themselves: "They proved to be a chink in the South's armor of unified resistance, voicing reason in a time when emotion seemed to rule the day" (12). Weill, too, explains how reckless it was for editors to espouse beliefs that ran counter to those who supported them economically:

Socially responsible editorship of the Mississippi daily press following the 1954 *Brown v. Board of Education* decision might have seemed, to
advocates of equal rights, an editorship that would have endorsed quality
education for all people. But to most of the white editors and reporters of
the Mississippi daily press in 1954, and to most white Mississippians, socially responsible editorship during that time meant the endorsement and
protection of Mississippi society as they had always understood and defended it—racially segregated with blacks in subservient roles as second-
class citizens. (Weill, "Conserving" 93)

McGill agrees with Weill and Wallace when he writes: "When the civil
rights movement came, most southern newspapers reacted like most southern churches; they reflected their environment, the homogeneity of their local customs and traditions" (Williams 27).

Before introducing the editors who are the focus of *Burning Crosses
and Activist Journalism,* it is important to provide a few statistics that help
to describe Mississippi during the time period that the editors lived and
worked. In *The Race Beat,* Gene Roberts and Hank Klibanoff describe both
the role of newspapers and the political climate during the early 1960s:

> There were only nineteen daily newspapers in the state—the largest city,
> Jackson, had 150,000 residents, and no other city had even a third of
> that—and the state of journalism was not highly developed. While the
> Hederman dailies were the most powerful in-state papers, they were not as
> dominant in north Mississippi as the Memphis *Commercial Appeal* or in
> south Mississippi as the New Orleans *Times-Picayune.* There were five
> times as many weeklies as dailies in the state, some of them quite influen-
> tial...
>   What mattered most...was that [Governor Ross] Barnett had caught
> the segregationist wind just right. Mississippi was the poorest state in the
> nation, with an average per capita income under $1,200 and its 900,000
> Negroes represented 43 percent of the state's population, the highest per-
> centage in the nation; in some counties, six or seven out of ten residents
> were black. It was not hard to play on whites' fears. Barnett sailed into the
> governor's office in January 1960 on the hot air of racial anger and dema-
> goguery. Now, more than two years later, most of the newspapers were
> solidly behind him, showing a mixture of racism and laziness. (277, 278)

When riots followed James Howard Meredith's application for admission to Ole Miss in 1962, Barnett was largely responsible. Meredith's "an-
tagonist was the region and its customs, the rabid, determined segregationist
South, embodied in Ross Barnett," write Roberts and Klibanoff. "To many
Mississippians, Barnett was the defiant leader they had been waiting for
since the end of the Civil War. He said it plainly: no integration at any time,
at any place, so long as he was governor. Never, never, never" *(Race Beat*
280). Roberts and Klibanoff also are correct that after Meredith was admitted, Oxford, Mississippi, with its 6,200 residents "would attract the civil
rights movement's largest gathering of journalistic firepower" *(Race Beat*
279).

James Meredith's admission to the University of Mississippi; the murder of three civil rights workers; the murder of Medgar Evers; the murder of Martin Luther King Jr. by James Earl Ray on April 4, 1968; the murder of Robert Kennedy on June 5, 1968; and other events made it essential that the white-owned press address the issues central to their communities. In Smith's case, the determination to tell the story of the civil rights movement in a fair and balanced manner would cost her a career she loved. Both King and Kennedy were Smith's heroes (Whalen 237); in turn, she was a hero to many others.

Historian James W. Silver of the University of Mississippi knew James Meredith, who would become the first black student admitted to his institution, and was on campus the night that riots broke out after the decision to admit Meredith. He also knew William Faulkner and heard him speak at the Peabody Hotel in Memphis in November 1955 at a meeting of the Southern Historical Association. There, Faulkner said, "To live anywhere in the world of A.D. 1955 and be against equality because of race or color, is like living in Alaska and being against snow" (Silver xi). But Faulkner's perspective was not that of others in his beloved state, and much would transpire between the SHA meeting and his death in 1962.

Silver's often-quoted first-person narrative *Mississippi: The Closed Society* has as its thesis what the former Ole Miss professor calls "the all-pervading doctrine, then and now" that is white supremacy, whether the dominance of white people is "achieved through slavery or segregation, rationalized by a professed belief in state rights and bolstered by religious fundamentalism" or not. "Violence and the threat of violence have confirmed and enforced the image of unanimity" (6), said Silver.

As noted throughout this study, Smith would pay dearly for her moderate stance in a turbulent region. Silver writes that in 1954 she enjoyed some victories against what he calls the "closed society," but "troubles were just beginning for the crusading editor, whose sins piled up" (38). Lauding her "magnificent courage," Silver states that "her dogged struggle for survival" was "grim indeed" (39) and cites from one of her editorials:

Today we live in fear in Holmes County and in Mississippi. It hangs like a dark cloud over us, dominating every facet of public and private life. None speaks freely without being afraid of being misunderstood. Almost every man and woman is afraid to try to do anything to promote good will and harmony between the races, afraid he or she will be taken as a mixer, as an integrationist or worse, if there is anything worse by southern standards. (39)

In spite of the cost, some white editors contributed positively to discussions about race and ethnicity and their impact on politics in the Deep South. Martin Luther King Jr.'s "belief that nonviolent resistance could overthrow white supremacy in the South was premised on the existence of an audience, the American public, whose conscience could be aroused and would be outraged at the brutality used to enforce racial segregation when it was challenged. That belief in turn depended on a press that would tell the story" (1991, 36), writes Anthony Lewis, a First Amendment scholar and former *New York Times* reporter in *Make No Law: The Sullivan Case and the First Amendment.*

According to John A. Whalen, author of a biography about Smith, the times could not have been any less conducive to a newspaper editor who wanted to relay the full story. What follows is his description of life in average Mississippi communities during 1964:

> Inflamed by the state's media, panic gripped the white citizenry. The spring session of the state legislature enacted a variety of anti-black measures, the highway patrol was nearly doubled in size and a wave of violence against blacks during the summer totaled at least six murders, eighty beatings, thirty-five shootings, 1,000 arrests, thirty-five churches and thirty-one homes and other buildings burned or bombed. On April 24 alone, crosses were burned in sixty-four of the state's eighty-two counties. (173)

Into this climate of fear, retaliation, and violence walked a handful of courageous editors who might not have chosen to live in such a time and place, but every morning during every work week, they left their homes, drove to their offices, and confronted the myriad problems that challenged and, no doubt, terrified them. In the introduction to the biography of one of those editors, Hodding Carter Jr., Ann Waldron writes:

> When I said I wanted to write a book about a southern white liberal during the civil rights revolution, more than one person asked me, "Were there any?"
> Indeed there were white liberals in those years from 1954 through 1964, when the South was the battleground for diehard white segregationists on one side and frustrated African-Americans at last demanding basic rights on the other. To defend their "way of life," a squalid, outmoded, totally reprehensible dehumanization of a whole race, segregationists used every weapon they could muster, from lunatic legal schemes such as interposition, to bombs. Backed up by the "law of the land," including the 1954 ruling of the United States Supreme Court in *Brown vs. Board of Education* that outlawed segregation in the public schools, black and northern white civil rights leaders battled on. Caught in the middle were southern white liberals. They were reviled by their white neighbors, scorned by northern liberals, and abandoned by the black activists who took over the civil rights movement. (xi)

I would argue that Hodding Carter Jr. was not a "southern white liberal." He certainly never used the word "liberal" to describe himself, and when the wrath of the segregationists was unleashed upon his friend and colleague Hazel Brannon Smith, he reacted with anger and surprise, at least partially because he considered her a "moderate," not a "liberal."

Although courageous, Carter Jr. was a product of his times. He challenged the status quo and encouraged others to do the same. He did not stand by like those on Mrs. McIntyre's farm. But he was not a social liberal compared to many of his contemporaries.

It is perhaps true that Carter Jr. and Smith were as close to being "southern white liberals" as there were in the journalistic community, but it is important not to be guilty of historical revision with respect to their personal lives and their chosen career. They were people of courage surrounded by citizens who too often behaved as a fearful collective, citizens who watched silently as wrongs were perpetrated. They were not passive, and in small but significant ways they challenged discrimination. And perhaps that is enough.

Chapter 1.
The Unlikely Heroism
Of Hazel Brannon Smith

The title of this study is *Burning Crosses and Activist Journalism: Hazel Brannon Smith and the Mississippi Civil Rights Movement,* a title selected in spite of the fact that Hazel Brannon Smith would almost assuredly object to being categorized as an "activist" journalist. As Arthur J. Kaul wrote, Smith wanted to be known as a newspaperwoman, not as a crusader: "I flinch every time I am called a crusading editor," she said. "But an honest editor who would truly serve the highest and best interest of the people will not compromise convictions to support a popular cause known to be morally wrong just to incur popular favor or support" ("Hazel Brannon Smith" 291).

Certainly, Smith's self-perception matched the opinion of those who interacted with her throughout her career. Recalling her interview with Hazel Brannon Smith, Maurine H. Beasley said of her: "I'm impressed by her courage. Based on my brief interaction with her, I think she was a thoughtful person, not a fire-eating type at all, and also a bit vulnerable" (18 October 2007 e-mail message).

Smith would most certainly not have considered herself a hero. While acknowledging that many of the newspapermen and women and the scholars who have written about her consider her to be just that, this chapter focuses instead on her "unlikely heroism," the inadvertent impact of a life spent believing in compassion and fairness and the power of the written word. Because a moral woman published four newspapers and ignored fears of losing the profession she relied upon, of being considered a pariah in the hometown she loved, and of being threatened with physical harm, the lives of Mississippians were changed.

The most interesting aspect of Hazel Brannon Smith's story is that she was such an unlikely person to inspire the adoration and the hatred she experienced during her lifetime. Having graduated from high school when she was 16, she worked for the *Etowah Observer* long enough to discover that she liked weekly newspapers. A beauty queen and member of a sorority, she received a journalism degree, worked on her campus newspaper, and decided after graduation to borrow money to purchase a fledgling newspaper in a town in which she might like to live.

The plan was simple, and with the exception of the fact that she was a woman living in the Deep South in the 1930s, her decision to pursue journalism was unremarkable. Given her interests and talents, the decision to write was logical, although few assumed that the charismatic young woman would remain single or that she would put her career first. Certainly, upon graduation, Hazel Brannon Smith did not dream of a Pulitzer Prize. She did not want to move to a large urban setting and work for an established newspaper, nor did she long to become a quintessential wife and mother in a community in the rural South. Instead, within a few years she would marry someone she loved, would not have children, and would commit herself to four weekly newspapers, which she believed could provide a public service. As she began her career, she would focus on local news and join several community organizations in order to contribute her energy to the social well-being of her chosen hometown.

Even when the trouble began, Hazel Brannon Smith considered her role to be clear-cut. She was not agitating. She was not pushing her readers to espouse social perspectives they were not ready to consider. Instead, her actions were in keeping with how she defined the responsibility of a small-town weekly editor: The editor should speak truth to power. The editor should write stories that advocate for the disenfranchised. Her goals were consistent with her Christian beliefs; they were also at the heart of what she perceived to be the reason for media to exist. Eventually, she told those close to her that she wanted to live in a Tara-like house. She wanted to have fun, as evidenced by her ready smile, her outgoing personality, and her celebration of life as she drove through town in her convertible, sporting the hats that began to identify her as glamorous and attention-seeking. But Hazel Brannon Smith could not have dreamed that she would turn her small community upside down or that her moderate social and political views would alienate her readers and ostracize the community she loved.

In sexist prose that is unfortunately typical for the 1970s when it was written, a biographer describes Hazel Brannon Smith as a "handsome, dark-haired, buxom woman" who "looks years younger than her age": "Her eyes, contrary to the title of her editorial column, are deep blue. Talkative and gregarious, she possesses a sense of hospitality which, according to Ann Geracimos of the New York *Herald Tribune* (May 10, 1964), 'oozes fried chicken and biscuits'" (Moritz, ed., 386).

Further illustrating the manner in which journalists referred to women, in the 1940s, Damon Runyon said of Smith, "The lady has soft brown hair, gleaming teeth and nice eyes and is just the right size" (Whalen 38). Wilson F. "Bill" Minor remembered Smith in the mid-1940s "floating through the lobby of Biloxi's once-luxurious Buena Vista Hotel...as lustful eyes of country newspaper editors followed her every move. There were the dons of the Mississippi press...bowing and fawning over her...She was the sweetheart of the Mississippi press corps" (Whalen 44). And, finally, Hodding Carter III said Smith was "an extraordinarily attractive woman when she was young and lit up the press association meetings. You talk to those guys who were a little older than she and contemporaneous and a sort of wistful tone comes into their voices talking about just how pretty she was" (Whalen 45). When Smith was 35, Dorothy Doan of the International News Service said of her, "Hazel Brannon has more suitors than a magnolia tree has blooms. As the folks in Mississippi say, 'Hazel sure is a looker'" (Whalen 63).

Although contemporary scholars no longer focus on a woman's beauty, voluptuousness, or age in serious academic prose, the fact is that Smith caught the eye of those in her community and enjoyed doing so. She did not plan for herself the life that followed, and it is perhaps the surprises she encountered that help to explain the interest that readers and researchers continue to have in her.

Few of us can predict the twists and turns life will take, and Smith's responses when events began to move out of her control highlight her humanity. From a few biographical entries during the past few decades to a substantive biography in 2000, the story of Hazel Brannon Smith remains central to our understanding of race and ethnicity and the role of media in America, and her life is a reminder of both the joys and consequences of making unpopular decisions that challenge the status quo.

An Inauspicious Beginning

Hazel Brannon Smith was not born into power or privilege. She would not enjoy an Ivy League education. Smith's gregariousness, her ready laugh, and her professional focus made her an interesting young woman, but they do not explain entirely the way others have been drawn to her story. Hazel Freeman Brannon was born Feb. 5, 1914, in Alabama City, Alabama, near Gadsden, the seat of Etowah County. Her father Dock Boad Brannon was an electrical contractor and a wire inspector for Gulf States Steel; her mother Georgia Parthenia Freeman Brannon worked in the home. Both were active Southern Baptists. A black woman tended to the family, and Smith loved and relied upon her, sentiments she shared with Harper Lee and Carson McCullers in their near-autobiographies *To Kill a Mockingbird* and *The Member of the Wedding,* respectively.

Graduating in 1930 from Gadsden High School at the age of 16, she wrote for the weekly *Etowah Observer* from 1930-32 until she was old enough and ready to go to college. She reported news and sold advertising, skills upon which she would later rely. According to one description of her time at the *Observer,* "The editor, impressed with her talent, quickly promoted her to front-page reporting" (Moritz, ed., 384). Smith completed her B.A. degree in journalism with a minor in political science at the University of Alabama in Tuscaloosa in 1935, having been managing editor of the campus newspaper *(The Crimson-White)* and having enjoyed a busy social life along with her sorority sisters in Delta Zeta. As often as possible throughout this study, Hazel Brannon Smith will speak for herself, as she does eloquently in an essay entitled "Looking At The Old South Through Hazel Eyes":

> There were about 125 students in the Gadsden, Alabama High School senior class of 1930. The editor of the yearbook had the bright idea of using three adjectives to describe each member of the class. Under the name of Hazel Brannon, it read: "Industrious, independent, indomitable."
>
> I've learned since that those three qualities are not only valuable for a newspaper editor and publisher, but absolutely necessary if one is to survive and succeed.
>
> It's too bad the members of the White Citizens' Councils who wanted me dead, or at least out of Mississippi, many years later did not know about those three "I" descriptions of me as a high school senior. It would have saved all of us a lot of trouble and heartbreak.
>
> At the age of 18—after having worked for a weekly newspaper for nearly two years—I made up my mind what I wanted to do in life: edit and publish a weekly newspaper of my own. But I had to get my college degree from the University of Alabama first. Then I had to find a paper that I wanted in a nice community with prospects for growth and development in the future. (n.p.)

After graduation, Hazel Brannon Smith looked around and considered what she might do next. Except for the fact that she lived in the Deep South, that she was a woman, and that it was 1935, one logical possibility was to purchase a small weekly newspaper, an idea that appealed to her because of the encouragement she received at the *Etowah Observer.* A woman in this region of the country at this time was certain to confront her share of challenges. Smith was unlike most of the editors of weekly newspapers because of her youth, but she also surprised county residents because of her gender. Matthew J. Bosisio writes:

> She was also different in the fact that she was a woman operating in what was clearly a man's world in the South in the 1940s and 1950s. Even

outside the rural South, women struggled to be accepted by their male counterparts. While a number of women were making a name for themselves, such as Lorena Hickok of the Associated Press and Mary Baker Eddy of the *Christian Science Monitor,* women "remained marginal figures in the newspaper world until passage of civil rights legislation in 1964 that outlawed discrimination in employment on the grounds of sex as well as race." (73)

According to the *Current Biography Yearbook,* the *Durant News,* the Holmes County weekly that caught her eye, was called the "Durant Excuse" by its critics and had "exhausted three editors in the thirteen months prior to the purchase" (Moritz, ed., 384). Billy Snider, Mississippi lieutenant governor, is said to have told her: "Young lady, Durant has long been known as the graveyard of Mississippi journalism. If you can make a go of this newspaper, you can have anything you want in Mississippi journalism, or anywhere else for that matter" (Kaul, "Hazel Brannon Smith" 291). According to Kaul, "Despite a decrepit Linotype and press that often broke down on publication nights, Brannon boasted that 'we never missed an issue and were always at the post office in time'" ("Hazel Brannon Smith" 291).

Smith was drawn to Durant, a small town 12 miles east of Lexington, which boasted only 2,500 residents. Having borrowed $3,000 from a bank, Smith purchased the newspaper and proceeded to make it pay for itself and—in time—make a profit. In 1936, she moved to Holmes County, Mississippi, and set up shop as owner, publisher, and editor. At that time Holmes County, population 27,000, was "desperately poor" (n.p.), according to Bernard L. Stein, and the character of the county influenced Smith's plans for her newspaper:

> Realizing that her small weekly could not begin to compete with the larger daily newspapers in the coverage of state and national news, Miss Brannon made the Durant *News* a truly local paper, printing news of particular interest to the citizens of Holmes County—births, deaths, marriages, graduations, family reunions, arrests. As circulation more than doubled, to 1,400 readers, advertising revenues increased, and within four years the young editor completely paid for her paper. (Moritz, ed., 384)

Smith's strategy worked: "The local-news formula doubled subscriptions to almost fourteen hundred, increased advertising revenues, and enabled her to pay off the newspaper's mortgage in four years to become sole owner" (Kaul, "Hazel Brannon Smith" 292).

As noted earlier, in 1935 Smith and a college boyfriend had gone to Durant to look at a newspaper that was for sale. She had no idea how important that visit would be. Years later, in the words of a mature woman who understood the significance of her choices, she said:

> At age 21, I became the owner, publisher and editor of *The Durant News.* Seven years later, I bought the larger weekly paper in Holmes County, *The Lexington Advertiser,* again with borrowed money—and paid it off ahead

of schedule. As the owner of the only two newspapers in a county without radio stations, I became the voice of Holmes County. I didn't consider myself all that important, but I considered it my responsibility to do what I could to promote a county in which everybody could live in peace and without fear. ("Looking At The Old South Through Hazel Eyes" n.p.)

The *Durant News*, a financial liability, began making a profit within four years of Smith's leadership, and she would own the *News* from 1936 to 1985. Smith also purchased the *Banner County Outlook* in Flora, Mississippi, in 1955 (she was forced to sell it in 1977) and the *Northside Reporter* in Jackson, Mississippi, in 1956 (she was forced to sell it in 1973). Smith also helped to edit the *Baptist Observer,* a monthly newspaper for the largest African-American Baptist association in Mississippi.

In 1943, Smith bought the *Lexington Advertiser* in the county seat of Holmes County, the second-oldest newspaper in Mississippi. Here, too, she committed herself to local issues, participating in organizations that promoted the social, political, and economic climate of the town where she hoped to live her life and covering those organizations for the newspaper. *Current Biography Yearbook* reports that the "most influential enterprise" in Smith's soon-to-become "little journalistic empire" was the *Advertiser,* which served a "rural population dominated numerically by poor blacks but socially, economically, and politically by white truck farmers, small businessmen, and an occasional cotton planter" (Moritz, ed., 385).

In 1949, Smith met a ship purser for American President Lines from Pennsylvania, Walter Dyer (Smitty) Smith, on a cruise, and the two married March 21, 1950, at the First Baptist Church in Durant, Mississippi. Anxious to develop a social circle in Lexington, the couple engaged in many community activities and built a strong network during the 1940s. However, in his biography of Smith, John A. Whalen writes that by the early 1950s, the invitations to parties and other gatherings were diminishing: "Formerly in the midst of such social whirl as Lexington could boast, the couple now found that invitations to parties, luncheons and teas were quickly drying up" (81).

Throughout her career, the best known and most controversial of Smith's newspapers remained the *Lexington Advertiser,* the tough-minded little independent weekly in Holmes County. (Smith would be forced to sell the newspaper in 1987.) When Smith bought the newspaper, Lexington, Mississippi, was a small, rural town with 3,981 residents. At the time Smith began to purchase small weekly newspapers, 19,000 black residents in Holmes County outnumbered whites three to one. They were not represented in the newspapers produced in their communities: Few photographs of African Americans were printed, and even older, distinguished blacks were referred to by their first names.

Largely because of Smith's activist editorials, a group called the White Citizens' Council pressured advertisers to boycott her, and the boycott lasted between 10 and 17 years, depending upon the historical source. "Despite her positive outlook, Smith's prolonged economic battle with the Citizens' Council put her further into debt with each passing year" (96), said David Wallace. Characteristically, Smith was outspoken in her opposition to the group, writing on June 30, 1963, that her opposition "has been vindicated time after time in the past nine years as one after another good Mississippian has been smeared, lied about and given the Citizens' Council treatment—many of them now living in other communities or states. That we have survived at all is a miracle that we attribute only to God" ("Mississippi: Determined Lady" 38).

One biographer states that Smith's enemies in Lexington, Mississippi, founded the *Holmes County Herald* in 1958 as a direct attempt to drive her newspaper out of business. Another source indicates that Smith was forced to mortgage some of her business and personal property, reduce her staff, and borrow money in order to continue to publish: "An opposition paper was founded in 1959 [the first issue appeared in 1959] to cut into Mrs. Smith's readership, but by mortgaging her business and personal property, paring her staff from fifteen to five, and borrowing money she continued to publish" (Moritz, ed., 385).

In spite of the fact that beginning in 1958 the White Citizens' Council supported a new weekly designed to drive her out of business, by 1964, Smith was owner and publisher of weeklies that had a combined circulation of 10,000. There is no doubt that the advertising boycott by the White Citizens' Council devastated her, but in spite of the organization's formidable efforts, Smith succeeded in a way no one could have expected. An October 1997 article by Barbara Isaacs and Kevin Nance in the *Lexington* (Ky.) *Herald-Leader* quotes June Durff, assistant director of the Holmes County Chamber of Commerce, as saying that Lexington, Mississippi, is important largely because Smith once lived there: "She's kind of put us on the map" (n.p.), Durff said.

Certainly, the stands Smith took profoundly affected her social life and her ability to maintain friendships in her community. In retaliation for editorials Smith wrote in support of a black man who had been shot by a white law enforcement official, Smith endured further ostracism: "Also, when her friends started avoiding her, failing to stop in at the office to leave a news item, a classified ad or to renew a subscription, and snubbing her when sending out invitations...Hazel suffered so much from the rejection that she avoided the office more than ever, delegating many lesser tasks to employees" (Whalen 87). Ironically, early in her career, she supported segregation and criticized President Franklin Delano Roosevelt's New Deal. That her neighbors ostracized her is an indication of their own prejudice; certainly, she was far from being a social liberal.

While the editor who enjoyed parties and reveled in being with people no doubt understood that she was living during a time in which the social order was undergoing a seismic shift, there is nothing in her papers or biographical essays that suggests she knew that her belief in the tenets of community journalism would begin to have a cumulative negative impact on her finances and her health. Certainly, she and Smitty could have no idea that in 1964 she would become the first woman to win a Pulitzer Prize in editorial writing.

But the seeds of discord had been planted. Beneath the hospitality, civility, and treasured system of manners in the Deep South, the ground had begun to shake. Protected by white privilege, Smith and her husband could hardly imagine in the early 1950s what would eventually occur. Fourteen years after their marriage, an explosion would rock the printing plant for Smith's suburban Jackson weekly, the *Northside Reporter*. (Smith would have won the Pulitzer Prize and would be attending the Democratic National Convention when the devastation occurred.) Also during the early 1960s, James Meredith would enroll in the University of Mississippi. President John F. Kennedy would be assassinated. And during Freedom Summer, Smith would invite civil rights leader Martin Luther King Jr. to her home, unaware of what would happen to him. None of these events would occur without context or without warning, but Smitty and Hazel Brannon Smith could not have imagined what lay ahead.

At the time Smith bought her first newspapers, the social hierarchy was carefully protected and racism was the word of the day. Whalen describes the specifics of small-town Southern society:

> There were "white only" and "colored only" signs on the courthouse restroom doors, "white" and "colored" drinking fountains in front of the courthouse. Blacks were barred from certain restaurants, churches attended by whites, the public library and public park, with the children attending inferior "black only" schools, to which they walked while the white children rode buses to their schools. Blacks were required to step off the sidewalk when meeting whites, were to address them as "Mister," "Madam," "Miss," and so on, the men were to take off their hats in greeting whites and were not to expect whites to shake hands with them. They were always to go to the back door of a white person's house and, if allowed to enter, were not to take a seat.
>
> White law enforcement officers could shoot blacks unconcernedly, knowing that there was little or no likelihood that they would be brought to trial, and that, if they were, they would be assured of acquittal by an all-white jury. Only registered voters could serve on juries, blacks being kept from registering at the artifice of white county officials, backed by threats and violence from other whites intent on preserving the status quo. Lynchings were commonplace; nearly 600 blacks suffered violent deaths at the hands of whites in Mississippi between 1880 and 1940. (42-43)

Although one might call Hazel Brannon Smith an "activist journalist," she was not what Beasley would call a "fire-eater," a historically dramatic term for those who angrily and tenaciously espouse a particular cause, or what others have called a "crusading editor." Smith's trouble in her community escalated slowly, and her crime was simply her determination to produce fair and responsible community journalism.

A Time of Conflict

In 1943, the same year that Hazel Brannon Smith bought the *Lexington Advertiser* and began to fulfill her professional dreams, she "ran afoul of local authority by chiding law enforcement officials about their winking at bootlegging and gambling violators" (303), said historian Sam G. Riley. Defining herself as an anti-communist and a supporter of Senator Joseph McCarthy and his witch-hunts, Smith opposed federal welfare policies and did not think of herself as a liberal in any sense of that word. She described herself as a political and social moderate. She was a Baptist, a law-abiding citizen, and an observant journalist; she knew that those responsible for upholding the law in Lexington were averse to doing so, and she knew her newspaper should address the community's concerns.

Bootlegging had become big business in the formerly peaceful county. Walter J. Murtagh of Pickens became sheriff and promised to enforce the law, but according to Smith, "bootlegging proliferated": "I began letting the people know that something was wrong. I wrote a warning in the newspaper. I said that I was adopting a policy effective the following week: If anyone was arrested and charged with a crime which involved drunkenness, or other serious offenses, I would print the name of the person arrested and what they were arrested for." Smith demanded that the sheriff earn the salary the people were paying him: "In the newspaper, I called on the sheriff to enforce the law. When he still didn't take any action, I wrote in my column *Through Hazel Eyes,* which ran on the left side of the front page, that I had talked to the sheriff and offered him space in the newspaper to make any kind of statement he'd like to make about his plans for the rest of his term. 'This is what he said,' I wrote. Then I left the rest of the column blank" ("Looking At The Old South Through Hazel Eyes" n.p.).

According to Mark Newman, pressure exerted by her tiny newspaper led to 64 indictments for organized crime by a grand jury in April 1946 (n.p.). According to Kaul, the investigation returned 52 indictments for "prohibition and gambling violations" the day after the *Advertiser* "suggested that the sheriff resign or enforce the law" ("Hazel Brannon Smith" 293). Although Kaul said Smith was "exuberant," the trouble had begun: "The Holmes County law enforcement establishment—judge, jury, prosecutor, county attorney, and sheriff—was unaccustomed to a thirty-two-year-old newspaperwoman's stinging editorial criticism. They retaliated" ("Hazel Brannon Smith" 293).

In 1946, probably as part of the retaliation, Smith was found guilty of contempt of court. The court case involved an African-American man who had been whipped to death. Without knowing that talking to the widow of the murder victim was prohibited by the court, she engaged the woman in conversation in a hallway in the courthouse. She was charged with attempting to "embarrass," "hinder," and "impair" the court's proceedings ("Hazel Brannon Smith" 294), according to Kaul. The judge issued the following statement:

I sympathize with you and am sorry you got in this mess, but you brought it on yourself. I realize you are putting on a great campaign for law and order but if you read history you will see that the only perfect being didn't make much of a hit with his reform. He reformed a few and left this advice, "Before you clean up someone else clean up yourself"...I have been around a long time and know the job...I don't believe you can do it. I am of the opinion that when Gabriel blows his horn and rolls back the scroll of Heaven he will find the world like it is today...I wish you had stayed out of this mess. It reminds me of what the Irishman said when he saw the bull run head-on into the train. "I admire your spunk but doubt your judgment." You have run head-on to this court. When called up you proceeded to give the Court a curt lecture as to his duties. (Kaul, "Hazel Brannon Smith" 294)

The details of the case are important, both because Smith was a model of courage so early in her journalistic career and because they illustrate the social climate of the day. Near Durant, someone had stolen a saddle from a white farmer named J.F. Dodd ; eventually, the community would learn that two children on his property had taken the saddle. However, Dodd accused Leon McAtee, a black man who had lived on Dodd's property all his life, of the theft, and he was put in jail. Dodd dropped the charges, McAtee was released into his custody, and a week later, McAtee's body was found in a bayou in Sunflower County. Six white men were jailed for the crime, including Dodd. All were later acquitted.

Smith carried the story in the *Durant News* and the *Lexington Advertiser*, and the Holmes County courtroom was crowded every day of the trial. When Smith interviewed Henrietta McAtee, the widow of the murdered man, outside the courtroom, she was told she had violated Judge S.F. Davis' order. "I apologized and told him that if I had committed a crime, it had been out of ignorance. But the next day he charged me with contempt, and fined me $50 and sentenced me to 15 days in jail...In open court, he chided me for carrying out a 'great campaign' to clean up the bootlegging and gambling in Holmes County...The judge clearly showed that he was punishing me not for contempt of court, but for my three-year crusade against the lawlessness of the local power structure" ("Looking At The Old South Through Hazel Eyes" n.p.).

Although she was devastated by the conflict with the judge, not everyone agreed with him. A day after she was charged with contempt of court, an editorial in the *Jackson Daily News* called Smith a "brave, lionhearted woman" who had waged a "gallant battle" against the "reign of lawlessness" in a place in which "she gets no aid or encouragement" from law enforcement. Smith then appealed to the Mississippi Supreme Court, which later dismissed the charges against her ("Looking at the Old South Through Hazel Eyes" n.p.). In the April 7, 1947, opinion, the court said there was "wholly insufficient proof" for the charge of contempt and overturned the decision against her (Kaul, "Hazel Brannon Smith" 294).

One of Hazel Brannon Smith's supporters during this time was Ira B. Harkey Jr., who is featured in the second chapter of this study. When he won the Pulitzer Prize for editorial writing in 1963, she wrote, "We should like to add our sincere congratulations to Editor Ira and this fine honor which he has brought to our state. Long may you live and prosper, Sir" *(Smell* 1967, 124). Their respect was mutual. In his autobiography, Harkey writes of Smith: "She is now a courageous and eloquent speaker for civil rights and in 1964 won the Pulitzer Prize for her long-time editorial opposition to misused official power" *(Smell* 1967, 80). Specifically, he refers to his colleague's having been "unmercifully persecuted for objecting to the killing of a Negro by a local law officer" *(Smell* 1967, 80).

The event to which Harkey refers involves a 1954 editorial in which Smith denounces a local sheriff, Richard F. Byrd, as unfit to occupy office. Hazel Brannon Smith did not intend to oppose Jim Crow laws; in fact, a few days after the Supreme Court ruled in 1954 that "segregated schools are not equal and cannot be made equal," she attacked the ruling of the high court in "Through Hazel Eyes," a column on the front page of her newspapers. She worried about intermarriage between people of different races, and she believed that blood banks should not risk mixing blood donated by whites and blood given by blacks. But, as journalist Stein later wrote, "on the Fourth of July weekend, 1954, Sheriff Richard Byrd shot Henry Randall and Mrs. Smith's life began to change" ("This Female Crusading Scalawag").

Telling Henry Randall (spelled "Randle" by Kaul and Whalen) to "get goin'," the sheriff shot the 27-year-old man in the leg as he fled. After investigating the case and interviewing eye-witnesses, Smith believed Byrd shot the young man in the leg without provocation and called for his resignation. In an editorial, the newspaper owner and publisher—who did not believe in integrated schools, in miscegenation, or in storing the blood of African Americans and of whites together in a blood bank—wrote on July 15, 1954:

> The laws in America are for everyone—rich and poor, strong and weak, white and black and all the other races that dwell within our land...
> This kind of thing cannot go on any longer.
> It must be stopped.
> The vast majority of Holmes county people are not red necks who look with favor on the abuse of people because their skins are black...
> [Sheriff Byrd] has violated every concept of justice, decency, and right in his treatment of some of the people in Holmes county. He has shown us without question that he is not fit to occupy that high office.
> He should, in fact, resign. (Kaul, "Hazel Brannon Smith" 295)

Byrd sued for libel. An all-male, all-white jury found in favor of Byrd in October 1954 and issued a $10,000 judgment against Smith for libel. The state supreme court overturned the ruling in November 1955, but the battle was costly. In the time between the judgment and the appeal, Smith refused to budge, calling the sheriff a liar and saying he had "no more remorse than an egg-sucking dog" (Kaul, "Hazel Brannon Smith" 295). Although at the time Smith did not know the price she would pay for her advocacy, others suspected. Dr. Arenia C. Mallory, president of all-black Saints Junior College, said that the case involving Henry Randall was the catalyst for Smith's professional demise: "This story reduced her from a woman of almost wealth to a woman who has had to struggle like the rest of us," said Mallory. "She defended a little boy who couldn't defend himself" (Moritz, ed., 385).

Conflicts with law enforcement and judicial officials led to Smith's financial undoing. One of the retaliatory acts that would affect her finances profoundly involved her husband, who was fired from his job as the Holmes County Community Hospital's administrator in January 1956. Kaul cites one hospital administrator, who told a *Jackson Daily News* reporter that Smitty was fired because his wife had "become a controversial figure" ("Hazel Brannon Smith" 296). To no avail, more than 40 local business leaders asked that Smitty be retained. In June 1957, nearly 18 months after Byrd's libel suit had been overturned by the state supreme court, she still owed her lawyers $2,538 (Whalen 105), and her financial situation would not improve.

In addition to her campaign against crime in Holmes County and her demand that a sheriff resign, Smith protested the police shooting of Alfred Brown, a mental patient and a black World War II veteran, in 1963. Witnesses said Brown pulled out a pocketknife after being hit with a crowbar by police, and he was shot twice and died as officers reportedly tried to arrest him for being drunk. (The event occurred just days before the murder of Medgar Evers.)

The two Lexington police officers involved filed and later dropped a $100,000 libel suit against Smith for the editorial she wrote in response to the event. "Senseless Killing," published June 13, 1963, deals with what she considered an avoidable act by angry law enforcement officers. Her passion for justice is clear, and the reporting is fair and balanced even in an opinion piece. Her suggestions about how to prevent such an occurrence in the future make it obvious where she believes the fault lies:

> Many Lexington citizens have expressed concern and regret that a 38-year-old Negro war veteran was shot and killed in our community Saturday night by city policemen.
>
> From all accounts of reliable eye witnesses, the killing was senseless and could have been avoided by officers who either knew or cared what they were doing.
>
> In these days of high tension and widespread racial strife, it would appear that officers sworn to uphold the law and protect all of the people would make a special effort to discharge their duties coolly and without bias; that they would go the extra mile to avoid giving even the appearance of oppressing any citizen of whatever color or status.
>
> No person blames an officer for defending himself when his life is threatened by a criminal when he is in real danger. We do not believe in coddling criminals or law breakers in any fashion. But such was clearly not the case on Saturday night.

The victim was a harmless sick man who had never been in trouble his whole life with anyone, a man who had served our country honorably in the armed forces. His natural resentment of an unprovoked arrest on a false and baseless charge, his instantaneous fear of being locked up in the Holmes county jail, was and is understandable.

If we are to continue to have racial peace here, the present situation needs a great deal of improvement from the standpoint of law enforcement—and spirit and attitude as well. Officers guilty of lawless or unbecoming conduct should be made to give an accounting of their actions, the same as ordinary citizens.

An honest and complete investigation should be made by competent authorities—and no whitewash attempted.

And officers should be ordered to treat with respect and dignity all people with whom they come in contact. (Beasley and Harlow 94)

Also in the summer of 1963, Smith championed the first African American in Lexington who tried to register to vote. In an interview with Beasley and Harlow, Smith said that Hartman Turnbow, 58, of Tchula was among several black men who tried to register to vote in Holmes County, but they were refused and sent home. A month after his attempt to register, his house caught fire. Smith became suspicious and launched an investigation. Three white men shot at Turnbow and his wife and daughter when they ran away from the burning house, and Turnbow was arrested, along with four voter-registration workers, and charged with arson:

So when I heard his house had been firebombed, well, my husband and I went over to his house and took pictures of the place. He had a nice little home and he had done all this work on his house himself and then of course they were saying that he fired it himself, when any fool would know that a man doesn't work there for months and months, screening the front porch and putting steps in and all that and then turn around and burn his own house. (Beasley and Harlow 89)

An FBI investigation followed, and during the trial, Smith testified that she heard Sheriff Andrew Smith say, "I don't intend that any Negroes will vote while I'm sheriff" (Kaul, "Hazel Brannon Smith" 298).

What is not in question is that during Smith's time as editor, "crosses were burned on her lawn, her husband lost his job as administrator of [Holmes County Community Hospital], her paper went $100,000 into debt, and her offices were firebombed" (274), according to an almanac. On Oct. 31, 1960, several teenage boys burned a cross in the yard at Smith's house. She identified them and published an editorial entitled "A Cross Burns— Symptom of a Community Illness." And on July 12, 1967, the *Advertiser* was firebombed. Whalen writes:

The blaze was brought under control about two hours later but the building was partially gutted by the fire which originated in the pressroom. As agents of the state fire marshal's office and the FBI began investigations later than morning, workmen removed loads of water-logged newsprint and newspapers from the building. The loss was estimated in excess of $10,000. Although most of the fire damage was confined to the pressroom, the entire plant and offices sustained severe damage from water and smoke. Valuable files and bound volumes were destroyed. (225)

Belated Recognition

In spite of the years of conflict and fear for her personal and financial survival, Hazel Brannon Smith eventually knew she was appreciated and held in high esteem by many in and outside of Mississippi. She knew who she was. "I've been liberated all my life" (Beasley and Harlow 85), Smith said, acknowledging her strength and determination. Although she died alone at the age of 80, by then she had received a Pulitzer Prize, had watched a made-for-television film about her life, and had heard from friends and relatives who recognized her contributions before, during, and after the civil rights movement.

One of her strongest supporters is Stein, formerly of the *Riverdale Press* in the Bronx. "Hazel Brannon Smith endured more than 20 years of violence, ostracism, and economic strangulation" in order to speak what she perceived to be the truth and in order to protect the freedom of the press and the people the press served, according to Stein. "Ultimately, however, the campaign succeeded in driving Hazel Brannon Smith out of business—but not before her name became a symbol not just of courage, but of honor. Her nationwide fame has faded, her name is unfamiliar to a new generation of journalists" (n.p.). Fortunately, Stein's final statement is no longer true; in fact, a biography and a substantial amount of research by historians have helped to insure that students of journalism will know about her.

Without accounting for the ideological chasm that often separates a conservative from another part of the country from one from the Deep South during the civil rights movement, Stein disagrees with those who consider Smith to be a moderate. Since he is far from alone in his assessment, this chapter includes his tribute as part of her formidable historical legacy. Of those who consider Smith a moderate, Stein said:

> None of them can have read and absorbed the body of Hazel Brannon Smith's writing during the civil rights era. From the time the Holmes County movement began with the arrival of SNCC [Student Nonviolent Coordinating Committee] organizers in Mileston and Hartman Turnbow's effort to register to vote in 1963, relentlessly, week in and week out, "Through Hazel Eyes" and her editorials advocate justice for African Americans. They burn with indignation...While most of Mississippi's journalists joined its politicians in denouncing "outside agitators," Mrs. Smith welcomed the 33 Freedom Summer volunteers who came to Holmes County to organize Freedom Schools and to register blacks to vote...Hazel Brannon Smith was no moderate. She was a wholehearted

supporter of integration and of black political power who loathed the inter-twined apparatus of the government, Citizens' Council and Klan that un-derpinned American apartheid. ("This Female Crusading Scalawag" n.p.)

In many ways, Hazel Brannon Smith's Pulitzer Prize was based on her extensive canon of editorials, but it was given in particular recognition of her 1963 work. The Pulitzer Prize committee awarded her their highest honor in 1964 for editorial writing, citing her "steadfast adherence to her editorial duties in the face of great pressure and opposition." Notified by phone on May 4, 1964, about the Pulitzer, she asked the caller, Rick Fried-man of *Editor & Publisher,* "Are you sure, Rick?" He said he was quite sure (Whalen 164).

The Pulitzer Prize was far from the only award Smith received during her lifetime. Others include the Golden Quill Award from the International Society of Weekly Newspaper Editors (1963) and the "Woman of Con-science" award from the National Council of Women of the U.S. (1964). (The first award had gone to Rachel Carson for her 1962 book *Silent Spring.)* In 1993, she won the Fannie Lou Hamer Award at a ceremony at Jackson State University (Smith's friends accepted the award for her).

Smith was a member of the Mississippi Council of Human Relations, a representative of the Mississippi Advisory Committee to the U.S. Civil Rights Commission, the secretary of the Holmes County Democratic Ex-ecutive Committee (1940-48), and a delegate to the Democratic National Convention (1940, 1944). Smith was a former director of the Mississippi chapter of the National Editorial Association and a member of the Missis-sippi Council on Human Relations and the Mississippi Delta Council. In 1964, she was named "Mississippi Woman of the Year."

She won the Elijah Parish Lovejoy Award for Courage in Journalism given by the University of Southern Illinois (1960), which is named for an abolitionist editor killed by a mob in Alton, Illinois, in 1837. In Stephen A. Banning's article about those awarded the Elijah Parish Lovejoy prize, he lists the following qualifications for winners: "1) all of the Lovejoy Award winners suffered severe economic hardship; 2) all, except for one, endured physical threats or attacks; 3) six tackled political machines; 4) four won the award for taking a stand on matters of race" (64). Hazel Brannon Smith qualifies on all four criteria.

She also won the Theta Sigma Phi National Headliner award (1962). Other recognition includes awards from the National Federation of Press Women (1946, 1955), the Herrick Award for Editorial Writing (1956), and a special citation from the Mississippi Press Association (1957). She also received accolades from Women in Communications and the National Edi-torial Association. She was president of the International Society of Weekly Newspaper Editors (1981-82).

A documentary entitled "An Independent Voice" (1973) featured her and other small-town editors. The 30-minute film premiered at the Henry R. Luce Hall of News Reporting in the Smithsonian Institution Museum of Science and Industry on May 3, 1973, in connection with a National Press

Club gathering. Smith was the featured speaker when the tribute to journal-ists from John Peter Zenger to herself was shown.

"A Passion for Justice: The Hazel Brannon Smith Story" (1994) starred Jane Seymour as Smith and D.W. Moffett as Smitty and brought her even more attention, although, according to Newman, the film was made without the help or consent of her family (n.p.). Perhaps because of the memory loss she was suffering during this time period, she showed little response to see-ing the film. "The movie made it look like there was a happy ending, but there just wasn't any happy ending" (Bosisio 80), said Minor.

There is no doubt that Smith underestimated her importance; in fact, she described herself as "just a little editor in a little spot." This litote may have seemed accurate to her, but it was not then and is not now an apt de-scription. "A lot of other little editors in a lot of other little spots is what helps make this country," Smith said. "It's either going to help protect that freedom that we have or else it's going to let that freedom slip away by de-fault" (Moritz, ed., 384). In this statement lies an indication of her aware-ness that the times were changing and that she and other editors had played at least a small part in the evolution of the society.

Kaul claims that by the time Smith began to suffer from memory loss in 1985 (perhaps due to the onset of Alzheimer's disease), she had filed for bankruptcy and owed $250,000, including $34,000 in newspaper printing bills ("Hazel Brannon Smith" 300). According to another scholar, during these difficult days, Smith "borrowed heavily and mortgaged her home to keep publishing but in the 1970s had to close the Banner County paper and sell the *Northside Reporter.* Eventually she found herself a pariah to whites and to blacks, an ally they no longer needed" (Riley 304). Smith filed for bankruptcy in the fall of 1985 and closed both remaining papers. "After 10 years of economic, legal, and social attacks, the one-time socialite was left deeply in debt and largely isolated in the local community" (18), writes Wallace. After foreclosure on Hazelwood, where her property and personal belongings were sold at auction, she moved to Gadsden, Alabama, to be with her sister. Kaul writes:

> She got lost en route from Lexington to a mandatory bankruptcy-court hearing in Jackson in November, and her bankruptcy case was dismissed for her failure to appear. The bank foreclosed, taking her newspaper and repossessing Hazelwood [Smith's home]; her furniture was auctioned. In February 1986 Smith's sister quietly took her back to an obscure and pen-niless retirement in Gadsden, Alabama. ("Hazel Brannon Smith" 300)

Smith's front-page column, "Through Hazel Eyes," which began in 1936 and ran throughout most of her career, earned her national recognition. In her column, Smith argued against social injustices and promoted causes that drew retaliation. Those causes included support for a local venereal disease treatment clinic and opposition to slot machine operators, bootleg-gers, gamblers, and corrupt local politicians. Arguing that newspapers in the South had "largely ignored our responsibilities to our Negro citizens"

(Newman, "Hazel Brannon Smith" n.p.), Smith grieved about the emotional and financial toll her beliefs had taken on her and her family. "God has been with me," said the lifelong Baptist. "If he hadn't, I'd be insane or dead" (Moritz, ed., 386).

Having been a hospital administrator and the executive director for Mississippi Action for Progress, which was responsible for establishing the Head Start program, Smitty worked alongside his wife throughout their marriage. Three years after he died in 1983, Smith moved to her sister's home in Gadsden and then later to Tennessee in order to be near her nieces. Smith died May 14, 1994, of cancer at a nursing home in Cleveland, Tennessee, and was buried in Forrest Cemetery in Gadsden.

In his article "In the South—When It Mattered to Be an Editor," Dudley Clendinen writes of the 11 of 15 Pulitzer Prizes for editorial writing from 1946 to 1971 that went to Southern editors. Only one of those recipients was a woman, "but none was any braver" (18), he said. "She had fought the back-shooting segregationist sheriffs and other dark lights of the Delta for 10 years before she won the prize in 1964. She endured personal ostracism, bombing and economic boycott until her husband's career and her own finances were ruined, until the unrepaired roof over her press fell in, until she ran out of money and finally lost her mind to old age" (18).

The traumatic events in her life and the tragic circumstances that surrounded her death are in some ways mitigated by her successes. It is still difficult, however, to deal with the physical reminders of her hardest times. With the last edition of the *Lexington Advertiser* on Sept. 19, 1985, Smith closed the second oldest newspaper in the state: "To this day, the derelict Advertiser building in the shadow of Lexington's town square sits open to the elements, as though to remind those with long-enough memories of the price of defiance" (n.p.), Stein said.

Her legacy of compassion and defiance, Stein argues, remains in the lives and tributes of those she left behind, including those in the African-American community. "A group of men passing the time this February in a small convenience store, near the spot where Alfred Brown fell, talked of the killing and of Mrs. Smith's exposé as though it had happened four days, not four decades, ago," Stein said. "Her newspapers 'let the peoples [sic] know what was going on and didn't hide anything,' said Odell Durham, who joined the movement in 1964 when a white Freedom Summer volunteer knocked on her door and asked, 'Don't you want equal rights?'" ("This Female Crusading Scalawag" n.p.).

Beliefs about Race and Ethnicity

In spite of Smith's notable achievements, it is important not to deify this hard-working woman of conviction. She would not tolerate it, and, in fact, it is in her struggle with moral issues that she most resembles the rest of us.

Although, as Kaul says, she "gloried in being a newspaperwoman" ("Hazel Brannon Smith" 291), Smith shared with many of her Southern neighbors a belief in the separation of the races.

Although late in her career she supported the influx of civil rights workers into her state—noting that they would not have needed to come if white Southerners had acknowledged their responsibility to their black neighbors—it is questionable how far Smith was willing to go ideologically in her quest for justice for all people.

In an editorial "The South's Racial Problem," published in July 1943, Smith revealed her early reluctance to accept African Americans as equals. Her benign expressions of compassion are troubling:

> The white man and the black man have dwelt together in peace and harmony in the south for many, many years, because each has known his place and kept it. Each has had his own ideals, customs, and habits and they have not conflicted...as some of our meddling friends would have us believe...
>
> The vast majority of the colored race in the south know that the white man is his friend; when he is in trouble the first person he goes to is a white friend. And the white friend doesn't let him down. He values highly the friendship of his negro friends...
>
> But the south and America are a white man's country and both races know it...
>
> Southern white people are at last beginning to recognize the existence of trouble incited by people from the outside who have made a second carpetbagging expedition into the south under the guise of the New Deal...
>
> We in our own way and in our own time as best we can will work out a better world for both ourselves and the negro in the south. But we will not be hamstrung nor dictated to by the group in this nation who would tell us how to run our elections and our state. (Kaul, "Hazel Brannon Smith" 292-93)

And later, on May 20, 1954, Smith responded to the *Brown v. Board of Education* decision by continuing to advocate for segregation even as she cautioned against over-reacting to the court's mandate:

> The Supreme Court may be morally right when it says that "separate educational facilities are inherently unequal."
>
> But we know, for practical purposes, that separate educational facilities are highly desirable in the South and other places where the two races live and work side by side. We know that it is to the best interest of both races that segregation be maintained in theory and in fact—and that where it isn't maintained trouble results...
>
> The present situation has all of the ingredients necessary for a bloody revolution—if people don't keep their heads. (Kaul, "Hazel Brannon Smith" 294)

Media critics and historians disagree about how significant were the changes in Smith's attitudes. Kaul cites a 1952 editorial in which Smith argued that the election of President Dwight D. Eisenhower would cause a "thorough housecleaning that will rid our national government of all the pinks and reds and the pro-Soviet sympathizers that have been feeding at the expense of the American taxpayers for so long" ("Hazel Brannon Smith" 294). She was in the beginning, as Kaul suggests, "an ultraconservative states' rights Dixiecrat" ("Hazel Brannon Smith" 294). Of even more concern are some of the contemporary assessments. For example, Riley argues in his dictionary of newspaper columnists that Smith eventually advocated equal rights for all American citizens but never became a "true integrationist" (304). On the other hand, in a feature for "Mississippi History Now," Newman calls her development a "transformation" and argues that it occurred because her belief in "Christianity, law and order, public education, and economic development increasingly conflicted with the attempt of leaders in both state and local governments to preserve white supremacy and segregation" (n.p.).

There is little doubt that Smith was conflicted about issues of race in the South. She argued for segregation but supported equality before the law; she could not understand how the two beliefs could be contradictory. Although she opposed the integration of schools following the 1954 ruling *Brown v. Board of Education* ("We know that it is to the best interest of both races that segregation be maintained in theory and in fact—that where it isn't maintained trouble results"), Smith also argued that the South should have worked harder to maintain and fund schools for blacks (Kaul, "Hazel Brannon Smith" 294).

Admittedly, Smith was capable of strong attacks on racist attitudes, even when she might have had trouble spotting similar attitudes in herself. For example, a week after the disappearance of three civil rights workers in Mississippi in the summer of 1964, Smith appeared on a panel for the American Newspaper Women's Club in Washington, D.C. There she said, "You don't have to have a sheet to belong to the Klan. It's as much a state of mind as anything else" (Whalen 171).

One reason for her internal conflict may have been what some critics consider her inability to reconcile segregation with her own Christian beliefs about love, tolerance, and justice. Kaul suggests that "her views moderated when her law-and-order brand of Christian morality confronted the racial bigotry and violence that erupted during the mid 1950s" ("Hazel Brannon Smith" 300-301). However, it is clear that throughout most of her writing, Smith argued for the separation of the races. As noted earlier, in one of the most extreme examples, Smith attacked the "half-baked ideas" of the New Deal and the abandonment of "white supremacy principles" in the South by advocating the separation of the blood donated by different races at blood banks: "Good negro citizens...no more want white blood in their veins than does the white man want negro blood. The communistic influences that would mix the two do not have the interest of either at heart" (Kaul, "Hazel Brannon Smith" 293), she wrote.

When integration became the focus of conversation in her hometown in 1954, Smith said she "wasn't for it and...wasn't against it": "I recognized that forced segregation creates an inherently unequal situation" (Beasley and Harlow 90). The white community feared that "school integration would be followed by social contacts and marriage...and the thought of Negro blood in white veins was repugnant and horrible to them" (Beasley and Harlow 90), Smith said. Because there were three times more blacks than whites, Smith said the community also feared the "blacks taking over the county completely" (Beasley and Harlow 91):

> The black man was going to get that vote and if in the interim they (the whites) acted so badly that they earned the undying hatred of the blacks, then there could never be an accommodation between the blacks and whites in the county and the county would, in fact, eventually become all black as they feared. (Beasley and Harlow 91)

In spite of the fact that she had never wanted to be called a "crusading editor" (Moritz, ed., 386) and in spite of the fact that she maintained racist beliefs through much of her career, Hazel Brannon Smith was praised in her *New York Times* obituary for her crusading spirit and for her "stance against racism." The obituary was published May 16, 1994, and was datelined Cleveland, Tennessee. Two paragraphs are cited here:

> For 20 years, she prospered as a country editor, crusading against bootleg racketeering and becoming known for her broad-brimmed hats and her Cadillac convertible...
> As a result of her stands, Mrs. Smith's newspaper became the target of an economic boycott, and the segregationist White Citizens Council started an opposition paper. The boycott lasted 10 years, drained Mrs. Smith financially and eventually forced The Advertiser to close. But she continued to speak out against racism and bigotry. (B8)

As always, it is important to let Hazel Brannon Smith speak for herself as much as possible. One of her essays is especially worth inclusion in this study, and it appears here in its entirety:

> LEXINGTON, Miss.—The years of trouble began in 1954.
> A prominent local man walked into my newspaper office one hot day in July and asked to talk to me privately. I owned and edited *The Lexington Advertiser,* the only newspaper in Lexington, a town of 2,500 that was 55 miles north of Jackson. He told me that a meeting was going to be held that night at the Lexington Elementary School. I naturally assumed that he wanted publicity for the meeting, but he said only men would be allowed to attend. He said he wanted my "cooperation" with something called a "Citizens' Council," to be organized that night. The U.S. Supreme Court had just weeks before handed down its landmark decision against school segregation. The Citizens' Council, he said, would work to maintain segregation in the public schools using legal, nonviolent tactics.

"If a Nigra won't go along with our thinking on what's best for the community as a whole," the man told me, "he'll simply have his credit cut off."

"What do you think the Negroes are going to think," I asked, "when they hear that the white men are organizing?"

"Well, it might be a good thing for them to be a little scared," he replied.

"No," I said, "It's not a good thing for anyone to be a little scared. People can't live under fear, and it will end up with all of us scared and it will be a big scare. What you are proposing to do is take away the freedom of all the people in this community."

Despite my protests, the meeting was a success. The Holmes County Citizens' Council, which soon signed up most of the white men in the county, joined the growing white Citizens' movement in Mississippi. Members donated money to fund private, white-only schools in the county. The Council said it would use economic sanctions against any blacks who tried to break the color barriers in the state, and if any whites should oppose the Council's objectives it proposed to use social and political pressures. Their slogan seemed to be: "You are for us or against us. There is no middle ground."

I was opposed to the Council from the start, and I spoke out against it in my two weekly newspapers. For the first time, we had the lawless element and the so-called elite of the community involved in one organization with a common cause. The idea was that "we" could present a solid, united stand. I dissented by presuming to say that the truth had to be printed. As a result, I became one of the Councils' chief targets.

The Councils said that if we buried our heads in the sand long enough, the problem would go away. It was the technique of the big lie, like Hitler: tell it often enough and everybody will believe it. It finally got to the point where bank presidents and leading physicians were afraid to speak their honest opinions, because of this monster among us.

Over the next 15 years, as the Councils' influence spread to the highest offices in the state, my newspapers were boycotted, bombed and burned, a new newspaper was organized in Lexington to put me out of business, my life was threatened, and my husband lost his job as county hospital administrator—all because of pressure brought by this professional hate-peddling organization.

In the beginning, delegations of Council members went around to all stores that advertised with me in Lexington and tried to influence those merchants to cancel their business. Each Monday morning when the Advertiser came out, Council members would canvas the town in groups of two. They would walk into a store and confront the owner with, "We see you had another ad in Hazel's paper this week." These were people who knew each other, who attended the same church or were members of the same Rotary club. The merchants wanted to retain their local business, both black and white. For three years, most resisted the boycott.

Then a small group of die-hard segregationists began a campaign to find someone who would come to Lexington and start a newspaper: "A paper that will think like we do," they told some local businessmen. One paper was started in a community some miles from Lexington. It published just long enough to be awarded a year's contract to print the proceedings of the monthly county board of supervisors meetings. I continued to publish the monthly proceedings without pay because I did not want anyone to be forced to subscribe to a newspaper just to keep up with the supervisors.

It was during this time that I bought two more small weekly papers in other parts of the state. I had made up my mind that I was going to live in Mississippi the rest of my life—and if Holmes County should get so bad that I couldn't stand it, then I would have two other papers to keep me busy.

One night about 9 o'clock, my husband, Walter B. Smith, and I were finishing that week's edition of one of our newly acquired newspapers in suburban Jackson. Smitty had been fired as administrator of the local county hospital, despite the petitions of the entire medical staff. Suddenly, the telephone rang. It was my shop foreman at the Advertiser. It turned out that Council members in Lexington had decided to form a corporation and start publishing a new newspaper in a community that could barely support the one it already had. They called it the Holmes County Herald and they offered my foreman the job of editor. He was only the first of many editors hired by the Herald, which was governed by a board whose principals were Council members—including two prominent state representatives—bent on maintaining forever an entirely white school system. The new newspaper was organized for one purpose—to put me out of business—principally because the Council could not control my news and editorial policies.

My life had always been comfortable in Lexington. My two papers in Holmes County were paid for. I wore good clothes, and drove a Cadillac convertible. I went to Europe on vacation for four months and had more money in my bank account when I returned than I did when I left. But the boycott and the hate campaign wore my business down. The Council-backed newspaper depleted my advertising revenues, and I fell into deep debt. I began mortgaging my property, and cut my workforce by two-thirds.

But with the Councils growing more vicious and dictatorial, and becoming more influential in the state with each passing year, I could not abandon my battle. In the early 1960s, I wrote in an editorial in *The Advertiser:*

We cannot hold down more than 42 percent of our entire state population without staying down ourselves—and all intelligent people know it.

This greatest of nations was not built by men who were afraid. The Magnolia State was not carved out of a wilderness by the fearful and timid. And we cannot live and truly progress in today's atmosphere of fear—an atmosphere engendered by the Citizens' Council and its professional agitators who apparently are now running our state and setting its policies, even to the point of intimidating the Legislature.

If we lose our personal freedom, what does it matter what our masters call themselves?

Gestapo rule in Mississippi? It is nearer than we think.

Hate handbills were distributed against me. "Her Communist holiday is just about over," one said. Vandals tore up my lawn furniture one night. Another night, after returning home from a 4-H Club dinner, I was drinking coffee in the kitchen when I heard what sounded like a firecracker. I ran to the window. It looked like my magnolia tree was on fire in the front yard. But it was a cross burning—set by local high school boys who were reacting to what they heard at home about me.

"This is the world of change," I wrote in an editorial. "The old way of doing things will not suffice in this day and age. We cannot stop the clock. We ignore these facts at our own peril."

The FBI told my husband they had information that a segregationist group was "going to kill me." Shortly after I appeared on the nationally televised "Today" show with two black Democrats who were prominent in national politics, one of my newspapers was firebombed. The darkroom and some photographic equipment was destroyed. A group called "Americans For the Preservation of the White Race" claimed responsibility.

Some weeks later, a fire started in the press room of the Advertiser, causing minor damage. State fire officials determined that it was arson, but the guilty party could never be found. Several hundred local people were drawn to the pre-dawn fire scene. During the entire time I was there, not one person came up to say they were sorry about my loss.

The era of terror and violence continued through the 1960's, but the South was changing. When civil rights activist Medgar Evers was murdered in Mississippi in 1963, I wrote: "Far from killing the freedom movement in Mississippi, the perpetrator of the crime only made it certain that interest will be increased tenfold. New leaders will arrive to take Evers' place—and they will not be as moderate in their views, or as patient, reasonable, and understanding of the white man's position and views as was our friend, Medgar. God help us when the Negro starts hating in Mississippi."

The Holmes County Herald was bought out by an independent newspaperman in 1970, and that was the end of the Council's heavy-handed reign. Now my problems are purely monetary because of the economic hardness of these times. Holmes County is poor. Farming is the main way of making a living. There is no way that two newspapers in Lexington can make a good living.

But the circle is now complete. One of the high school boys who participated in the cross burning on my lawn recently came back to ask my pardon. He is now head of a large government agency in Mississippi. And when we buried my husband Smitty, who died in an accidental fall, our old enemies were there to express their sorrow at his death. (n.p.)

The essay "Bombed, Burned, and Boycotted" illustrates Smith's conviction, represents her professionalism, suggests her determination to fulfill her responsibilities as a journalist, and underlines her humanity and her compassion even for those who attacked her. Her activism encompassed more than issues of race and ethnicity. In 1966, Smith condemned the Vietnam War; a year later she said the war "diverted money" needed to fight poverty in the United States (n.p.), according to Newman. Much of what she believed was a direct result of her understanding of the life of Christ. "As a child I was taught to love everybody and not to hate anyone," she said. "Respect and consideration for the rights of others were engrained in me for as long as I can remember" (Kaul, "Hazel Brannon Smith" 291).

Her spirit and sense of humor remained. When she was in her 70s, she was still the woman who, as Kaul writes, "[indulged] a penchant for expensive designer clothes and white Cadillac convertibles." "Honey, I had the most eligible bachelor in Durant and the most eligible bachelor in Lexington," she said, "and my only trouble was that I couldn't have them both. That's true. I was something" (Kaul, "Hazel Brannon Smith" 294). Unlike Ira B. Harkey Jr., she never lost her love for the South: "The South is my home and my love and I don't ever expect to leave it" (Whalen 26).

Hazel Brannon Smith is a reluctant hero: She believed that what she produced was more important than who she was. As much as she could, she believed in equality. She lived a life committed to journalistic principles. She was especially loved and respected by her husband, members of her family, African American readers, and, as we will see—in "Hazel Brannon Smith and Editor Ira B. Harkey Jr." and "White Civil Rights Editors and Hazel Brannon Smith"—by influential white male editors of newspapers throughout the South. "The community newspaper profession has hundreds of leaders, as well as admirable journalists and hard workers beyond counting," said Garrett Ray, retired professor of journalism at Colorado State University and a former community newspaper editor. "Truly heroic figures? They are harder to come by. Hazel was one of my heroes" (Whalen 327).

It is no surprise that Dr. Arenia C. Mallory, Smith's steadfast friend, provides one of the final testaments to Smith's life: "Can you imagine Lexington without the *Lexington Advertiser* or Holmes County without Hazel Brannon Smith?" (Whalen 209), Mallory asked. Although it was not enough to save Smith from having to foreclose and sell her newspapers, black readers did what they could. Headlines for two stories say it all: "Holmes County Negroes Chip in for Prizewinning Editor" is the title of a story that appeared Nov. 23, 1965, in the *Memphis Commercial Appeal*. The story ran only a day after the headline "Negroes Raise $2,800 to Aid Hazel's Paper" on Nov. 22, 1965, in the *Jackson Daily News.*

Hazel Brannon Smith may have been a reluctant hero, but she was a person of courage at a time when citizens of Mississippi lived in fear and hesitated before taking a stand. Two chapters in this collection deal with other editors who, like her, crusaded for what they believed was right and who dealt with some of the same challenges. "White Hate Groups and Mississippi Newspapers" provides more detail about the White Citizens' Councils and the Ku Klux Klan, two of the more public and well-known hate groups that impacted the financial well-being of the editors of small town Mississippi weeklies.

Chapter 2.
Hazel Brannon Smith
And Editor Ira B. Harkey Jr.

Ira B. Harkey Jr. and Hazel Brannon Smith were not close friends, but they were affectionate and mutually supportive colleagues during a time in which they needed to rely upon each other. An essay in *Burning Crosses and Activist Journalism* is devoted to Harkey because he and Smith won Pulitzer Prizes for editorial writing within a year of each other, because they were editors of Mississippi newspapers covering the same controversial events, because they were profoundly affected—both personally and professionally—by white supremacist groups, and because they experienced ostracism and endured threats to their lives and careers.

A chapter is also devoted to Harkey because comparing him with his fellow editor teaches us a great deal about each of them. In spite of their similarities, Harkey was an ardent integrationist; Smith was not. Harkey was not in danger of bankruptcy; Smith lived on the brink of financial ruin and eventually was forced to sell her newspapers and lose Hazelwood, her elegant Southern home. Harkey left the South; Smith said she would never leave her home and moved to Tennessee only when her health began to fail. Harkey could be brusk, taciturn, and occasionally sarcastic, as evidenced in his most passionate editorials. Smith relied upon her Southern system of manners unless pushed too far.

When Harkey won the Pulitzer Prize in 1963, Hodding Carter Jr. and Hazel Brannon Smith were two of the colleagues who congratulated Harkey in their newspapers. "We would like to add our sincere congratulations to Editor Ira for this fine honor which he has brought to our state," Smith wrote in a personal note. "Long may you live and prosper, Sir" (Whalen 281). The two interacted in professional circles throughout their careers, and when they reconnected during a reunion of Pulitzer Prize winners, Harkey spoke affectionately about her. In his autobiography, Harkey said that Smith was "unmercifully persecuted for objecting to the killing of a Negro by a local law officer": "She is now a courageous and eloquent speaker for civil rights and in 1964 won the Pulitzer Prize for her long-time editorial opposition to misused official power" (2006, 78).

Theirs was an important collaboration, especially when one considers a statement Harkey made in *The Smell of Burning Crosses: An Autobiography of a Mississippi Newspaperman* (The subtitle was later changed to *A White Integrationist Editor in Mississippi.)* In the book he acknowledges how alone he felt during his time as an isolated voice for integration in a state in which the majority opposed him. Harkey believed he had few advocates, and he is effusive about only two people who came to his aid. He appreciated the support of Claude Sitton of the *New York Times,* especially an article published Jan. 23, 1963, because Sitton's coverage of Harkey's contributions to civil rights helped increase the circulation of the *Pascagoula Chronicle.* Closer to home, Claude Ramsey, president of the Mississippi Labor Council of the AFL-CIO, collaborated with Harkey. Since the *Chronicle* maintained a pro-labor stance during the time Harkey was editor, the relationship between Ramsey and Harkey was a mutually supportive one.

However, it takes more than the passive support of a few and the active support of two to give a person a sense of security and safety. Harkey would not have been one to differentiate among those such as Mr. Shortley in Flannery O'Connor's short story "The Displaced Person"—who actually pulled the brake and put the tractor in gear—and those such as Mrs. McIntyre and the other farm workers—who simply stood by and watched the tractor crush someone. It mattered little to Harkey whether a person were passively or actively racist. "I was a pariah," said Harkey in an interview with Maurine H. Beasley and Richard R. Harlow. "Nobody would be seen talking to me...all the people I thought were with me had evaporated at the time that I needed them" (74). This sentiment, of course, is familiar to Hazel Brannon Smith and other activist editors as well.

Although Harkey expresses gratitude to the AFL-CIO and the FBI in his autobiography, he ultimately did not survive the hatred expressed by many of the residents of Mississippi. He resigned from the newspaper in July 1963, exhausted, beleaguered, bitter, and alone. Having separated from his wife in 1959, Harkey had nothing to tie him to the region. He moved to Ohio. In *The Smell of Burning Crosses,* he writes:

I won, but I lost, too.

When it was all over, after we had welcomed back the defecting advertisers and had increased circulation to 8500—fifteen percent more than it ever had been—I found I could not remain in Pascagoula, could not bear to exist in the vacuum of an ostracism that remained in force even after victory, could not function in a silence of total isolation as if I were underwater or in galactic space. I was a pariah...

At home in Pascagoula, the silence was deafening. I had been since the Ole Miss riots a pariah. My company was avidly unsought, the stream of favor seekers, publicity seekers and advice seekers that long had lapped against my door trickled off to nothing. (2006, 18, 127)

Although Harkey left the South and entered academia, his commitment to journalism remained strong. He became a faculty member at Ohio State University in 1965, teaching a course in editorial writing and advising the campus newspaper. He received his master's degree in journalism in 1967 and his doctorate in political science in 1973 at Ohio State University. Harkey also taught at the University of Alaska, the University of Montana, and the University of Oregon. In 1993, Harkey was inducted into the Mississippi Hall of Fame. According to David L. Bennett in "Ira B. Harkey, Jr., and the *Pascagoula Chronicle,*" Harkey was a "widely sought speaker" (204) and continued to have significant impact even after he sold the newspaper into which had poured 14 years. He continued to write. In 1967, he published *The Smell of Burning Crosses,* and in 1974, he published *Pioneer Bush Pilot,* a profile about a pilot in Alaska.

In addition to his time in journalism and academia, Harkey also worked as a vice president and director of the Oklahoma Coca-Cola Bottling Company and as a director of Sequin Aviation. He married three times and was the father of seven children. He is best known, of course, as one of the few integrationist editors in the Deep South during the 1950s and 1960s.

A Life Well Lived

From 1949 to 1963, Harkey was editor and publisher of the daily *Pascagoula Chronicle.* He happily settled into Pascagoula, a shipbuilding and fishing town that lies on the Gulf Coast between Biloxi and Mobile. In his autobiography, Harkey introduces his first chapter discussing the origin of "Pascagoula," "the lovely Indian name of a small industrial city on Mississippi's Gulf Coast 100 sandy miles east of New Orleans and 40 marshy ones west of Mobile." He then writes:

One hundred years later the lovely name Pascagoula stung bitter on the tongues of most Americans who read it as a dateline in their newspapers. For four months in 1962-63 Pascagoula citizen leaders abdicated their duty and allowed their community to be ruled by fear imposed by an organized gang of white supremacists. This was an aftermath of the entrance of Negro Mississippian James Meredith onto the campus of his state university. The Pascagoula gang was cloaked in a quasi-legality lent it by the office occupied by its leader, the Jackson County sheriff, a bloated hard-drinking semiliterate ruffian. The nucleus of the gang was a group of men who had gained local fame by taking part in the riots at Oxford after Meredith's admittance September 30. These, numbering about thirty, had been called out over the Pascagoula radio station to be led by their sheriff in cars and a chartered bus to the University of Mississippi campus, arriving in time to enjoy the bone cracking and property destruction. (2006, 11-12)

His editorial policies for dealing with breaking news were so shocking to white Mississippi readers that one irate subscriber said that Harkey "calls niggers 'Mr.' and 'Mrs.'" and "writes news stories so you can't tell who's a nigger and who ain't" (2006, 13). Harkey writes:

> I know about these things and what the 600-member Jackson County Citizens Emergency Unit intended to do in Pascagoula because I was editor and publisher of *The Chronicle,* the despised "niggerlover" who "ridicules our great Governor Barnett," "calls niggers 'Mr.' and 'Mrs.,'" "writes news stories so you can't tell who's a nigger and who ain't." For four months—from October, 1962, to February, 1963—my newspaper was the target for a campaign of vilification, boycott, threats and actual violence. A rifle slug was fired through my front door and a shotgun shell blasted out the windows in my office. Hate spewed into *The Chronicle* telephone and mail box, grown men grabbed and shook and cursed our carrier boys on the street, advertisers were threatened and dropped their space in *The Chronicle,* a high sheriff himself chased a Negro carrier boy off his route and warned him not to return—part of the Negro boy's route traversed a "white" area—and so thoroughly did the poison of hate permeate upward from the gutter that a lady library worker, supposedly a dispenser of culture and learning, could bring herself to write to me and pray that "instead of a bullet through your door I hope you get a bullet through your stupid head." *(Smell* 2006, 12-13)

Harkey's campaign against the Jackson County Citizens Emergency Unit continued as the organization threatened the existence of his newspaper: "We fought back through editorials, the only weapon at our hands, striving to save not only *The Chronicle,* into which I had poured 14 years of life's energies and all my material wherewithal, but striving also to save my own personal skin...We covered as best we could the Unit's meetings—of course our reporters were not welcomed—and in an editorial explaining the widening evil of the Unit's objectives (the first editorial I had ever placed on page one) I tried to bring home to Pascagoulans that this was not my fight alone but theirs as well" *(Smell* 2006, 15-16).

When Harkey moved to Pascagoula, he said he had counted on those on the Gulf Coast being more "liberal and intimate" than residents of other counties. He also believed in the positive influence of a large Roman Catholic community. In an interview with Beasley and Harlow, Harkey said later,

"I realize it was ridiculous...because it simply was not possible" (70). Losing his faith in the influence of the churches in the South, Harkey said churches had become "clubs" for white people (Beasley and Harlow 72). But Harkey never lost sight of the world that could exist if human beings could follow teachings of Jesus and behave in ways that were supportive and honest. One of his most powerful editorials, "How Many Kinds of Christianity?" was published during the Christmas season in 1962:

> Well, certainly, the governor's cousin is correct when she complains that the racial attitudes of her native state's leaders make more difficult her job as a missionary in Nigeria.
>
> "You send us out here to preach that Christ died for all men," wrote Antonia Canzoneri to a Mississippi Baptist newspaper, "then you make a travesty of our message by refusing to associate with some of them because of the color of their skin."
>
> This is the basic cause of the Mississippi schizophrenia, the incredible disease that allows us to claim that we are at one and the same time Christians and white supremacists, when there are no two attitudes more incompatible than these.
>
> The racists would have you believe that the teachings of Christ, the lessons you learned in Sunday school, are like the Santa Claus myth, just something to kid around with. The Sermon on the Mount, the brotherhood of men in God, the great philosophy of kindness and compassion, all of this just words to listen to on Sunday and then forget at the door of the church.
>
> Christianity is a white man's fraternity, they impute. There is only one God, but he is God only for certain people, people who look and think like we do. There is a heaven, but there would have to be a sign by the pearly gates that says "All Colored Angels Step to the Rear," where they will find a heaven-annex marked "For Our Colored Patrons Only."
>
> Christianity is a philosophy of tolerance, a philosophy that makes bearable through hope the wretched lives of the unprivileged. It is a philosophy of love and understanding and turn the other cheek. It is a philosophy that makes no sense on a once a week basis, that is barren and futile if shucked at the door of the church and not carried out into the world and practiced there.
>
> In Mississippi, a person who attempts to carry Christianity out the church door, who dares to practice the Christian virtue of tolerance outside the church, is cursed as liberal, a leftist, a communist, a niggerlover. Christ was the greatest champion of the underdog the world has ever known. If He were to visit us here, now, by whose side would He stand, beside the brick-throwing, foulmouthed, destroying, profaning, slavering members of the mob and their "nice-folk" eggers-on, or beside the trembling victims of their hate?
>
> There cannot be one answer for Sunday between 11 a.m. and noon and another for the rest of the week. And there cannot be one brand of Christianity for Mississippi and another for Nigeria and the rest of the world. (Beasley and Harlow 81)

Late in his career, Harkey took solace in the fact that he lived what he believed, even when it cost him dearly. He had grown up believing in compassion toward all, and he could not reconcile the manner in which some in Mississippi saw no conflict between the teachings of Christ and segregation. "I was a wide-eyed kid who believed what he heard in Sunday School about brotherhood" (69), Harkey told Beasley and Harlow.

Harkey argued that heaven is not segregated, and in his dealings with African Americans in his community, he relied upon what he remembered from his time as a lieutenant in the U.S. Navy in World War II. In the military, African Americans often gave their lives for a country that discriminated against them. When a bomb exploded Jan. 22, 1945, 52 soldiers of several racial and ethnic identities died together. "It was ironic for me to see that we buried 52 people at one time—tossed them over the side (of a Navy ship on which he served)—and some were black people" (Beasley and Harlow 69), said Harkey. The memories of that event recurred years later, when he wrote in his autobiography about the years he spent as a newspaper editor in Mississippi: "These feelings led me to fourteen years of what is sneeringly known in the white South as starry-eyed idealism, fellow-traveling do-goodism and treason to our nice little old way of life" (1967, 207).

However, although Harkey attended Sunday School as a child and later worked alongside African Americans in the Navy, he also described the family members and friends who reinforced the stereotypes of the day and the impact they had on him. "All my friends were typical white Southerners, and...there was no other word, no other way to refer to a black man, but 'nigger'" (70), said Harkey in an interview with Beasley and Harlow. Focusing on the lack of economic privilege and lack of education that afflicted a large number of white people, Harkey said of the white supremacist in the South, "He has almost nothing else he can look down upon," adding that the average member of the Ku Klux Klan "is the typical guy who didn't go beyond the third grade and he sometimes can't spell cat" (Beasley and Harlow 70).

Harkey's life was rich; his experiences, varied. Born in 1918 in New Orleans, he graduated from Tulane University. He was a reporter and feature writer for the *New Orleans Times-Picayune,* where editors insisted on a policy that prohibited African Americans from appearing in photographs. Later, Harkey wrote about this editorial absurdity in his autobiography:

> Photographs of Negroes rarely appeared in Mississippi newspapers until late in the 1950s, after the sins of the Mississippi press had become notorious throughout the land because of interest focused on them through the civil rights struggle. Before then, photos of Negroes appeared only when someone in haste sent up a mat and cutlines without studying the accompanying proof. Sometimes, in this way also, a Negro woman was referred to as Mrs., and the apologies to white womanhood followed. Their efforts in the late Fifties to adopt the appearance of true newspapers that cover all the news were piteous. Wire service photos of well-known Negro athletes from the world at large were sparingly used, but the hometown colored boy—even if he happened to be Ralph Boston, the greatest broad-jumper in the world—received no calls from the local press on his visits back to the old place. (2006, 45-46).

The dearth of photographs of blacks in Mississippi newspapers is but one battle Harkey would fight throughout his career, beginning in 1949 when Harkey bought the *Pascagoula Chronicle* and made it a daily newspaper. Not one to be fearful and not one to back down, Harkey explains the title of his book in the following excerpt:

> No one not rooted in the South can understand the full terror of a cross burning...It is like the voice of doom, the sentence of death, the placing of the victim beyond the pale...I hailed the year's new season with, "Ah, autumn! Falling leaves...the hint of a north breeze stirring in the night...the smell of burning crosses in the air." (2006, 103)

When Harkey won the 1963 Pulitzer Prize for editorial writing, the selection committee applauded him "for his courageous editorials devoted to the processes of law and reason during the integration crises in Mississippi in 1962." But his celebration was short-lived. In December 1963, six months after receiving the prize, Harkey sold the newspaper to Ralph Nicholson of Tallahassee, Florida, for $1 million, having paid $106,000 for it 14 years earlier. He moved to Reno, Nevada, before deciding where to go and what to do next. "Friendless, emotionally spent and separated from his wife, he sold out the paper that he had built from a weekly and left the state the year after he won the Pulitzer," writes Dudley Clendinen. "Harkey went on to earn a master's and doctoral degrees, to write two books and teach at several universities. He did not return to Mississippi" ("In the South" 17).

When Harkey left the newspaper business, he did so with characteristic bravado; however, when he talked about the awards he had amassed, he said the honors had come "at the forfeit of a life's work I had loved" (2006, 19). His description of an interview he gave—in which he was less than honest about his sense of loss and betrayal—appears in his autobiography:

> There had been no applause in Pascagoula for the winning of any of these. Recognition from "Yankees" only proved my perfidy. Time enough has not yet passed to allow me a judgment on whether or not I had made an even swap—these honors earned at the forfeit of a life's work I had loved, a newspaper into which I had siphoned my juices, nurturing it from a frail weekly into a semi-weekly and then a daily, reversing the mid-century trend of American journalism. A national news magazine asked a quote from me regarding the sale. "All bad things must come to an end," I told the reporter. I did not really feel so fly about it. *(Smell* 2006, 19)

In the next section of this chapter and in "White Hate Groups and Mississippi Newspapers," it is important to address the cause of the greatest damage to the careers and reputations of both Harkey and Smith. By the 1950s and 1960s, white supremacist groups such as the Ku Klux Klan had proliferated and were overtly threatening. But another group of organizations was emerging that were in some ways more dangerous than the Klan because of their benign rhetoric and their membership, which included the most prestigious politicians, businessmen, and law enforcement officers in their respective communities. As we have seen, the White Citizens' Council harassed Smith and took a toll on her advertising revenues; Harkey would feel the wrath of the Jackson County Citizens Emergency Unit.

The Jackson County Citizens Emergency Unit

From October 1962 to February 1963, Harkey was the target of threats and violence, much of it initiated by a segregationist group called the Jackson County Citizens Emergency Unit. The group had been organized in the early 1960s after the admittance of James Meredith to Ole Miss. Between 400 to 600 people attended the Unit's weekly meetings, and the group included the local sheriff. According to Beasley and Harlow, "The announced purpose of its 'action committee' was to 'take care of nigger-lovers so that we're not embarrassed like the people of Oxford were'" (67). What Beasley and Harlow call "maneuvers" took place on Saturday mornings under the direction of a "training officer" (67), but eventually, some officers resigned and the attendance shrank to "less than 30 hard-core haters" (68).

Harkey dealt often and directly with the Unit, a group established to oppose integration, prevent African Americans from voting, and control African Americans through economic discrimination. Its opposition to Harkey affected him personally and professionally. On October 29, 1962, he published an editorial entitled "If Goons Threaten You, Here Is What to Do":

> Four Chronicle advertisers report that they have been instructed not to do business with the newspaper. Others may be afraid to report.
> This is what the Jackson County Citizens Emergency Unit said it would do—"put the pressure on Chronicle advertisers."
> If they continue to advertise, the businessmen reported, the goons said they "will not be responsible for anything that happens to your business."
> One strongarm man threatened an advertiser by saying he represented "a union of 300 families" that would boycott the store.
> For the reassurance of Chronicle advertisers we offer this:
> Threats of physical violence are illegal and evidence is being gathered that will take care of goons that make such threats.
> There are not 300 families in Jackson County so low in morals that they would condone much less participate in such an attack against anyone. If there are 300 such, their economic status is so depressed that their buying-power is nothing.
> If you are threatened or even talked to about dropping your advertising in the Chronicle, call the Chronicle immediately and give us the name of the goon, his description and a report of what he said.
> Decent, law-abiding businessmen...have nothing to fear. Right is on your side, help is coming and we assure you that our community will not be allowed to succumb to dictation by evil elements that would destroy all that is good in our lives. *(Smell* 2006, 168)

Although there were many crises that fueled the hatred of the Jackson County Citizens Emergency Unit members, nothing shook them like the admittance of James Meredith into Ole Miss. In him, they saw a symbol of all they stood to lose. Although Smith reacted to Meredith's courage in her newspapers, Harkey took a personal and intense interest in the case; the riots that followed Meredith's request for admission proved to be Harkey's worst nightmare come true.

James Meredith and Ole Miss

According to Beasley and Harlow, Harkey was one of the few editors in the South who supported James Meredith's admission to the University of Mississippi. In fact, Harkey became the "chief target" of the Jackson County Citizens Emergency Unit, organized to support segregation (65) in all its forms, because of his advocacy for African Americans and his belief in essential equality.

The United States Supreme Court on September 10, 1962, ordered that all colleges and universities be desegregated. Mississippi Governor Ross Barnett gave a statewide address September 13 and said, "No school will be integrated while I am your governor." A state resolution supporting Barnett was adopted by the state legislature, and the *Jackson Daily News* officially opposed Meredith's admission. When the Air Force veteran walked onto the campus September 30, 1962, the first known black student at the university, the reaction was swift and violent. Riots in Oxford, Mississippi, on the nights of September 30 and October 1 followed. They lasted more than eight hours, and two people were killed. According to Susan Weill, Ole Miss was "littered with burned-out automobiles, tear gas canisters, and broken glass" ("Mississippi's Daily Press" 37). Between the time the Supreme Court ordered that the university had to accept Meredith and the time he graduated in August 1963, he would endure turmoil.

In his autobiography, Harkey said he grieved for Mississippi during 1962 and 1963 more than at any other time. "I thought I would lose my mind," he wrote. "I remained in misery, overwhelmed by shame and guilt, viewing the wreckage of Mississippi's soul" (2006, 144, 146). Soon after the riots in Oxford, shots were fired at Harkey's office, his life was threatened, and he bought a .38-caliber pistol and hired a bodyguard. Much of the incentive to do so came from Hodding Carter Jr., who recommended that Harkey move to a hotel, purchase a weapon, and hire a bodyguard. Carter Jr. said his situation was not as dangerous as Harkey's, but Harkey writes: "Nevertheless, [Carter Jr.] said he and his sons had been patrolling their grounds at night" *(Smell* 2006, 160).

More devastating than anything that occurred to him personally, Harkey was forced to watch as Governor Barnett damaged the reputation of his beloved state. He was embarrassed by the state's leadership and anxious about the violence that was sure to erupt. Like Smith, he knew no state could stand against the federal government. He said the options were "compliance or physical defiance":

> Mississippi, to its everlasting shame, allowed Ross Barnett and the Citizens Council puppeteers to whose jerks he danced to choose the latter for them. Barnett denounced Justice [Hugo] Black's order—he actually called it "illegal"!—and vowed again that he would not allow Meredith to enter Ole Miss. He announced that he would address the people of Mississippi—meaning the white people, of course—over statewide radio and television the night of September 13.
>
> Many men in Mississippi—deluded idealists—had long thought that despite Barnett's campaign oratory of hate and his daily anti-Negro pronouncements since his inauguration, he must, when the moment came, elect to do the American thing and allow justice to be done peacefully. Defiance that inflamed the mobs and kept them inflamed down to the very moment of truth was unthinkable. Barnett could have saved face by issuing a plea for law and order and preceded by a statement that he had done everything he possibly could to stave off the awful event, but that now the state of Mississippi must either bow to or take up arms against the United States without hope of prevailing. He could have saved himself politically even while surrendering, as later did Alabama's cynical little Governor George Wallace in the skit he acted out while denying a Negro's entrance to his university and at the same time allowing him to enter. *(Smell* 2006, 135-36)

Harkey's world had shattered. In a particularly emotional excerpt from *The Smell of Burning Crosses,* he writes of his response to Mississippi after Governor Barnett illustrated for the nation the worst of the South:

> I thought I would lose my mind. Despite the unassailable facts, my mind rejected what had happened at Ole Miss. I could not reconcile all I had been taught and believed about the ultimate goodness of men with what the newspapers and television reports showed that men—the leaders of my state—had done at Oxford. And what came after October 1 was as bad. There was no recoil or remorse. Instead, from the Gulf to the Tennessee hills, from the Mississippi River to the Tombigbee, Mississippians exulted in rebellion, hailed murder, raised Barnett to sainthood and assigned John Kennedy to perfidy with Tojo, Hitler and Castro. Confederate flags—cheap, soon-faded renditions of the Confederate battle flag—plastered the state and flapped from the radio aerial of every redneck's automobile. This was the symbol of defiance and brave indeed was the man or woman who dared hang an American flag on his car.
>
> Politicians, editors, judges and educators blamed John Kennedy and his brother Robert for the riots—like hoodlums cursing the police—and their bitter incessant words kept the public hate white hot. I nearly drowned in shame. And guilt. It was the worst time of my life. (2006, 144)

According to David Wallace, in spite of Harkey's integrationist stance, the *Chronicle* had remained surprisingly successful until 1962. Harkey's support of Meredith opened the floodgates of rage. Meredith, 29, a U.S. Air Force veteran, wanted to transfer his credits from all-black Jackson State College and complete his degree at Ole Miss. His decision to seek admission was momentous and directly affected Harkey's newspaper. Wallace writes:

> Although a six-foot cross was burned in Harkey's yard after he publicly lauded the Supreme Court for its *Brown* ruling, the Pascagoula *Chronicle* surprisingly continued to find success and by 1961 had expanded into a daily. It was not until the controversy surrounding James Meredith's admittance to Ole Miss in 1962 that Harkey felt the full brunt of segregationist force. Up to that point, many Mississippians had been convinced that desegregation could be avoided, or at least postponed for several more years through legal maneuvering. Meredith's admittance quickly brought this wishful thinking to a halt. For months after voicing his support for Meredith, it seemed the entire community of Pascagoula had turned against Harkey. Yet he confronted the opposition head on and continued to express his opinions without restraint, earning him the Pulitzer Prize in 1963. The attacks on Harkey eventually subsided and the *Chronicle's* circulation returned, but not before convincing the editor to sell the paper and leave Mississippi. (14-15)

The actions that precipitated these dark days were simple enough. Meredith was not oblivious to the firestorm his action would bring down on Mississippi, but after talking with Medgar Evers, Mississippi NAACP field secretary, and Thurgood Marshall, head of the Legal Defense and Education Fund (an extension of the NAACP), Meredith submitted his application. In a letter to the admissions office, Meredith wrote, "I sincerely hope that your attitude toward me as a potential member of your student body reflects the attitude of the school, and that it will not change upon learning that I am not a white applicant. I am an American—Mississippi—Negro citizen" *(Race Beat* 270-71). The office of the registrar sent a telegram to Meredith saying his application had not arrived by the deadline. What followed, according to Gene Roberts and Hank Klibanoff, were 20 months of "defiance" against the integration of Ole Miss *(Race Beat* 271)

Enraged white Mississippians began to discuss the possibility of closing the university in order to avoid integrating it. With characteristic vigor, Harkey published an editorial entitled "Perfectly Capable of Closing Ole Miss":

> Anywhere else in the United States, the suggestion that a state university be closed down for any reason at all would not rise to the level of public discussion. Such a suggestion could not originate outside a lunatic academy.
>
> But in our state—where the leaders for eight years led us to believe we would not be required to obey the same laws that others must obey, whose leaders called out the mobs to let blood in senseless opposition to the will of the nation, where American GIs and marshals are referred to in terms of hate formerly used only for Huns who ravished Belgium in the

World War and Japs who tortured prisoners in World War II—in this state we had better discuss the possibility. Now.

For the people who could do and say the things that have been done and said in our state during the past six weeks have proved themselves perfectly capable of closing down a university.

The suggestion has been made that Old Miss be closed. It has been offered by the same group of false prophets who deluded the people for eight years into believing that we could maintain school segregation in Mississippi while all about us other Southern states were failing in their attempts to prevent integration. Somehow, in the face of all that is sane, they managed to convince most white people that they had a secret unknown to other Southern leaders.

If we now let them convince us that it is proper to close Ole Miss and destroy a century of cultural advancement, then maybe we do not deserve any better than to be led by owners of grammar-school intellects and of attitudes that most humans left behind somewhere in history.

It is heartening to note a resurgence of manhood on the part of the Old Miss staff and faculty and the rallying of alumni support to keep the institution going. All alumni, all parents of present students, all Mississippians who care a hang about their state—we will exclude moral and religious considerations here and mention only the economic—all should also rally behind the university and let our leaders know that we do not regard suicide as a solution. *(Smell* 2006, 176-77)

As noted earlier, the U.S. Supreme Court ordered that Meredith be admitted, and the trouble in Oxford, Mississippi, began in earnest. On September 11, 1962, a cross near the fraternities at the university was burned, and on September 13, 1962, Governor Ross Barnett became irrevocably involved: "On Sept. 13, Barnett went on statewide television and radio to declare that the state of Mississippi was a sovereign power and that he was interposing himself between the federal government and the university to nullify the federal court's desegregation order" *(Race Beat* 274). On September 30, mobs fought U.S. marshals, soldiers, and Mississippi National Guard Troops at Ole Miss. The *Chronicle* claimed the blame lay with Mississippi politicians and with the "jungle of hate they had cultivated" (Beasley and Harlow 67).

In response to Barnett's address and his fear about what would occur in Oxford, Harkey published an editorial entitled "Confusing Times, Dangerous Times" on September 20, 1962. It reads:

A pall of contradiction covers our state as if everyone of us had developed schizophrenia.

The newspapers and politicians who hailed Governor Barnett's address call upon citizens not to resort to violence. "Do they really mean it?" is the question, for these same papers and people have long been advocates of a "fight to the finish" and now they may see just what it is they have raised up. How can we defy the law "to the finish" without resorting to violence?

Then there is the call upon the United States of America not to send marshals into our state to enforce the law. How can we make such a demand without appearing devoid of all sense? Does the burglar announce to the police that he will not observe anti-burgling statutes because they violate his way of life and then expect the police to issue him an exemption?

Governor Barnett knows full well how laws are enforced when the lawless are defiant. He himself has sent troops into counties to search out a bottle of whiskey here, to shatter a crap table there. Federal marshals enforce the law except in rebellions which are tended to by troops. How do we think that the United States will enforce the law now? By sending in the Peace Corps? Postmen? Soil conservationists? When orders are ignored, force is applied. Governor Barnett knows that.

A Sunday editorial in a state capital paper is titled "Future Economic Growth Hinges on State Income Conditioners," as if there will be any growth but of hate, any conditions but strife, any state income but grief in the turmoil of anarchy we are approaching.

At a luncheon meeting Monday in Pascagoula a group of local leaders heard a talk by a Mississippi State University official. He spoke on plans the university has for its educational program in Jackson County—as if there will be any education after Ole Miss has been padlocked or burned down or whatever it is Governor Barnett has planned for it.

Meanwhile, the first Mississippian to decline Governor Barnett's invitation to go to jail is Judge Sidney Mize of Gulfport. The day after the governor's speech, Mize issued an order directing Ole Miss to admit James Meredith without delay. Mize followed instructions of the federal circuit court of appeals rather than Governor Barnett's call to suicide.

In a madhouse's din, Mississippi waits. God help Mississippi. *(Smell* 2006, 141-42; *Race Beat* 275 [texts are slightly different])

As much as possible, it is important to let Harkey speak for himself. In direct response to the governor's actions, Harkey penned an editorial entitled "Governor Reaches Point of No Return" in which he wrote, "He will drive Mississippi to chaos." The remainder of the editorial published September 14, 1962, appears here:

> Mississippians are mature enough to recognize the inevitable, to accept it and adapt to it with good enough grace. The political faction that rules them, however, is not.
>
> We had always thought deep down inside that when the moment arrived even Ross Barnett and his blazing advisors would make the best of it.
>
> Instead, the emotional nature of Barnett's address last night left little doubt that he intends to make the worst of it. He will drive Mississippi to chaos.
>
> True, the exact "moment" has not yet arrived. Barnett last night invoked the "doctrine of interposition," attempting to place the sovereignty of the state between state officials and the U.S. government, thus removing the necessity of their complying with federal orders to admit James Meredith to Ole Miss.
>
> If the governor had stopped there, perhaps there would still be hope that ruin could be avoided. But he went far beyond an invocation of interposition. He called upon officials to defy the United States and he vowed again that Old Miss would not be integrated. This can mean only one

thing, that when interposition is brushed aside in the courts—as the bogus contention surely will—Barnett either will back down or will destroy our educational system. His words last night make it virtually impossible for him to back down.

It is too early yet to attempt an analysis of Barnett's address to determine what else was in it. This was in it, though: a dangerous use of the century's most inflammatory issue in an attempt to solidify Brand X power in Mississippi. This attempt was proclaimed when he dragged in his whipping boy, "the Kennedy administration," and said "the Kennedy administration is lending the power of the federal government to the ruthless demands of…agitators."

But it is not "the Kennedy administration" that is making demands upon Mississippi. It is the United States of America, it is democracy itself, it is the whole of humanity. These surely will not back down either. Barnett has asked them to force us to comply. They will, and the process can ruin Mississippi. (Beasley and Harlow 78; *Smell* 138-39)

There was, of course, no middle ground between Harkey and Barnett. According to Roberts and Klibanoff, "Harkey, who had been at ideological odds with the Mississippi mainstream for years, stayed on the subject for days, crafting passionate commentaries" *(Race Beat* 275). According to Harkey's autobiography, Barnett and the majority of newspaper editors wanted Mississippians to believe that if the university and the state refused to admit Meredith, then Kennedy and the federal government would leave them alone (138). In his article "In the South—When It Mattered to Be an Editor," Dudley Clendinen writes that when Harkey stood up to Barnett, he "condemned him as a demagogue leading the state to disaster" (16). But Harkey's constituents did not encourage or support him. According to Clendinen, "One man in a county of 54,000 people came to his support. Harkey faced gunshots, falling circulation and threatened advertisers. A cross was ignited on his lawn" (16-17). Barnett had done significant damage to what remained of Mississippi's reputation by the time he gave his farewell address Jan. 8, 1964.

Attorney General Robert F. Kennedy directed the Justice Department to intercede. Soon, 200 military policemen from Memphis arrived, and 13,000 soldiers "began taking control" *(Race Beat* 297). "They evacuated the wounded…and, amid sniper fire, waded into the mobs and began arresting people; the number would reach three hundred, only a third of them Ole Miss students. Half the marshals were wounded" *(Race Beat* 297). The evening after Meredith attended class for the first time, NBC aired a report on the Ole Miss crisis:

In a live interview by newsman David Brinkley, Robert F. Kennedy said that the previous night had been his worst ever because he'd asked marshals to hold their fire while being fired on. States, he said, can't pick and choose which laws they'll obey, any more than citizens can legally decide to quit paying income taxes just because they dislike them. He decried the lack of leadership in the state. The reason Georgia had been able to desegregate its university without problems, he said, had been leadership from politicians and the press, namely *Atlanta Constitution* editor Ralph McGill. *(Race Beat* 299)

Although one of the most powerful and articulate voices, Harkey was not the only editor who was horrified by Barnett's response to Meredith's request to attend Ole Miss. In his biography, John A. Whalen quotes Smith as having been "saddened" by the rioting at Ole Miss. "There is no such thing as state sovereignty," she said. "The state was never meant to be supreme. That question too was settled a hundred years ago in a bloody conflict" (142-43). Certainly, her reference to the Civil War is a powerful analogy.

Social and Political Activism

For Harkey, the discriminatory practices in the South were anti-Christian and counter-intuitive. Segregation was one of the institutions that enraged him most: "It was an economic stupidity to have duplicate school systems for blacks and whites and each to be not worth a nickel" (71), Harkey told Beasley and Harlow. Statements he made—such as "I was possessor of an un-Southern and radical opinion that Negroes were human beings. I held also a quaint belief that the white people of Mississippi, Arkansas and Louisiana—the old darkest South—needed to have this truth revealed to them" (Whalen 277-78)—illustrate both his courage and the sense of moral superiority that alienated some of his readers.

The fear spawned by the Jackson County Citizens Emergency Unit affected Harkey's financial well-being, but he was undeterred in his advocacy for the disenfranchised. Even when he was directly and physically attacked, he stood firm. He also expanded his own experience and suggested to the community how dangerous the Unit's activities were for all residents:

> Having learned that the group's first target was to be the *Chronicle,* and after a pistol shot broke out a section of the *Chronicle's* plate glass door, Harkey wrote a front-page editorial declaring that "a terrorist group" had been organized in the county and calling on the responsible leaders of the community to "organize and notify our sheriff in no uncertain terms that he is leading our country and himself to disaster...We are under no illusion that anyone here cares what happens to Ira Harkey. But think long on this: what happens to him can happen to you. You may be next. (Whalen 279)

After the 1954 *Brown v. Board of Education* decision, Harkey addressed the prejudice that underlay the desegregation of schools. The next two excerpts illustrate his commitment to equality in the schools and to improvement in the facilities for all children. His rage is barely contained as he ridicules the caste system in his region. In his autobiography, Harkey writes:

Most Mississippians could not conceive of black and white children sitting
side by side in schools and they honestly believed, and were supported in
this belief by their press, that when the time came all they had to do was to
show up at the school house door and Uncle Sam would back down. Further, it was inconceivable that any Mississippi "nigger," any *good* darkey,
would agitate to send his child to a white school. Everybody knows that
we love our niggers and that they love us and that they wouldn't have it
any other way. They are the happiest people in the world and they know
they are better off here in their sheltered world where we can see that they
are taken care of. They don't want to mix with us any more than we want
to mix with them. They're proud of their race and want to preserve it.
"Never!" This was Mississippi's religion until the very minute James
Meredith arrived at Oxford to contaminate the hallowed halls of Ole Miss.
(2006, 96-97)

And later, he discusses the way in which integration of colleges and universities was proceeding peacefully throughout the South and how it could lead
to equality in other social arenas. Much of the hope he saw for the South resided in fair and equal judicial processes and well-funded educational institutions:

The fiction that the black man is a lower order of human is furthered
in much of the South by the fact that few whites have ever met an educated black man. Many, therefore, involuntarily reach the fallacious conclusion that the black man is uneducable because he is black. By beginning at the top of the educational structure and over a 20-year period ef-
fecting a gradual integration downward, the whites at the end of two decades would have accepted the blacks simply as human beings like themselves, differing only in accidental and irrelevant physical characteristics,
even as they themselves differ physically from one another.

Our politicians are doing the state of Mississippi a grave disservice
by their white supremacist cheerleading, waving the ancient and phony
bugaboos of "miscegenation" and "social equality," arousing the hoary
fears in ignorant whites. Social equality has nothing to do with equal education. Social equality will not only never be legislated between black and
white, but it never this side of Heaven will be effected in any community—even if the community is populated only by people of identical skin
hue, height, weight, reach, hair color, collar size and everybody is named
Oswald or Ophelia. The only question before the state is this: should all
persons in a democracy who obey the laws, are subject to taxes and the
military draft, receive from their government the same fruits?

Our answer is yes. Logic and justice demand it. *(Smell* 2006, 99)

Harkey did not perceive his social message to be radical. For him,
equality in every social sphere was rational and inevitable. In addition to his
support for judicial fairness and educational equality, Harkey simply advocated one of the tenets of good journalism: fair reporting. A chapter of his
autobiography entitled "Two Men Hurt and a Nigger Killed" is a possible
allusion to an often-quoted line in *The Adventures of Huckleberry Finn* by
Samuel Clemens. In the excerpt from the novel, Huck tells Aunt Sally that

there has been an accident. Huck says, "It warn't the grounding—that didn't keep us back but a little. We blowed out a cylinder-head." Aunt Sally replies, "Good gracious! Anybody hurt?" It is Huck's response that reveals Clemens' mastery of wit, parody, and irony. Huck answers her question by saying, "No'm. Killed a nigger." In a classic example of dramatic irony, Aunt Sally, the proud Christian woman, tells Huck, "Well it's luck; because sometimes people do get hurt" (280).

The chapter title also refers to an incident Harkey relates in his autobiography. It is the most incendiary and horrific description of racism Harkey provides. In 1950, soon after Harkey had bought the *Pascagoula Chronicle*, he asked a deputy sheriff about the casualties that followed an explosion at a local shipyard. The deputy responded, "Two men were hurt and a nigger was killed." Harkey writes, "A few moments later, at the scene, I stood beside Mayor Wilbur Dees and inspected the wreckage. 'Look at that stuff,' said the major, pointing to some bloody matter smeared on a jagged edge of steel. 'Brains. That's where the nigger was. I didn't know niggers had any brains!'" (2006, 42-43).

But it was not just the manner with which law enforcement officials, politicians, and local businessmen referred to African Americans that appalled Harkey. In addition to his concern about the widespread hatred and racism in Mississippi, Harkey complained vehemently about the journalists who labeled the African-American citizen in what was supposed to be balanced news coverage:

> In print he is never a man. He is a Negro, negro or colored. His wife is not a woman. She is colored, Negro, negro, Negress or negress. Indeed, she is not even allowed to be his wife in most Southern newspapers, being denied the title of Mrs. no matter how legally married she may be, and is referred to on the streets, in the courts and in the newspaper as Bessie Lou or Willie Mae or Mandy.
> "Mandy Price," reads a story in the Collins, Mississippi, *News-Commercial*, "was arrested last Saturday when raiding officers found a jug of homemade whiskey in her home. Mandy was fined $350." The state's dry laws were a favorite weapon for police who preyed on the Negro, and $350 is more than the yearly income of many Mississippi Negroes, but these are not the injustices over which we weep here. The practice of refusing to apply Mrs. to Negroes goes back, of course, to slavery days when Negroes were allowed to breed and propagate as biped livestock but were not permitted to marry and had no last names. Today's redneck believes that application of the title to a Negro woman somehow will impart respectability and social status to her and this he will not tolerate. *(Smell 2006, 40-41)*

In an interview with Beasley and Harlow, Harkey discusses at length more examples of astonishing lapses in journalistic ethical practice:

> The newspaper I bought used to say, "Billy Jones, colored," so on and so forth, "Maggie Jones, colored" and such things as "two people and a colored maid were killed in an automobile accident." Anyway, I dropped

the tag. Another thing, there never was a story in this paper about a black man that wasn't a police story...I started doing little features about them...I started Negro with a capital N. Now, this was revolutionary...Then I started using "Mrs." for married Negro women and this was considered awful. (71)

One of the most egregious examples of racism cited in Harkey's autobiography was written by fellow editor E.G. Sellers in the *George County Times* of Lucedale, Mississippi. There is no apology offered to black readers after black babies are listed with white babies in the regular birth announcements:

There are times, in running a newspaper, when you would like to crawl into a hole, and last week's issue was that time—again, with us. Last week in the Birth announcements, the names of William C. and Bessie Lee Fairley, and Cephus C. and Vencila Taylor, and their baby, both colored, somehow got above a number of the white couples, with new born babies. Our apologies to these couples listed below the colored section, who should have been included in the White section...Incidentally, we are running a corrected list, on Page Eight, for the benefit of the mothers who wish to keep a scrap book for their child. (2006, 49)

Harkey also includes in his autobiography news articles and excerpts from Mississippi newspapers to illustrate the inherent racism involved in daily newspaper coverage. One article that appeared in the *Gulfport* (Mississippi) *Daily Herald* reads: "Three persons were killed—a Keesler airman, a Negro private, and a Wiggins Negress—and eight others were injured in two weekend traffic accidents on US Highway 49 in the Wiggins area" (1967, 47). A headline in the *Deer Creek Pilot* of Rolling Fork, Mississippi, reads, "White Man, 2 Negroes Hurt/Near Here as Cars Collide." In second references to subjects of stories, a black man named "Willie Jones" becomes simply "the Negro." A story in the *Gulfport Daily Herald* referred to a "young colored elevator girl," and the *New Orleans State* included the phrase "seven Negro youths" (1967, 48). Such phrases were common.

Other examples of racism appear in *The Smell of Burning Crosses,* and allusions to people are not the only problematic references, according to Harkey. For example, he includes headlines from various newspapers such as "Colored Residence Damaged by Fire" and "First Colored Paved Streets Realized." Falstaff beer, Harkey said, became "nigger beer" in newspapers after the company made donations to the NAACP in the mid-1950s. Readers in Mississippi commonly referred to "nigger news," and the newspapers ordinarily had columns entitled "Colored News," "News for Our Colored Friends," etc. (1967, 49-50).

Because of what he had read in the state newspapers, Harkey began to break five unwritten rules of Mississippi journalism. None of the changes he makes is particularly "heroic." All are examples of what was considered balanced reporting by newspapers in other regions of the country, and in one case, Harkey's own racial prejudice emerges. However, these new practices were enough to stun his readers:

1. Harkey dropped the word "Negro" unless the physical description was important to blacks and whites in the story. For example, if law enforcement officials were searching for someone, Harkey included the person's race and ethnicity. That policy continues in American newspapers today.
2. Harkey employed a courtesy title in addressing *some* African-American women. (Usually they were professional women.) Harkey said later that it was a "weak-chinned decision" on his part: "I wanted to be certain that the word was used only with patently respectable Negro women known as such to all the community" *(Smell* 2006, 49).
3. He published no Jim Crow lists. (The newspaper "did away with jim-crow lists and in its news columns segregated people only in accordance with news value and not by race"—*Smell* 2006, 50).
4. He mixed the birth announcements of black couples in with those of white couples until the registrar at Jackson County Hospital stopped supplying them.
5. He covered news of particular interest to African-American readers.

Awards and Accolades

In *The Smell of Burning Crosses,* Harkey describes receiving the Sidney Hillman Foundation Award for editorials in New York in April of 1963. The same year, he also won an award for editorials from the National Conference of Christians and Jews and from the Society of Professional Journalists. In addition, he was given recognition from the Paul Tobenkin Memorial Award Committee of the New York chapter of the American Newspaper Guild for "editorials opposing Governor Barnett" (18-19). A portion of his speech during the Hillman acceptance is a clear indicator of the level of emotion he felt after having been vilified by his community and lauded by strangers:

> I have committed many foul *un*-Southern crimes in the past 14 years. I have willfully agreed with the Negro Mississippian that he should be granted the rights of citizenship. I have maliciously tried to persuade other white persons that the Negro is entitled to the same fruits of citizenship that they themselves enjoy.
> And now here, today, at this very moment, I commit the darkest, most inexcusable crime of all as, with an abandoned and malignant heart, I aid and abet Yankees in recognizing and honoring my *un*-Southern villainy. *(Smell* 2006, 9)

On May 7, 1963, the day Harkey accepted his Pulitzer Prize, stories in the *Vicksburg Evening Post* were published with these headlines: "Liberal Writers Selected Again for Pulitzer Prizes" and "Anti-State Editorials Win Prize." Writing in the *Jackson Clarion-Ledger,* Tom Ethridge said: "This award for distinguished editorial writing is made each year under auspices of New York's Columbia University, a fountainhead of race-mixing ideologies and one-world radicalism." In Hazel Brannon Smith's back yard, the *Holmes County Herald* called Harkey a "traitor" *(Smell* 1967, 117-18).

Other stories were just as condemnatory. In the *Starkville Daily News,* an editor referred to William Faulkner (who received the Pulitzer Prize posthumously) and Harkey when he wrote that "two Pulitzer Prizes were awarded to Mississippians this week...Ira Harkey received an editorial award for his work in the Pascagoula *Chronicle.* The editorials all dealt with the Meredith case—and most of them critical of Mississippi. It seems that Pulitzer journalistic awards now deal more with subject matter than quality of writing. And, as we see it, the distinction is not nearly so great as it once was" *(Smell* 2006, 118). A *Charleston News and Courier* editor wrote, "A Mississippi editor who is out of step with Mississippi hardly could escape an award" *(Smell* 2006, 119), and Jimmy Ward, editor of the *Jackson Daily News,* wrote, "It takes a lot of naked bravery, unflinching courage and steely grit to write one of those editorials about the backward South. Gracious peace, the KKK may come after you the very next day and tar and feather you. Sure! If you're lucky enough to have THAT happen to you, you're a virtual cinch to win a Pulitzer Prize with enough Oak Leaf Clusters to start your own arboretum" *(Smell* 2006, 119-20).

Harkey was hardly oblivious to the criticism. With sarcasm, he told Beasley and Harlow that any more attention from the Northern media could get him killed: "And Barbara Walters wanted to get me to come up to do the *Today Show,* and I said 'That would get me killed for sure'" (75).

The Final Days

Harkey's brand of reporting and editing was too radical for his readership. On June 4, 1963, Harkey wrote his farewell to the Mississippi press and the citizens of his state. Fourteen years after he bought the *Chronicle,* he published the editorial "Spewers of Hatred Aren't Mississippi." Then, brokenhearted, he moved on. The editorial was one of Harkey's most passionate; its publication follows his being compared with the most loathsome of historical figures:

> Now that we have established the Caligula, Hitler and Lucifer prizes for hateists unworthy of Pulitzer Prizes, we take up another part of the situation—the idiot charge that it is "un-Mississippian" to win a Pulitzer Prize.

The contention has been advanced, of course, only by persons doubled-over with sour grapery, but it is believed nevertheless by many retarded people who do not have mind enough to discount the self-discredited sources.

Envious hacks have charged that the writing that won this year's Pulitzer Prize for editorial writing was "against Mississippi"…when in truth the editorials did exactly 180 degrees the opposite. The editorials were against race hate, against the un-Christian doctrine of white supremacy, against the demagoguery of political leaders that nailed Mississippi's name at the top of the western hemisphere's infamy list. The writing was "against" those who have come very close to destroying Mississippi.

The writer of those editorials believes what he learned of Christianity in Sunday school and what he learned of Americanism in history and government classes. He believes that he is no better before the law than any man, entitled to no rights that all other Americans are not entitled to. He believes it the primary mission of every man to help advance the welfare of every other man and never to stand in the way of self-advancement of anyone.

The winner of the 1963 Pulitzer Prize for editorial writing denies that foul-mouthed haters are "Mississippi," denies that ignoramus newspaper editors who promote hatred are "Mississippi," denies that politicians who make Mississippi detested wherever justice is loved are "Mississippi," denies that leaders who push demagoguery to the extreme of homicide are "Mississippi."

The writer of those editorials loves Mississippi as those leaders never have, as those carpers never could, as race hateists never would, else he could not since September 30, 1962, have been burdened with shame and guilt because of what those leaders, carpers and hateists perpetrated at Ole Miss.

The writer of those editorials feels his heart swell with sad pride when he hears the strains of Dixie, but the grand tune does not conjure up to him a scene of ignorance, disease, poverty and hatred, but a picture of compassion, honor, nobility and the code of gentlemen that the hateists know nothing about but by which Robert E. Lee lived.

The lowest elements in our society are ruling our state. But there will come a day when the hateist press will be ignored, the hateist politician will spew his venom to empty spaces and Mississippi's fair name will be extricated from the disgrace into which the hateists have thrust it. *(Smell* 2006, 132-33)

Harkey was revolutionary in ways that today seem unthinkable. He believed African Americans are human beings equal in every way to whites. This belief determined his editorial decisions, and he ran photographs of African Americans and addressed them with titles of respect in print.

Other editors were slow to follow his lead, even when they eventually shared Harkey's views about equality. Hazel Brannon Smith, for example, waited until Harkey and others altered journalistic practice before joining them in making historic changes: "In her early days as a publisher, Hazel Brannon followed her peers in the handling of news of blacks, separating the admissions, discharges and births in the hospital notes under 'white' and

'colored' subheads and referring to blacks in similar fashion in such stories
of them as were run" (Whalen 31). In fact, Whalen reveals that Smith joined
several other white editors "in taking issue with Ira Harkey...when he told a
Mississippi Press Association convention audience that he had dropped the
tags 'Negro' and 'colored,' had begun using the title 'Mrs.' for married
black women and had sought out favorable stories about blacks" (32).

Harkey was one of the first journalists to use courtesy titles for blacks
and to print their photos. As noted earlier, he did not use the word "nigger,"
nor did he write headlines such as "Two Men and a Negro Killed in Auto
Accident." Harkey said the headline "Two Men Hurt and a Nigger Killed"
remained in his mind: "For years a phantom headline—Two Men Hurt and
a Nigger Killed—has appeared in my dreams as a sort of apothegm for the
State of Mississippi, translated into Latin and wrapped around the state's
arms, cryptic but profoundly suggestive" *(Smell* 2006, 43).

Because of his policies, in only two months time, the *Chronicle* lost
five large advertisers, and its circulation plummeted. "The threats were
equally intimidating: A bullet through the newspaper door; a shotgun blast
through the window of his home; hate-filled letters; and the classic Klan
warning, a cross burning on his lawn" (Beasley and Harlow 65). In *The
Smell of Burning Crosses,* Harkey describes the horror of the cross burning:

> Not so easily brushed aside was an expression from another quarter,
> the Knights of the Ku Klux Klan. On the early evening of September 1, a
> few days before the opening of local schools for the new year, the Klan
> burned six-foot crosses at select locations around the city—before the Ne-
> gro schools, the largest Negro church and the Beach home of editor Har-
> key. One of my startled children first saw the blaze in front of our home
> and ran screaming to his mother. White-faced, round-eyed, she called me.
> I went out and hosed the evil thing. A message had been left, painted on a
> piece of brown corrugated cardboard. "We do not appreciate niggerlovers.
> We are watching you. KKKK." A few weeks before, Tommy Harper, the
> local Klan head, had stopped by for a chat. His unblinking snake-eyes
> fixed on mine, he had told me, "If any niggers try to register at white
> schools next month, we're not gonna bother them. The one we'll get is the
> white man that's behind them and we know who he is." (2006, 102-103)

In addition, the members of the Jackson County Citizens Emergency
Unit had dedicated themselves to putting Harkey's newspaper out of business, calling the newspaper itself "the leading niggerlover in the State"
(Smell 2006, 12). Within two months, the *Chronicle* lost five advertisers,
and circulation declined from 7,000 to 6,200, a devastating loss for a small
newspaper. As noted earlier, members of the racist group also fired shots
through the door and windows of Harkey's newspaper office: "On the night
of November 1, a shotgun blast blew out four windows in my private office" *(Smell* 2006, 173), Harkey said. Because the Unit was headed by the
county sheriff, Harkey could not ask for or expect protection.

Harkey was not opposed by radical groups alone; some of the most
startling examples of antagonism toward him come from unlikely places

and people. According to Beasley and Harlow, when someone shot out the two-foot section of the *Chronicle's* plate glass door, the *Chronicle* ran a front-page editorial and "continued its counterattack" (67). However, as noted earlier, one Jackson resident who worked as a librarian then wrote a letter saying, "[Instead] of a bullet through your door I hope you get a bullet through your stupid head" (68). That comment drew little protest, according to Beasley and Harlow, who write, "As no protest was voiced that a woman in such a job could hold and express such a sentiment, it may be assumed that she spoke the mind of the city" (68).

In his autobiography, Harkey explains that the letter from the librarian was a response to an editorial about Christianity and its teachings about equality. Uttered as a threat against Harkey if he chose not to publish the full text of her letter, the letter reads: "If you do not publish the enclosed copy of the letter...it will prove to the people of Pascagoula and Mississippi you are truly an integrationist and I hope you not only get a hole through your office window but through your stupid head. You deserve it if this answer does not appear in *The Chronicle*" *(Smell* 2006, 182). Harkey published the letter by the librarian, whom he refers to as "Mrs. Lott," and the messages that supported her.

The disappointment in his townspeople and the isolation that engulfed him took a terrible toll. As his neighbors and members of the Jackson County Citizens Emergency Unit continued their campaign, Harkey continued to write what he believed would lead Mississippi to a new day. Beasley and Harlow write:

> Although several leading citizens privately deplored the Emergency Unit's purposes, none would make a public statement. The sheriff's sponsorship of the Unit made it almost impossible for the *Chronicle* to obtain help from other local police organizations. But despite this isolation, a flood of hate mail and phone calls, personal ostracism of the *Chronicle* editor and staff, a boycott placed against the paper's advertisers, threats to carrierboys, and a shotgun blast that blew out the windows in the editor's office, the *Chronicle* continued to speak. (67)

Ira Harkey is no more influential than the editors to be discussed in "White Civil Rights Editors and Hazel Brannon Smith," nor was he a close friend of Hazel Brannon Smith's. He merits extensive coverage in a study that features Hazel Brannon Smith and the civil rights movement because he was an integrationist when even Smith herself would not use the word to describe herself. He merits coverage because he survived financially when Smith and others were forced out of business. He merits coverage because, unlike Smith, he was not averse to leaving the South when he felt his work there was complete. And he merits coverage because, like Smith, he won a Pulitzer Prize for editorial writing in a time and a place that made such an achievement nothing short of remarkable.

It is his courage in the face of insurmountable odds that makes Harkey memorable. When Harkey said that he did not champion revolutionary thought—in fact, when he said he believed in "routine American doctrine, the stuff heard at every Rotary Club meeting, the words of brotherhood spoken in every Mississippi church every Sunday morning, the spirit evoked in every declaration of allegiance to the flag uttered in every schoolhouse every schoolmorning and by grownups before every meeting of every civic club in the state" *(Smell* 2006, 54)—he was acknowledging how mainstream he believed himself to be.

Draping himself in the flag of the United States and the Constitution it represents, Harkey stood his ground. When he discusses the difference between himself and others who preach Christianity and espouse the tenets of the Constitution, he writes: "The only difference was that I meant it, every word of it, literally, unequivocally, and would practice it as well as recite it, applying it to all people, not just to white people, which is what the Southerner means when he says 'people'...Readers of *The Chronicle* were soon astounded to learn that among the 'us' *The Chronicle* actually proposed to include Negroes" *(Smell* 2006, 55). Harkey understood that racism involved hypocrisy and dishonesty. In response to one particularly harrowing expression of hatred toward others, he wrote, "That is one of the ironies of the Southern way of life. Integration has always been practiced between the sheets and in the bushes" *(Smell* 2006, 22).

The next chapter in *Burning Crosses and Activist Journalism* deals more fully with white supremacist groups and their impact on Mississippi editors such as Harkey. The editors, like Harkey, would eventually prevail. In the shadow of those who acted on their hatred of others, Harkey responded to discrimination with a simple and effective formula. In *The Smell of Burning Crosses,* he writes with pride and hope:

> *The Chronicle* still survived, strong with a new confidence born of having weathered perhaps the cruelest attack a newspaper can suffer, one stemming from race hate and sanctioned by its community's constituted authorities. Had we not fought back, had we not fully informed the people of Jackson County of the evil being planned by the Unit, we would have gone down.
>
> The moral here for newspaper editors is: Fight back without delay. Hit them, hit them, hit them. They are yellow and they are stupid, but only a well-planned, immediate and all-out counterattack can save you. (2006, 186-87)

As "White Hate Groups and Mississippi Newspapers" suggests, white supremacist groups held sway in the American South, but the days when they would terrify residents of Mississippi were numbered. Before they lost their ability to create fear and chaos, however, they would impact not only Harkey but other editors such as Hazel Brannon Smith and Hodding Carter Jr.

Chapter 3.
White Hate Groups
And Mississippi Newspapers

This section provides a transition between two essays about Hazel Brannon Smith and her colleague Ira B. Harkey Jr. and a discussion of the white civil rights editors who provided financial aid in an effort to protect Smith. The role of these well-known editors cannot be exaggerated.

Books such as *The Mississippi State Sovereignty Commission* by Yasu-hiro Katagiri and sections of books such as *Race Beat* by Gene Roberts and Hank Klibanoff deal in detail with the white supremacist movement in Mississippi. Because extensive works address the growth and intimidation of White Citizens' Councils, this essay provides instead an overview of their development and impact on individual editors.

White hate groups during the 1950s and 1960s were a potent force in the backlash against federal legislation outlawing discrimination in voting and employment. A thorough analysis of the origins and impacts of White Citizens' Councils and the Ku Klux Klan would, of course, require ex-tended studies, and others have accomplished far more than will be at-tempted here. However, the topic is essential to a discussion of Ira B. Har-key Jr. and Hazel Brannon Smith, and the impact of racist organizations is alluded to here and in other chapters in *Burning Crosses and Activist Jour-nalism.*

For a more complete understanding of white hate groups, readers may want to seek out book-length studies. One of those studies is Neil R. McMillen's *The Citizens' Council: Organized Resistance to the Second Re-*

construction, 1954-1964. In it, he suggests that members of the councils believed that "the threat of desegregation could be effectively minimized by
the removal of those who would 'stir up discontent'" (251). Although sup-
pressing the voices of African Americans was their first challenge, the
White Citizens' Councils soon turned to those in the white community who
stymied their plans: "The ways and means whereby moderate voices in the
white community could be suppressed were among the organization's first
concerns" (251).

White Editors and the Councils

Harkey and Smith spoke out often and passionately against the White Citizens' Councils, which separated themselves from the Ku Klux Klan by pre-
tending to protect the safety of white Mississippians and by enlisting the efforts of the most powerful and privileged white professionals in their communities. The pretense was that the White Citizens' Councils would not engage in violence but would maintain law and order by economic threat.
"This was the pitch of the Citizens Council, the white-collar Ku Klux Klan,
but it really did not work that way," writes Harkey. "So violently did the
Council speak out its defiance, that before an obstreperous 'nigger' could be
economically subdued, he usually was physically (and permanently) subdued by rednecks inspired to terrorism by the Council tirade, the only contribution that the inarticulate could make" *(Smell* 2006, 97-98).

Like Smith, Harkey was far-sighted enough to know that the councils
would gain strength and could succeed by intimidation. Because of their
development, he wrote the first page-one editorial of his career entitled
"You May Be Next":

> A terrorist group has been organized in your county. Its first targets
> are this newspaper and any white persons designated by the group's "ac-
> tion committee" as "niggerlovers."
> The group has been given a quasi-official status because it was spon-
> sored by the chief law enforcement officer of your county.
> It will attack the Chronicle initially by "putting pressure" on its ad-
> vertisers. Only a few of its members are people of any moral or economic
> standing in the community. The rest can apply pressure only through
> threats, intimidations and, ultimately, destruction. Among its members are
> a dozen men whose lives have been dedicated to participation in violence.
> Ten days ago the Chronicle called upon the decent element in our
> county to announce publicly that it wants law and order and to insist that
> our officials maintain law and order. We received an immediate response
> to that appeal—a bullet fired through our front door that night, blasting a
> two-foot section from the plate glass.
> Now this.
> If the responsible leaders of our community—its company presidents,
> club and fraternal heads and Christian churchmen—do not recognize the
> evil nature of this threat, do not organize immediately—tonight—and no-

tify our sheriff in no uncertain terms that he is leading our county and himself to disaster, they can say goodbye right now to their investments and their hopes and dreams for their future and that of their children.

We are under no illusion that anybody here cares what happens to Ira Harkey. But think long on this: what happens to him can happen to you. You may be next. *(Smell* 2006, 157-58)

According to John A. Whalen, Hazel Brannon Smith was almost immediately forced to deal directly with the formation of White Citizens' Councils in her county and others. "In mid-July of 1954, white citizens of Indianola, fifty-five miles northwest of Lexington, formed a Citizens' Council, the first unit in a movement that would mushroom quickly throughout Mississippi and surrounding states," Whalen writes. "With their primary purposes the maintenance of school segregation, the prevention of voting by blacks and opposition to 'moderates,' the councils publicly rejected Ku Klux Klan type violence. In its place, they ostensibly substituted social, political and economic pressure in the atmosphere of fear and unrest that permeated white society in the wake of *Brown v. Board of Education"* (83). In their attempt to set themselves apart and to identify groups that supported integration and equal rights, the councils called several legitimate organizations "subversive," including the American Red Cross, the Methodist church, the Federal Bureau of Investigation, the National Lutheran Council, the Interstate Commerce Commission, and the Young Women's Christian Association (Whalen 83-84).

Over time, the councils boasted as many as 60,000 members in more than 200 groups (Weill, "Mississippi's Daily Press" 22). These statistics indicate the influence the organization would have in the lives of white and black citizens of the state and suggest the dire impact its members might have over the circulation and advertising of small newspapers. It would not be long before Smith felt the sting of the new and increasingly influential organization.

The White Citizens' Council was born July 11, 1954. The first council in Mississippi was founded by Robert Patterson, manager of a plantation in Leflore County, and met in a home in Indianola, where blacks made up 68 percent of the 56,000 residents. Only .03 percent of the black residents were registered voters. The 14 men who gathered were mayors, dentists, druggists, bankers, farmers, sheriffs, lawyers, hardware store owners, auto dealers, and planters. By October 1954, there were 30 White Citizens' Councils in the state *(Race Beat* 66).

Harkey and Smith were not alone in their fear of the White Citizen's Councils. Hodding Carter Jr. and his wife Betty "feared that the Citizens' Councils could force the South into another Civil War" (Waldron 266). Carter Jr. remembers the challenges of being a newspaper editor during this time in *First Person Rural*. September 1954 was especially frightening because, he said, the "public can be aroused to a high and dangerously emotional pitch by demagogues and the causes demagogues espouse" and because the newspaper itself began to feel the "temper of the mob" (206):

In the wake of the Supreme Court's decision on the public schools, there have been organized in Mississippi widespread and still loosely bound groups which are called Citizens' Councils. Their avowed purpose is to fight integration of the races in Mississippi's public schools by non-violent means, including economic pressure. By and large, the Councils have been led by well-known and law-abiding men, though their operations have been quasi-secret.

But the organization of these Councils has emboldened bigoted and violent men, within and outside the Councils. So it is that in September 1954 there were circulated in our county and elsewhere three anonymous circulars. One threatened a boycott of Greenville because the directors of our baseball association had leased the ball park to a Memphis promoter who proposed to put on an exhibition ball game between Negro and white barnstorming clubs. Two of the directors are Jewish. The second circular was violently anti-Semitic. We had said editorially that we saw nothing wrong in such a game. The third circular was a crudely versified attack on me personally, in which racial fears and personal innuendoes slimily competed.

I am not so sure that the Citizen's [sic] Councils can keep their members within the announced bounds.

Which makes me feel that this is where I came in. We thought back in 1929 that the Klan had just been laid to rest. Newspapers and newspapermen must remember that the enemies we fight are never stilled. (207)

The first article about the White Citizens' Councils in Mississippi appeared September 9, 1954, in Carter Jr.'s *Delta Democrat-Times*. Reporter David Brown quoted those who characterized the group as "trying a peaceful and intelligent approach to a very difficult problem" and as wanting to provide "responsible, sincere and effective leadership in maintaining segregation" (Waldron 236). According to Ann Waldron, Brown also wrote freelance articles for *Time* magazine, which published a story based on his research. According to him, White Citizens' Councils "claimed a membership of 25,000 in twenty-four of Mississippi's eighty-two counties" during this time (237). Waldron writes:

Council membership played a leading role in December of that year in the passage of two state constitutional amendments, one intended to prevent black voter registration by requiring more difficult qualifications for voting and the other empowering the state legislature to abolish the state's public school system "as a last resort"—which meant if integration ever appeared unavoidable in Mississippi...

Mississippians voted two to one in favor of both the amendments that the Citizens' Councils wanted. In fact, the Councils won every battle they entered, and by the beginning of 1955 they were organizing in other southern states. The Councils were able to silence all vocal black opposition to segregation in Mississippi. When fifty-three blacks in Yazoo City signed a petition asking for an immediate end to segregation, the local Council outlined brutal economic retaliation: employers of the signers were to fire them, and landlords to evict them; retailers were to refuse credit to black customers who had signed, and wholesalers to cut off credit and supplies to black retailers who signed. When Clinton Battles, a black doctor in Indianola, registered to vote, urged other blacks to vote, and publicly supported the Supreme Court's decision, Council members warned his patients to find another doctor or lose their jobs. Most of Dr. Battles's patients deserted him. (237, 238-39)

The White Citizens' Councils used economic pressure against blacks to intimidate those who signed petitions in favor of desegregated schools. In 1955, the *Yazoo City Herald* "sold a full page of advertising to the Citizens' Council so that it could list the names and addresses of fifty-three local Negroes who had petitioned the school board there to desegregate. All but two were bullied into withdrawing their names—and still they lost their jobs, their credit, their interest in staying in Mississippi" *(Race Beat* 73).

Hoping for Smith's support in founding a local chapter of the White Citizens' Council locally, a citizen of Lexington approached Smith soon after the Indianola White Citizens' Council was formed. He said the group would renounce violence and would control blacks in the community through economic intimidation. When he said it might do the blacks good to be "a little scared," Smith responded in a manner that is characteristic of her and that created immediate and permanent divisions between herself and some local residents. "No, it's not a good thing for anyone to be a little scared," she replied. "People can't live under fear, and it will end up with all of us scared and it will be a big scare. What you are proposing to do is take away the freedom of all the people in this community" (Whalen 84).

Nonetheless, the Holmes County Citizens' Council was founded. The intellectually and socially "elite" and the law-breakers were now members of the same organization. Instead of public support for violence and intimidation, the Holmes County Citizens' Council relied at first on more subtle forms of discrimination and established itself as though it were as legitimate an organization as the Boy Scouts of America or the Chamber of Commerce. Smith said, "It finally got to the point where bank presidents and leading physicians were afraid to speak their honest opinions, because of this monster among us" (Whalen 85).

In *First Person Rural*, Carter Jr. details the ways in which Smith was targeted by the White Citizens' Councils. Since his description provides chronology and specifics, it is perhaps more helpful in a study of Hazel Brannon Smith than the editorial she wrote that punctuated the furor. Several paragraphs of his essay follow:

> The year 1954 was a tense one in Holmes County for another and more significant reason. In the wake of the United States Supreme Court's decision on school desegregation, the citizens of little Indianola, less than fifty miles from Lexington, organized the first White Citizens' Council, the white-supremacy group which, while abjuring violence or masking, pledged itself to hold down Negro voting, fight "moderates," and prevent school integration by economic and social pressures. A second unit was almost immediately organized in Holmes County. Among its leading

members were men actively aligned with the sheriff in his feud with the editor and suspicious of her advocacy of equal justice.

That summer a respectable Negro woman, a teacher for twenty years, was shot in her own home by a leading Lexington white man after she had remonstrated with him for driving his automobile into her yard and damaging it while turning around.

White Citizens' Council members and others tried to persuade Hazel Smith to kill the story. She printed it. Telling the story did no good, for no arrest was made. The wounded teacher was dismissed from the school and her husband was fired by the filling station operator for whom he worked. The pair then moved to Chicago.

The White Citizens' Council gathered momentum. County and state and Southern politicians began to cash in on the fear and unrest of the white people over the Supreme Court's frontal assault. Tensions in Holmes County increased...

Clearly she was becoming far too much a problem of the atavists to be dealt with lightly. The White Citizens' Council leaders began organizing a concerted advertising boycott. Her local advertising volume shortly fell off some fifty per cent, a loss which she has never recovered. She kept and even gained readership; but without the necessary advertising and commercial-printing volume, her papers began to suffer.

And in 1958 her enemies organized a new weekly paper at a meeting at which an officer of the local Citizens' Council presided and asked for stock subscriptions from those present—mostly Council members. The new weekly, the Holmes County *Herald,* has been subsidized from the beginning by well-to-do Council leaders. It couldn't have lasted three months without pressure in its behalf from county politicians and White Citizens' Council leaders, generally the same persons and all of the same readily recognizable stripe. (221, 223-24)

As noted earlier, the White Citizens' Councils were, in some ways, more dangerous than the Ku Klux Klan because they masqueraded as legitimate organizations and counted educated professionals and law enforcement officials among their membership. They intimidated both blacks in the community and whites who knew they had to work with bankers, law enforcement officials, and political leaders in order to prosper. As Roberts and Klibanoff write:

In marked contrast to the Ku Klux Klan, members of the Citizens' Councils wore their affiliation proudly. The councils, in an effort to allay fears about their mission, were quick to contrast their membership and tactics to those of the Klan; indeed, they said, they were the nonviolent alternative willing to work within the system to maintain segregation. The organizers made their appeals to the finest white people in town. Mayors, legislators, police chiefs, bankers, school superintendents, and other white-collar power brokers and major employers in town after town fell into line with the Citizens' Councils. So did some newspaper editors. *(Race Beat* 66)

"A Long Walk Home"

The impact of the White Citizens' Councils and the Ku Klux Klan on the lives of progressive newspaper editors is undeniable. Few examples of the role of White Citizens' Councils exist in popular culture, although the topic emerges in several lesser-known films and documentaries. In the 2002 film "A Long Walk Home," for example, a black woman and a white woman build a friendship in the cauldron of racial hatred during the 1955 Montgomery, Alabama, bus boycott. Narrated by Mary Steenburgen, the film is a reminiscence of childhood.

Seven-year-old Mary Catherine Thompson (Lexi Faith Randall) draws conclusions about the "cradle of the Confederacy" from her early experiences in her hometown and from her parents and their divergent reactions to issues of race and ethnicity. Her mother Miriam Thompson (Sissy Spacek) is passively tolerant of the racism around her; her life is devoted to keeping order in her home, and she wants to believe that all is right with the world. Although she intercedes when her black housekeeper is evicted from an all-white park while caring for the children of white residents of Montgomery, her call to the sheriff's office is motivated by her own sense of violation rather than her identification with or advocacy for her housekeeper.

As is true for child protagonists in Harper Lee's *To Kill a Mockingbird* and Carson McCullers' *The Member of the Wedding,* Mary Catherine forms a deep connection with the housekeeper, Odessa Cotter (Whoopi Goldberg). Cotter has worked for the Thompson family for nine years and is a nurturing mother figure for Mary Catherine. As in *To Kill a Mockingbird* and *The Member of the Wedding,* the black caregiver is considered a member of the family, but, in fact, like Calpurnia and Berenice Sadie Brown, Odessa Cotter has her own family and little time to spend with her own children.

When Rosa Parks quietly and determinedly alters the way black people are perceived throughout the nation, the narrator of "A Long Walk Home" is speaking of Parks, Cotter, and Miriam Thompson when she says, "I guess there's always something extraordinary about someone who changes and then changes those around her." Mary Catherine and her mother have grown to love Cotter; in fact, Mary Catherine says early in the film that Cotter was the "first woman to rock me to sleep," a statement that belies her mother's inability to express her love for her child and that testifies to the bond between white children and black caretakers and house servants throughout Southern history.

Although "Mississippi Burning," "Ghosts of Mississippi," and other films about the 1950s and 1960s in the South do not focus on the White Citizens' Councils, "A Long Walk Home" does. In it, Norman Thompson (Dwight Schultz) joins his brother Tucker Thompson (Dylan Baker) and other white men of the community in a council meeting. Miriam Thompson is stunned, saying to her husband, "These are the people that you said couldn't count to 10. You're going to go to one of their meetings?"

Her husband informs her that he'll join whatever organization he pleases. He says he'll join the White Citizens' Council or the Ku Klux Klan because everything is "out of control" in Montgomery. He also tells his wife that the community leaders are already members and that she cannot influence his commitment to the cause. Although Tucker Thompson jokes with his brother that there are "no white sheets" and "no secret oaths," the White Citizens' Council was, of course, devoted to making certain that black citizens remained powerless. Viewers learn that over half the small business owners in town are members of the council and that law enforcement officials are involved with its activities.

As her husband begins to attend meetings of the council, Miriam Thompson becomes introspective. When she peruses a worn photo album—presumably of her own childhood—she realizes how close she, too, was to her own black housekeeper. The bus boycott has affected her well-ordered life directly, since Cotter refuses to take public transit and must walk nine miles to Thompson's home and back at the end of the work day.

Ostensibly apologizing for her husband's refusal to let her drive Cotter to work, Miriam Thompson is actually apologizing for the racist infrastructure of the Deep South. In a quiet moment in her living room, she says to Cotter: "The rest of the world around you is living that way, and so you just don't question it." She tells Cotter about going to Portland, Oregon, when she was a teenager and watching as two black boys jumped into the swimming pool with the white children. She and her Southern friends immediately left the pool, but the residents of Oregon continued to play in the pool as though nothing out of the ordinary had occurred.

Miriam Thompson realizes that this memory of another society in which other rules prevailed changed her life. She also understands consciously, perhaps for the first time, how essential her black caregiver was to her own emotional well-being. With great feeling, Miriam Thompson tells Cotter that Cotter "does the mothering" in the home. She recalls a time when Cotter held Mary Catherine, who was ill with the chicken pox, without any apparent concern for her own health. Cotter had not had chicken pox, but her affection for the child overcame her own fears. Miriam Thompson says to Cotter, "I wonder. Would I have done that for your daughter?" Cotter does not respond because she, Miriam Thompson, and the viewers already know the answer. However, that Miriam Thompson would raise the issue is, of course, a signal that a seismic change has occurred in her own self-awareness and that she understands the significance of her home life as a microcosm of the larger society.

Miriam Thompson tells Cotter that she wants to drive in the car pool of volunteers helping black residents of Montgomery go to and from work and home. Cotter warns her that the bus boycott is just the first step; soon, she says, black citizens will insist upon their rights to visit all-white restaurants, to have integrated schools, and to vote. In spite of Cotter's warnings about retaliation, Miriam Thompson risks divorce and ostracism from her white community and begins to work on behalf of black residents of Montgomery.

At the end of the film, viewers learn that 50,000 people participated in the bus boycott and that on December 20, 1956, the Supreme Court made it illegal to force black citizens to ride in the back of any bus. Subsequently, four black churches and two homes were firebombed. Odessa Cotter's walk back and forth to work was a long journey home, but by implication, so was the civil rights effort by blacks and some whites in Alabama.

The History of the Councils

The story of white hate groups runs parallel to the resistance against school desegregation in the 1950s and and 1960s, James Meredith's admission to Ole Miss in 1962, the murder of Medgar Evers in 1963, and Freedom Summer in 1964.

White Citizens' Councils were for their constituency a kind of preemptive strike. The idea for such groups surfaced as early as 1953 in anticipation of a ruling by the U.S. Supreme Court on desegregation, and white members were correct to be concerned because the tide was turning and they would be required to make immediate and significant changes in the social and political structures that provided white citizens with significant advantages. In 1954, blacks faced "intimidation, restrictive poll taxes, and violence by the Ku Klux Klan and other groups" (Weill, "Mississippi's Daily Press" 21).

Even in 1954 when the Supreme Court voted to end segregation in the schools and in 1965 when Congress approved the Voting Rights Act, white hate groups in Mississippi refused to see that their time for intimidation and violence had come to an end, and many whites who supported equal rights lacked courage and/or opportunity to address the racism around them.

In "A Long Walk Home," Miriam Thompson volunteers to drive those who are striking against the transit company in support of Rosa Parks. But it is important to understand that in 1955, women relied for their very economic well-being upon their husbands. Her eventual commitment to social justice seems long in coming, but Miriam Thompson and women like her had much to lose. Fear of her husband was real to Miriam Thompson, and he hits her when she announces her intention to work on behalf of Cotter.

Fear of the White Citizens' Council is even more real to Miriam Thompson. When her husband becomes a member of the council, Miriam risks not only her marriage but custody of her child and physical injury or death at the hands of the white mob who prevent her from driving black residents to and from work and home.

One of the most dramatic case studies of the impact of the White Citizens' Council involves James Meredith, 29, an U.S. Navy veteran, who sought admission to the University of Mississippi in 1962. His attempt led to the integration of the campus, yes, but it also led to several days of rioting and the most difficult time in Mississippi for editors such as Harkey.

The White Citizens' Councils were, in many cases, at least passively supported by newspaper reporters and editors. So, for Meredith, the wall of hostile white faces in government, law enforcement, education, and journalism must have been terrifying. When Governor Ross Barnett promised that no school in Mississippi would ever be integrated, the federal government responded. According to Roberts and Klibanoff, the community response to the intervention is swift and angry: "The next day, amid rumors that federal agents were going to sweep into the Governor's Mansion in Jackson and arrest Barnett, the Citizens' Councils issued a call for supporters to come to the mansion and encircle it with 'a wall of human flesh.' More than two thousand people showed up and ringed the mansion. There was an air of celebration as they sang Dixie and fight songs, waved flags, honked their car horns, followed Ole Miss cheerleaders in cheers, and booed the Kennedy name" *(Race Beat* 289).

Further underscoring the relationship between racist groups and local newspapers, the *Jackson Daily News* published a fight song entitled "Never No Never" on its editorial page. The battle hymn of the small republic of Oxford was a song of defiance, rage, and racist rhetoric. The references to Barnett and Robert Kennedy are obvious:

> Never, Never, Never, Never N-o-o-o Never Never Never
> We will not yield an inch of any field
> Fix us another toddy, ain't yielding to no-body
> Ross's standing like Gibraltar, he shall never falter
> Ask us what we say, it's to hell with Bobby K
> Never shall our emblem go from Colonel Reb to Old Black Jo.
> *(Mississippi: The Closed Society* 119; *Race Beat* 289)

The events of September 30 and October 1, 1962, at Ole Miss also point to the failure of local law enforcement officials, who—because of their involvement in the White Citizens' Council—were often conflicted about their role. Since some were racists themselves, they responded to crises only because they were required by law to protect order. In Oxford, they were largely ineffectual against the horde of racists from all over the South who converged on the campus and the town. As Roberts and Klibanoff write:

> Soon the sheer number of outsiders coming onto the campus became too much for police, and they let down all barriers. Clusters of hostile white men who had driven from Louisiana, Alabama, Tennessee, and Arkansas streamed onto the university grounds; the growing mob soon approached 2,500 noisy, angry people who came ready to fight. Chanting, yelling, firing bullets and pellets, throwing bottles, sticks and cans, the mob seemed capable of overpowering the federal forces. Before the night was over, state and local law officers would quietly slip away from the campus, abandoning their positions and their public trust, leaving the feds to fend for themselves. *(Race Beat* 291)

The strength of the White Citizens' Councils eventually dwindled to nothing. As noted in "Hazel Brannon and Editor Ira B. Harkey," as many as 400 to 600 members attended meetings at the height of the Jackson County Citizens Emergency Unit. By February 1963, that particular organization had only 25 members. Before they lost their prominence, however, the members left terror and chaos in their wake, and they directly affected the livelihood of Mississippi editors, especially those who stridently opposed them, such as Harkey, and those who gradually came to speak out more publicly against them, such as Smith.

Escalating Conflicts with the Councils

Smith's issues with the White Citizens' Councils escalated during her time as editor of the *Lexington Advertiser* and her other newspapers. In January 1961, Smith criticized the Mississippi Sovereignty Commission for giving $5,000 per month to the White Citizens' Council. Later, Governor Paul Johnson ordered the practice to stop, but this did not occur until 1964 (Whalen 122).

Some of the attacks by the White Citizens' Councils were more than personal. On January 2, 1962, Mississippi Sovereignty Commission Director Albert Jones and an investigator, A.L. Hopkins, reported a meeting among Smith and her husband, "both white," and Medgar Evers, a field representative for the NAACP in Mississippi. The meeting, they said in an affidavit filed with the secretary of state's office, occurred at the offices of the *Mississippi Free Press,* a black newspaper, on December 15. The paper was founded by Evers, and Smith printed the newspaper on a contract basis (Whalen 135, 137).

Unsurprisingly, given the fact that White Citizens' Council members were also politicians, the attacks on Smith and her husband moved from the Mississippi Sovereignty Commission to the state legislature. Sen. T.M. Williams called attention to the affidavit in the state legislature, saying, "If you read her newspaper you would know why we have this attitude toward her. We are no longer proud of her paper." He accused her of being "smart, shrewd and—we later found out—scheming" (Wallace 30). Smith responded in an editorial January 11, 1962: "The question Holmes County citizens must decide now is whether they want to continue to have a newspaper open to all the people of the county, a newspaper that will honestly protect and defend their right to know, a newspaper that will not bow down to a boss-controlled clique which uses economic pressure, reprisals and intimidation of all kinds to hold an entire county in terror" (Wallace 31).

After local teenagers erected and burned a cross on her lawn, Smith became "more outspoken in her condemnations of the Citizens' Councils and called for the abolition of the Mississippi State Sovereignty Commission, a state agency she likened to 'a Gestapo' for subsidizing the councils and gathering files on dissenters" (n.p.), Mark Newman said. Although Smith had always condemned trespassing and intimidation, perhaps having high school boys involved—boys who were responding to the opinion their parents no doubt expressed about Smith—gave her a clearer understanding of how terrifying a burning cross in the middle of the night had been to black people throughout history.

In spite of opposition from editors such as Harkey and Smith, the Mississippi State Sovereignty Commission held sway from 1956 to 1973. On March 17, 1998, the commission papers were opened to the public, revealing the "fear, hysteria, and bigotry" that had characterized the organization (*Mississippi State Sovereignty Commission* 240).

On June 20, 1963, Smith published "Do Mississippians Today, As Sir Winston [Churchill] Put It So Beautifully, Have the Habit of Liberty?" It in, she alludes to the intimidation and control exerted by the White Citizens' Councils:

> There was a time, almost a decade ago, when we Mississippians were free...we did have the habit of liberty. Newspaper editors were free to write editorially about anything in the world, giving our honest opinions, and there was no fear of economic reprisals or boycott. Today a newspaper editor thinks a long time before he writes anything that can be construed as controversial...
>
> The editor of this newspaper has opposed the racist Citizens' Council from the very beginning—not because we oppose racial integrity and constitutional government they now claim to foster—but because in 1954 we recognized it as a serious threat to the personal freedom, peace and security of every living Mississippian—and its potential as a real Gestapo to take over the state. It is the individual freedom of our friends and readers we have and are fighting for...
>
> Our personal opposition to the Citizens' Council (although we have a large number of personal friends who belong to it) has been vindicated time after time in the past nine years as one after another good Mississippian has been smeared, lied about and given Citizens' Council treatment— many of them now living in other communities or in other states.
>
> That we have survived at all is a miracle we attribute only to God— but if He is for us then it makes no difference who is against us.
>
> God willing, we shall endure. (Beasley and Harlow 95)

When Smith alludes to the personal friends she had who were members of the White Citizens' Councils, she makes an important point. Educated, accomplished white professionals were the cornerstone of the councils in Mississippi, and as Smith wrote her editorial, she no doubt saw the faces of her friends and colleagues and envisioned their response. That she persisted in denouncing the organization is a tribute to her character and her courage.

As mentioned throughout the study, Smith's colleague and friend Harkey also was profoundly affected by the actions of the White Citizens' Council. And although the White Citizens' Councils were never able to drive Harkey into bankruptcy, the Jackson County Citizens Emergency Unit did significantly affect the financial stability of the *Pascagoula Chronicle* and made it impossible for Harkey to expand his operation and establish another newspaper. David Wallace writes:

> Although the plans for a second paper never came to fruition, the Unit's efforts soon began to affect the *Chronicle's* business...Harkey recalls that seven of the paper's newsboys quit without any explanation and circulation dropped 12 percent. Advertising was also affected, and there was reason to suspect that organized pressure was responsible. Similar to Smith, Harkey received word that several local businesses, including two department stores and a grocer, had been warned that if they continued to advertise in the *Chronicle,* they would be boycotted. (101)

Not one to be silenced, Harkey published his October 29 editorial entitled "If Goons Threaten You, Here is What to Do" and recommended that his readers not let their decisions be ruled by fear of the Jackson County Citizens Emergency Unit.

The fact remains, of course, that the White Citizens' Councils during the civil rights movement provided a legitimate avenue for white educated professionals to express racist ideology and hide behind an organization. The councils did great and irreparable damage to editors committed to covering all sides of the civil rights issues. Wallace writes about the victims of the White Citizens' Councils and the rage of their members:

> Included in these victims were the newspapers of Hodding Carter, Hazel Brannon Smith, P.D. East and Ira Harkey, among other "liberal" editors. Be it through organized boycotts or the collective effect of individual subscriber reactions, these journalists often experienced drastic drops in circulation and advertising. Paired with the economic backlash from the legal and social attacks, these boycotts created a significant financial burden for many newspapers. Hodding Carter publicly expressed his concern over this issue during a Joseph Pulitzer Memorial Lecture at Columbia University in April 1958. He warned, "The pressure groups frighten advertisers, and the papers come under the gun of the local merchants and local political bosses...Any threat to the more than 10,000 weekly newspapers also endangers the democratic concept of individual dignity and individual worth." No matter how steadfast these liberal journalists appeared in the face of social ostracism or litigation, this economic pressure posed a more immediate threat. Although certain journalists like Hodding Carter had built a financial foundation strong enough to weather these attacks, others were pushed deeply into debt and to the verge of bankruptcy. (90)

It would be inaccurate, of course, to portray all the editors of the Deep South as opposing the White Citizens' Councils and being victimized by them. In fact, the editors were sometimes members of the councils; in other cases, they were simply sympathetic to the views of council members and catered to them in their news and editorial coverage. In the capital city of Mississippi the *Jackson Clarion-Ledger* and *Jackson Daily News* were published by brothers Thomas Hederman and Robert Hederman. Whalen is among those who characterize them as racists:

> Their papers were available statewide and largely set the pattern of thought for white Mississippians. As the civil rights struggle gained momentum following the United States Supreme Court's school desegregation decision, the Hederman papers took the lead by means of editorials, personal columns and outright distortion of the news, in opposing activists and in kowtowing to the Citizens' Councils, established in 1954 to maintain segregation in the schools. Later, the papers became a powerful tool of the State Sovereignty Commission, established by the legislature in 1956 "to prevent encroachment upon the rights of this and other states by the federal government." (Whalen 31)

In spite of the influence of the White Citizens' Councils and the reluctance demonstrated by some of her colleagues to challenge their power, Smith decided issues on the basis of her responsibility to her readers, not on her own opinion. She understood her role to be that of providing residents with essential information as they decided for themselves how to respond to the civil rights movement, to the increasing involvement of the federal government, and to legislation that would eventually lead to a New South. "Ours is the only paper in the county," Smith said in 1964, "and I just cannot permit Citizens' Councils to tell me how to run my newspaper" (Moritz, ed., 385).

The editors whom we will meet in "White Civil Rights Editors and Hazel Brannon Smith" also opposed the White Citizens' Council and the argument by council members that they were not racist but were concerned citizens interested in maintaining law and order. In March 1955, Hodding Carter Jr., editor of the *Delta Democrat-Times,* published "A Wave of Terror Threatens the South" in *Look* magazine. As we will learn, the 89 members of the state legislature wasted no time attacking him. His response, entitled "Liar by Legislation," ends by telling the legislators what he thinks of them and their attempts to intimidate others: "I am hopeful that this fever like the Ku Kluxism which rose from the same kind of infection, will run its course before too long a time. Meanwhile, those 89 character mobbers can go to hell collectively or singly and wait there until I back down" *(Race Beat* 74).

Carter Jr. was far from alone in his experiences, although too few editors went public with their concerns for fear of alienating their readers and losing their livelihoods. (Certainly, those fears were realistic.) Ralph McGill, editor of the *Atlanta Constitution,* and Buford Boone, editor of *The Tuscaloosa* (Alabama) *News,* also attacked the White Citizens' Councils. However, as Roberts and Klibanoff write, "The councils and their like had found solid footing across the South—due in part to newspapers and local television stations that threw their full editorial weight behind them, but due in greater part to a larger number of quiescent editors who failed to take a stand against them" (74). As in "The Displaced Person" by Georgia writer

Flannery O'Connor, those who watch the murder are at least as dangerous as those who commit it.

"White Civil Rights Editors and Hazel Brannon Smith" deals with editors who gradually grew less cautious and more committed to equality for all citizens of the South. Their development may appear painfully slow to those reading their stories in the twenty-first century, but both their impact on the society and the risk they faced—even when their views seem moderate—are significant.

Chapter 4.
White Civil Rights Editors
And Hazel Brannon Smith

Although it might be more accurate to entitle this chapter "White Mississippi Editors During the Civil Rights Movement and Hazel Brannon
Smith," it is important to understand the continuum on which editors found
themselves. The editors featured in this chapter would not have called
themselves activists or crusaders, and if the phrase "civil rights editors"
suggests that they were all integrationists before their time, then the phrase
is inaccurate. Ira B. Harkey Jr. advocated unapologetically for equal rights
for African Americans, but other white editors—including those who
championed Hazel Brannon Smith—often were more conflicted about issues such as segregation (as was Smith herself).

Hazel Brannon Smith had the good fortune to be beloved and celebrated by many of her colleagues during the civil rights movement. There
were few women editors in Mississippi during the 1950s and 1960s, and she
faced a unique set of obstacles. Logically enough, most of those who came
to her aid—both personally and professionally—were white male editors
whose financial situations at their respective newspapers were more stable
than hers. One of those editors was Ira B. Harkey Jr., discussed at length in
Chapter 2, but others played pivotal roles in Smith's resistance against racism and discrimination in Holmes County.

In spite of a list of powerful opponents, Smith was not without friends
and supporters during her time as a Mississippi editor. Several prestigious

Southern editors—Mark Ethridge of the *Louisville Courier-Journal,* John Netherland Heiskell of the *Arkansas Gazette*, Ralph Emerson McGill of the *Atlanta Constitution,* and Nelson Poynter Jr. of the *St. Petersburg Times*— were among those who banded together to try to protect Smith. Chief among them was Pulitzer Prize-winner Hodding Carter Jr., publisher of the *Delta Democrat-Times* in Greenville, Mississippi, who formed a committee in 1961 to help raise money to offset her losses in advertising. That committee included Ethridge, Heiskell, and McGill. In addition, the *Columbia Journalism Review* established a fund to insure the survival of her newspaper, the *Lexington Advertiser,* and black subscribers collected almost $3,000 to help her remain in business.

In spite of their help, Smith "borrowed heavily and mortgaged her home to keep publishing," according to Sam G. Riley, and in the 1970s she had to sell two of her newspapers. In the fall of 1985, she filed for bankruptcy and closed her last two newspapers. "Eventually, she found herself a pariah to whites and to blacks, an ally they no longer needed" (304), Riley writes. Nonetheless, in 1961 when her colleagues became aware of her trouble, Smith's financial problems did not seem insurmountable.

In July 1961, Hodding Carter Jr. formed a group to address Smith's plight and called it the Tri-Anniversary Committee. This effort was more than a gesture to raise money to help offset the loss of revenue by Smith's newspapers. It was also a strong statement of support for her commitment to causes that he, too, espoused. The name of the committee came from Carter Jr.'s celebration of three milestones in Hazel Brannon Smith's life: her 25 years as an editor, the centennial of the *Durant News,* and the 125th year of the *Lexington Advertiser.* Francis S. Harmon, editor of the *Hattiesburg American* from 1926-31, was secretary. Nelson Poynter sent Smith a full-page ad for the "opening salute" in the Tri-Anniversary campaign. Smith ran the ad October 19, 1961. The competing newspaper, the *Holmes County Herald,* lost no time in attacking the committee, calling it a "group of out-of-state agitators, masquerading as do-gooders and moderates" (Whalen 130).

Although little documentation of the committee's work exists, there are letters between members, memorandums, and progress reports. According to a confidential memorandum circulated among the members on October 26, 1961, the committee "estimated that $16,400 was needed over the course of one year" to adequately address Smith's immediate needs (Wallace 122). The memo suggested that the funds "would be raised through the sale of individual advertising space in the *Lexington Advertiser* and *Durant News* for $164 per full page" (Wallace 122).

By the end of October, the group had raised between $6,000 and $8,000, depending on the source and depending upon whether advertising dollars or individual contributions are included. "The bulk of the contributions were used to pay off portions of Smith's bank notes and overdue interest, but part was used to take care of local debts and demonstrate to her opposition some signs of economic recovery. Afterward, the committee continued to solicit contributions, expanding its reach to several other editors and publishers, while also focusing on acquiring local and national advertising," according to a progress report (Wallace 124). In the October 26 memorandum to the committee, Harmon wrote: "I realize that this gal is trying to do the work of three people. She has so many problems it is a wonder she is still able to stay in the ring and fight. Above all, she *is* making progress!" (Whalen 132).

John A. Whalen writes in his biography of Hazel Brannon Smith that the Tri-Anniversary Committee members reviewed information about Smith's career and excerpts from her column and editorials so that they could be informed supporters during her most difficult time. They wrote letters asking that fellow publishers and editors buy ads in the *Lexington Advertiser* and the *Durant News*. The ads could be designated for the Red Cross, American Cancer Society, Boy Scouts of America, Girl Scouts of America, National Conference of Christians and Jews, the National Safety Council, or any organization dedicated to charity and/or education. Contributors could also simply provide funds "in appreciation of Hazel Smith's efforts in behalf of a free press" (Whalen 126). In fact, Norman E. Isaacs, managing editor of the *Louisville Times,* said:

> We're doing it because we believe so firmly in the right of free speech, because we want to show our appreciation of Hazel Smith's gallantry under economic fire, and because we want to see her courageous papers survive. As I said, we consider it our own private little battle. But freedom is never an exclusive battle and any and all who want to join are warmly welcomed. (Whalen 127)

Money came from newspapers in Boston, Chicago, Cleveland, Detroit, Honolulu, Houston, Little Rock, Los Angeles, Minneapolis, New York, San Diego, San Francisco, Seattle, Spokane, and Washington. According to Whalen, newspaper and magazine editors and reporters who donated money—both while the committee was in operation and after it disbanded—include Oveta Culp Hobby, *Houston Post;* John Denson, *New York Herald Tribune;* John Cowles, *Minneapolis Star and Tribune;* John W. Sweeterman, *Washington Post;* Alicia Patterson, *Newsday;* Paul Miller, Gannett Newspapers; William Maxwell, *Chicago Tribune;* Leonard Davidow, *Family Weekly;* Harry Ashmore, *Arkansas Gazette;* James Linen III, *Time;* Frank Stanton, CBS; Roy W. Howard, Scripps-Howard Newspapers; and Gardner Cowles, *Look.*

Others include John A. Clements, Hearst Magazines; Robert McLean, Associated Press; Palmer Hoyt, *Denver Post;* DeWitt Wallace, *Reader's Digest;* John Knight, Knight-Ridder Newspapers; Tom Vail, *Cleveland Plain Dealer;* Don Maxwell, *Chicago Tribune;* Katharine Graham, *Washington Post;* Mike Cowles, Cowles Communications; and Abigail Van Buren, the columnist also known as "Dear Abby" (Whalen 127-28, 198-99).

Clearly, efforts by these people and others were polarizing and controversial. Some editors and other donors, such as Jonathan Daniels of the *Ral-*

eigh News and Observer, sent checks but asked Smith to withhold their names. The request usually had nothing to do with protecting themselves but with protecting her. Daniels recommended that she not mention him publicly because of the backlash she might experience, "since along with Hodding and Ralph McGill I'm listed by Citizens' Councils as among the devil's disciples" (Whalen 129).

Hodding Carter Jr. was direct and emotional in his plea for his fellow editors to come to the assistance of his friend and colleague Hazel Brannon Smith. One of the most dramatic statements issued on her behalf reveals anger toward the moral people who failed to risk exposure and do what they believed to be right: "Maybe the brave bigots will stop putting up. Maybe the now silent, decent people will begin speaking up," Carter Jr. said. "If not, another light will have gone out in a shadowed state" (Whalen 200).

Several paragraphs from his 1961 essay "Woman Editor's War on Bigots" are worth sharing here. The cited section follows two paragraphs in which Carter Jr. describes the stereotypical Southern belle and Southern gentleman and questions whether or not gentility and manners are dead in Mississippi. Certainly, Carter Jr. believed that there was no chivalry, compassion, or fairness in the treatment Smith received. He writes:

> Working day and night, learning the art of printing as well as of publishing, tirelessly striving to make Lexington, Durant, and all of Holmes County better and more profitable places to live, Hazel wrought miracles in the old shop in Lexington in which the papers were printed...
>
> So what will happen next? There is no real wealth in Holmes County. It is unlikely that the *[Holmes County Herald]* will survive if Hazel's friends begin to speak out, as some already are doing. Men get tired of indulging their prejudices at the expense of their pocketbooks. And this is exactly what is happening in the case of the Holmes County *Herald,* a travesty of a newspaper which is only an instrument devised to destroy a brave woman, who twenty-five years ago came to Mississippi with eyes shining and dreaming a dream that had to do with the rights of all men and the freedom of newspapers to speak their pieces...
>
> And perhaps the supreme irony is that nowhere outside the Deep South would Hazel Brannon Smith be labeled even a liberal in her racial views. If she must be categorized, then call her a moderate; a churchgoing, humanity-loving newspaper woman who takes seriously her responsibilities toward her fellow men. But that doesn't fit well in Holmes County where the most benighted are today also the most powerful. *(First Person* 218, 224-25)

Although the committee had a limited life span, when its work ended, Carter Jr. set up the "Hazel Brannon Smith Fund" in 1965 with help from Edward W. Barrett, dean of the Graduate School of Journalism at Columbia University. Both in 1959 and in 1965, Carter Jr. called Barrett to ask his help in publicizing the problems with which Smith was dealing. Barrett and Carter Jr. launched a national campaign to raise money, and in 1965 after they wrote a column in the *Columbia Journalism Review,* contributors provided $2,000.

Historians comment often on Carter Jr.'s unwavering support for his friend. "Carter's most ardent—and longest standing—support was on behalf of Hazel Brannon Smith, the editor of the *Lexington Advertiser,*" writes Ginger Rudeseal Carter. "Smith—also a Pulitzer Prize-winning editorial- ist—had been threatened nearly out of business, her newspaper fire- bombed, her daily existence threatened at every turn" (283-84).

Hodding Carter Jr.

The life and contributions of William Hodding Carter Jr. are discussed more prominently in this chapter than those of his peers because of his special commitment to Hazel Brannon Smith and her reliance upon him. Hazel Brannon Smith and Hodding Carter Jr. were moderates. Among other Mis- sissippi editors—including Harkey and Smith—Carter Jr. was by far the best known editor and publisher inside and outside the state. In the 1950s, he was "one of the two most celebrated Southern spokesmen" (286), ac- cording to Ginger Rudeseal Carter. The other, she said, was McGill.

Whether as well known or not, there is little doubt about the talent and tenacity of all the editors celebrated in this essay, several of whom won Pul- itzer Prizes. Carter Jr. won a Pulitzer Prize in 1946; McGill, in 1959; Har- key, in 1963; and Smith, in 1964.

By contemporary standards, it is difficult to think of Carter Jr. as pro- gressive. Understanding that he was considered liberal by some residents in Mississippi is the best indicator of how powerful racist rhetoric was in the 1950s and 1960s. For example, for a time Carter Jr. favored integration at the college level, but not in earlier grades (Weill, "Mississippi's Daily Press" 28). At first, he simply called for "equalizing the conditions in sepa- rate schools," saying this was a "human rights issue" (Ginger Rudeseal Car- ter 277), and this position earned him the wrath of many of his readers and neighbors, who considered even this balanced stance too radical.

When Carter Jr. published *First Person Rural* in 1963, the book jacket lauded him as the "foremost integrationist in the South," and Carter Jr. re- called the book. The new jacket called him "one of the South's leading spokesmen" (Ginger Rudeseal Carter 281), and he was satisfied with that description. "While his journalistic peers honored him, the segregationist establishment of his home state vilified him" (275), Ginger Rudeseal Carter writes.

Although Ann Waldron calls Carter Jr. a liberal throughout her biogra- phy, it is important to read her argument and understand her definition; otherwise, the title is debatable. His tendency to defend his homeland by suggesting that African Americans were better off in the segregated South than in a "grisly Northern ghetto" is not a liberal sentiment, although Wal- dron suggests Carter Jr. was "moving toward a slightly more progressive stance" when he championed a "purposeful liberalism" that was "lighting up dark and tragic corners of a harried region" (222). Waldron writes:

> Defiant reactionaries at home branded the liberal a communist, a nigger-lover, a Yankee tool, Hodding said, and he was at the same time a target for the militant, all-or-nothing crusaders who fought their war at a distance. If he advocated or praised local equal hospital facilities, or pushed for equal pay and facilities in the separate school systems, or for the inclusion of blacks on trial juries, northern liberals who believed in the immediate ending of segregation "at the point of a bayonet" would denounce him for endorsing the status quo, while people who yearned for the good old days would whiplash him for endangering it. (223)

It is difficult to read editorials by Carter Jr. and find evidence of the fear that plagued other small-town editors. However, in her biography, Waldron confirms that Carter Jr. was often under fire and anxious about his livelihood. In a section on his life from 1947 to 1954, Waldron writes: "While he was never physically afraid, Hodding was assailed by fear that his whole enterprise could go under at any time. His anxiety became acute, his son Philip remembered, as the racial situation worsened" (174). And Waldron writes that the Carters "installed an alarm bell that would ring from the big house to the little house, so whoever was staying there could get help" if it was necessary and that they "kept guns in every room of the house and in the glove compartments of the cars" (250).

Greenville, Mississippi, was home to Carter Jr.'s *Delta Democrat-Times*. At the time Carter Jr. was editor, Greenville was a small town in Washington County and had the largest proportion of blacks in the state. Carter Jr. loved his community and loved Mississippi, and it is perhaps his affection for his home that sometimes blinded him to the intense problems there. In "I'll Never Leave My Town," he writes:

> I am not concerned here with segregation. It is a fact in Greenville and largely will remain a fact for a long, long time. But, within the pattern, Greenville has been extraordinarily fair. Ours was the first Mississippi community to provide a public swimming pool for Negroes, a counterpart of the one constructed for whites. Our new General Hospital houses Negro and white patients in identically equipped wings. The operating rooms are common to both races; qualified Negro doctors can operate there—a privilege that is rare in more places than Mississippi.
>
> I cannot say that our separate school systems are truly equal. But, since the war, we have built a new Negro high school and two new Negro grammar schools and have remodeled two others. Most of this was done before the South was prodded by the courts into trying to live up to the separate but equal principle, if only as a deterrent to integration. Also, we had moved a long way toward equal pay for equally qualified teachers, regardless of race, before our state recognized that principle.
>
> Too many of Greenville's Negroes live in substandard houses—so do too many of our white citizens. We are now trying to do something about our slums with a proposed building code and clearance projects. Yet more

than half of our Negro families own their own homes, and some of these are as good as or better than most of the white dwellings.

We have discrimination in labor. But 1100 Negroes are employed in skilled and semiskilled categories in our industries. Almost as many Negroes as whites work as carpenters, masons, electricians, plumbers, and mechanics. A Negro is one of our principal masonry contractors. Another is a house mover whose equipment is worth more than $75,000. And if this is still a long way from perfection, it is an even longer way from the imperfection that challenges the national conscience. (236)

Assessments such as this one characterize Carter Jr. as someone from a particular generation and as someone who never espoused integration wholly or enthusiastically. Incremental steps toward equality suited him, and he focused as much on the progress he perceived had been made as he did on the goals to which the community should dedicate itself. In the same chapter, he writes:

I believe that a publisher should quit a community he does not embrace. I love my town. If I should ever feel otherwise, and if my three sons should decide in turn that our newspaper is not something they want to hold, I would sell the *Delta Democrat-Times*. And however bright a picture I have honestly tried to paint, I know that Greenville is far from perfect. In our newspaper we continually make known our awareness that we have our cheats and chiselers and free-loaders, our bigots and Scrooges, our slums and slum profiteers, our juvenile delinquents and pettifoggers and our shirkers and haters and just plain inert citizens. But I also believe that such civic aberrations haven't shaped the direction of Greenville. (243)

Carter Jr.'s positive sentiments about Greenville carried over into his opinion about his job and the profession he had committed to serving. The final line of his book *First Person Rural* reads: "I would rather be a small city newspaper editor and publisher than anything I know" (249).

The life of Hodding Carter Jr. is worthy of detailed attention such as that provided by Waldron in *Hodding Carter: The Reconstruction of a Racist*. For our purposes, it is important to focus primarily on the way in which his ideas evolved and on the central role he played in encouraging editors and reporters throughout the nation, especially Hazel Brannon Smith. In spite of the fact that Carter Jr. changed his attitudes slowly, he is now remembered as an editor who promoted the civil rights movement. "He didn't believe the haters should be allowed to succeed in silencing any newspaper," Carter III said (Ginger Rudeseal Carter 284).

The Development of a Southern Editor

Carter Jr. was born February 3, 1907, in Hammond, Louisiana. He attended Bowdoin College in Brunswick, Maine. While in college, Carter is said to have gone to "great lengths to avoid a black student, moving into a different dorm room to distance himself" (Ginger Rudeseal Carter 268). He then attended the Columbia School of Journalism and Tulane University. He describes his early newspaper days in "A September to Remember":

> In September 1929 I got my first newspaper job on the New Orleans *Item*, to which, after five years of college and one year of college teaching, I was worth $12.50 for a fifty- to sixty-hour work week. In September 1936 my wife and I came to Greenville to establish a then competitive and now monopolistic afternoon daily after selling the tiny tabloid daily which we had established four years before in Louisiana and had somehow kept alive. In September 1954 my son returned to college from his own first newspaper job, also on the *Item*, where his starting pay was roughly four times as much as his father's had been. *(First Person* 204)

Carter Jr.'s rise to fame is nothing if not colorful, and his southern sensibility is obvious throughout his development as a writer. In this reference from his autobiographical collection of essays, the Louisiana newspaper he founded and sold was the *Hammond Daily Courier.* During his time in Louisiana, Carter Jr. gained experience challenging authority by fighting corrupt Governor Huey P. Long and his political machine. He received national attention for a series of articles in *The New Republic,* the first of which was entitled "Kingfish to Crawfish" and was published January 24, 1934.

In 1936, he moved to Greenville and founded the *Delta Star* to compete with the *Daily Democrat-Times.* In 1937, he startled his readers by running a photograph of a black man, Olympic athlete Jesse Owens, on the front page. As Ginger Rudeseal Carter notes, "But it is significant that the subject—Jesse Owens—was a national, not a local figure; it would be years before he made similar, and riskier, moves in his paper for local blacks" (271).

Carter Jr.'s career took off when he moved to Mississippi and became invested in the life of the state socially and politically. His ability to make friends easily served him in good stead and connected him with those who were and would become well known in America's literary and political circles, including historian Shelby Foote, who worked for Carter Jr. in 1936. In 1938, Carter Jr. bought the *Daily Democrat-Times,* merged it with his paper, and called the new entity the *Delta Democrat-Times.* In 1939, he was awarded a Nieman Fellowship at Harvard; in 1945, a Guggenheim Fellowship in creative writing; and in 1946, a Pulitzer Prize for editorial writing.

During his lifetime, he published 20 books, published articles in national magazines, conducted numerous speaking engagements, and was affiliated with Sigma Delta Chi (now the Society of Professional Journalists), the Pulitzer Prize selection committee, the Nieman Fellow alumni group, and the American Society of Newspaper Editors. He is remembered for having defended Japanese Americans who served in the military or who were forced to live in relocation camps during World War II. Carter Jr. also worked for the United Press and Associated Press, assignments that provided him with a sense of fairness and balance in the coverage of hard news stories.

Carter Jr. was at the forefront of the support system for Smith. His "diversified media operation left him more immune to segregationist attacks and in a position to take on a support role for several journalists," Wallace writes. "He had stood by Smith personally and financially since her troubles began" (120). According to Ginger Rudeseal Carter, even more than other editors in the South, Hazel Brannon Smith "found Carter to be an inspiration and a help in her own newspaper struggle" (267). One of the reasons he was so effective an advocate was his willingness to publicly endorse those with whom he agreed. For example, Whalen describes a speech Carter Jr. gave in 1958 in which he featured Smith:

> Hodding Carter, in delivering the third annual Joseph Pulitzer Memorial Lecture at Columbia University Graduate School of Journalism on April 26, 1958, warned that pressure groups in small communities were threatening the independence and survival of weekly newspapers, endangering the "democratic concept of individual dignity and individual worth." Citing the case of Hazel Smith, he noted that "her papers have been subjected to advertising boycotts, her windows have been broken, and she and her husband have been taunted by students in the street." (108)

In addition to founding the Tri-Anniversary Committee and the "Hazel Brannon Smith Fund," Carter Jr. looked for seemingly small ways to reinforce Smith in her efforts. On February 21, 1957, for example, Carter sent Smith a $500 prize he had won in the American Traditions Project Contest sponsored by the Fund for the Republic, "an organization concerning itself with civil rights." In the letter he wrote to compete for the prize, he said, "Hazel Brannon Smith has had to pay as high a price in relative financial loss and in personal harassment to uphold the principle of freedom of the press as anyone I know in the United States" (Whalen 104).

Carter Jr. advocated for others, but he was not immune to having to confront problems in Greenville and elsewhere himself. He was a cordial, outgoing person who enjoyed being with other people, and he never made peace with being attacked personally for his views. Hodding Carter III said his father "hated being seen as the enemy within almost as much as he hated the bigotry, the overt racism, the dehumanizing results of segregation, the corrupted political process produced by rigid adherence to white supremacy as the guiding principle of principles" (Ginger Rudeseal Carter 266).

In one of his most provocative pieces, entitled "A Wave of Terror Threatens the South," Carter Jr. compared the White Citizens' Council to the Ku Klux Klan and warned of its potential for violence. The piece was published in *Look* magazine March 22, 1955. A few weeks after the piece ran, he learned that the Mississippi legislature had voted 89 to 19 to call his comments in *Look* a lie. Before and after the vote, members of the Mississippi House of Representatives had called him a "nigger-lover editor," a "scalawag," a "lying newspaperman," a person who "as far as the white people of Mississippi are concerned, should have no rights" (Wallace 25).

As noted earlier, in "Liar by Legislation," Carter Jr. writes about the Mississippi legislature and its most virulent attack on him. At the time the legislators were meeting, he was hunting with friends 40 miles from Greenville. When a friend dropped off a press association report and a note from his wife, Carter Jr. learned that the Mississippi House of Representatives had written a resolution April 1, 1955, stating that Carter Jr. had "lied, slandered [the] state, and betrayed the South" in the March 22 *Look* magazine article (208). In *First Person Rural,* he writes at length about the experience:

> Then I read the wire service report. It was like being kicked in the stomach by eighty-nine angry jackasses. That number of state legislators, with nineteen opposed and thirty-two others not voting, had officially branded me a liar. During two hours of angry debate preceding the vote, I had been described in terms not often used by lawmakers. I was a Negro lover and a scalawag, a lying newspaperman, a person who "as far as the white people of Mississippi are concerned, should have no rights." I had sold out the South for 50,000 pieces of silver. (Note to *Look*: You owe me money.)...
>
> I am hopeful that this fever, like the Ku Kluxism which rose from the same kind of infection will run its course before too long a time. Meanwhile, those 89 character mobbers can go to hell, collectively or singly, and wait there until I back down. They needn't plan on returning. *(First Person* 209-210)

The action by the legislature was not the only retaliation Carter Jr. faced during his career. Another incident led to white supremacists burning a five-foot effigy of him in Glen Allan, Mississippi. The Indianola, Mississippi, mayor and board of aldermen attacked Carter Jr. for advocating for freedom of speech for Oliver Emmerich, a fellow editor. Carter had argued that Emmerich should be protected by force if necessary. On December 9, 1961, the *Jackson Daily News* ran the following headline: "Hodding Carter Urges Force to be Used to Integrate State." According to David Wallace, there was rarely a lull in the anger directed at Carter:

> The ramifications of his opinions appeared in ways both large and small. In 1962, as a result of his stand against the White Citizens' Council, he was voted off the board of the Delta Council, an economic development group for the region. In addition, that same year, he was not re-elected to the vestry of St. James Episcopal Church after voicing his opinion that no one should be turned away from services, regardless of race. (22)

Throughout Carter Jr.'s career, the home he shared with his wife Betty in Greenville was a refuge for reporters and editors weary with covering the civil rights struggle. "Feliciana became a shelter and a community for an eclectic, exotic mix of national and local newspaper, television, and newsmagazine reporters, foreign journalists, field representatives from progressive organizations in the South, an occasional FBI agent and a few enlightened souls of the Delta who subscribed to *The Atlantic Monthly, Harper's Magazine, Saturday Review of Literature,* or *The New Republic" (Race Beat* 203).

In her biography, Waldron writes that "Hodding was a mentor to a host of younger journalists in Mississippi" and that "everyone perked up" when he and his wife walked into meetings of the Mississippi Press Association (170). And throughout the roller coaster ride that was Mississippi journalism in the 1950s and 1960s, the Carters continued to give parties that cheered up their friends. One of those whom they encouraged said, "Hodding gave me a reason to think what I was doing was worthwhile. He made me want to continue in journalism. If it hadn't been for him I would have left. He gave us hope" (Waldron 251).

It is in "Liar by Legislation" that Carter Jr. makes plain his position as a moderate in a time of chaos and fear. His middle-of-the-road stance is unacceptable to some of his contemporary critics; ironically, his middle-of-the-road stance was wholly unacceptable to the racists of his day as well. Carter Jr. wrote about the changes that occurred during his lifetime and those his sons discussed with him. Unfortunately, references to "numerical pressures" and "Negro migration" suggest Carter Jr.'s own racial biases and his mistaken belief that African Americans should begin to leave the region in order to lessen the fears of white citizens. Nonetheless, a section from *First Person Rural* is essential to our understanding of his editorial position and his role in advocating for editors such as Hazel Brannon Smith. He writes:

> I don't mean that many white Southerners are willing to have public schools integrated now, especially in the Deep South where numerical pressures are greatest. But they know that inflammatory political behavior and the formation of vigilante groups aren't the answer any more than would be a Supreme Court edict ordering complete integration next fall. There must be a middle ground.
>
> That brings up something personal. I've been pretty much a middle-of-the-roader all my life. Some of my fellow Southerners think otherwise. They've been conditioned largely by political demagogues to believe that anybody who challenges extremism in the South is in league with the Supreme Court, the N.A.A.C.P., the Communist party, the mass-circulation magazines, and everybody north of the Mason-Dixon Line to destroy the Southern way of life. There's a lot of it I do want destroyed. There's a lot I want to keep.
>
> And some of my non-Southern correspondents have been wrong also, though in a kindlier way. They envision a dangerous life for the Southern dissenter, or, at the best, a social and economic martyrdom. That, I am glad to say, just isn't so, though it could have been twenty years ago...
>
> The gradual adjustment will be aided by accompanying improvement in the Negro's economic status; by Negro migration which will reduce the pressure of numbers; by the tolerance of those who today are our young; and by the persistent growth of the idea that democracy and Christianity

and man's responsibility for his brother are all facets of the same bright dream.

I know that, against these forces, the South's braying demagogues, its Klans and Councils and Southern Gentlemen, Inc., cannot forever stand. As our eldest son, who is twenty, disdainfully told our ten-year-old, who has been delighted with all the excitement:

"If you think this is something, you should have been around when I was in the fifth grade..."

Or when I was. (214-16)

A Legacy of Hope

Some argue that Carter Jr.'s philosophical evolution was admirable and was all that could be expected of him during the dark days in Mississippi. In the introduction to her biography, Waldron said she "marveled at Carter's long, spectacular journey from his childhood in a segregated Louisiana to the lonely place where he was almost the only voice of reason in Mississippi during the early days of the racial revolution and eventually the South's most celebrated spokesman for racial justice. I could hardly believe the day-to-day horror of his life—threats, ridicule, insults, boycotts—as he conscientiously goaded fellow Mississippians on racial matters and they, in turn, tried to isolate him socially and run his newspaper out of business, and even threatened to kill him" (xii).

Although it is difficult to argue that Carter Jr. (or anyone else during this unsettled period) was not a product of his or her time, Carter Jr. was one of the bright lights in a dark place. And his support of editors such as Hazel Brannon Smith was one of his most compassionate and wise acts. Certainly, he is one of the best known white editors during this time period.

As noted, Carter Jr. published more than 20 books during his time as a Mississippi editor. Since most deal with the South and his evolving perceptions of the region, they are listed here: *Lower Mississippi* (1942), *Civilian Defense of the United States* (with Ernest Dupuy, 1942), *The Winds of Fear* (1944), *Flood Crest* (1947), *Southern Legacy* (1950), *Gulf Coast Country* (with Anthony Ragusin, 1951), *Where Main Street Meets the River* (1953), *John Law Wasn't So Wrong: The Story of Louisiana's Horn of Plenty* (1952), and *Robert E. Lee and the Road of Honor* (1955).

Others are *So Great a Good: A History of the Episcopal Church in Louisiana and Christ Church Cathedral* (with Betty Carter, 1955), *The Marquis de Lafayette: Bright Sword for Freedom* (1958), *The Angry Scar: The Story of Reconstruction* (1959), *First Person Rural* (1963), *Doomed Road of Empire: The Spanish Trail of Conquest* (with Betty Carter, 1963), *The Ballad of Catfoot Grimes and Other Verses* (1964), *So the Heffners Left McComb* (1965), *The Commandos of World War II* (1966), *Their Words Were Bullets: The Southern Press in War, Reconstruction, and Peace* (1969), and *Man and the River: The Mississippi* (1970). He edited a book entitled *The Past as Prelude: New Orleans, 1718-1968* (1968).

In addition to books, from 1947 to 1954, Carter Jr. wrote articles for *The Saturday Evening Post, Reader's Digest, Look, Collier's, Holiday, The New York Times Magazine, This Week,* and *Ford Times.* He wrote book reviews for the *Times* and the *New York Herald Tribune.*

Like Smith and Harkey, Carter Jr. knew he was beloved by many, and he won his share of tributes. In 1971, Carter Jr. received an alumni association award for lifetime achievements from the Columbia University School of Journalism. Betty Carter and Willie Morris went to New York to accept the award on his behalf. Carter Jr. died April 4, 1972, and by then must have known that Smith's career had plummeted.

But Hodding Carter Jr.'s legacy continued with his son, Hodding Carter III. The younger Carter wrote his dissertation about the White Citizens' Councils, which later was published as *The South Strikes Back.* Carter III became managing editor of the *Delta Democrat-Times* in 1960 and editor and associate publisher in 1966. He remained at the newspaper until 1977. Invested in social issues during the civil rights movement, he reactivated the Mississippi Young Democrats and co-sponsored a new Head Start agency, Mississippi Action for Progress (1966).

In addition, Carter III was one of the editors who stood by Harkey when he won the Pulitzer Prize. Like his father, he encouraged those who faced racial and ethnic prejudice, and he championed their publications. In his autobiography, Harkey records the defense Carter III wrote on his behalf:

> "A Jackson publication which appears daily," young Carter wrote, "has published the scribblings of one of its crew making light of the Pulitzer Prize earned by Pascagoula's Editor-Publisher Ira Harkey. Even to the non-journalist, the Pulitzer is known as one of the highest, most honorable awards that can be received, a fact that is recognized around the world. In Editor Harkey's case, he had the intellectual courage to attack the idiocy which prompted some extremists to demand closing of Ole Miss rather than admit James Meredith. For this, he endured personal abuse, and escaped injury from gunshots. To sensible people, Harkey needs no apology, in any case." (125)

Betty Carter sold the *Delta Democrat-Times* in 1980 when it became clear that neither Hodding Carter III or Philip Carter was interested in stepping into his father's shoes. The newspaper sold to California chain Freedom Newspapers for between $14,000 and $16,000. At the time, it had a circulation of 17,000 (Waldron 327).

Carrying on the family's level of accomplishment, Carter III won a Nieman Fellowship in 1964, worked for President Lyndon Johnson, was assistant secretary of state for public affairs for President Jimmy Carter, and headed the John S. and James L. Knight Foundation in Miami, Florida. Although not interested in carrying on his father's legacy as a newspaper editor for more than a few years, he wore his family name proudly and has worked in journalism and public service throughout his career.

Other Editors Who Championed Smith

Although Hodding Carter Jr. led the charge, other editors were instrumental in supporting Hazel Brannon Smith as well, and she could not have survived financially as long as she did without their assistance. The Southern editors who were most invested in her cause include Mark Ethridge, J.N. Heiskell, and Ralph McGill.

Ethridge, who at one time was editor of *The Telegraph* in Macon, Georgia, saw promise in a young sportswriter named Ralph McGill and began to mentor him. When McGill returned from Europe in 1938, he became executive editor of the *Atlanta Constitution:* "Still shaken by the racism he had encountered in Germany and having drawn parallels in his mind with the treatment of Negroes in the South, his first directive to department heads was that henceforth the *Constitution* would capitalize the word 'Negro' whenever it was used. He may have been the first editor in the South to abandon the common practice among journalists in the region of writing the word with a lowercase *n" (Race Beat* 29-30).

As noted earlier, it is important to realize that the editors who lined up to support Smith in her determination to promote freedom for both blacks and whites in the South would not be considered liberals by today's definition. The Mississippi-born publisher of the *Louisville Courier-Journal,* whom Gene Roberts and Hank Klibanoff call "the dean of the handful of liberal editors in segregated states" (23), was Mark Ethridge. Certainly, neither Ethridge nor Jonathan Daniels of the *Raleigh News and Observer* was an integrationist. Neither Carter nor McGill was an integrationist either. "Those Negro newspaper editors who demand 'all or nothing' are playing into the hands of the white demagogues," Ethridge said. "There is no power in the world—not even all the mechanized armies of the earth, Allied and Axis—which could now force the Southern white people to the abandonment of the principle of social segregation" *(Race Beat* 23).

Daniels and McGill are said to have "muted their criticism of Negro editors but said publicly that Negro progress could be made without ending segregation" *(Race Beat* 23). In 1942, McGill said he believed the "Negro problem" was economic and not social: "Anyone with an ounce of common sense must see...that separation of the two races must be maintained in the South" *(Race Beat* 23). The same year, Daniels wrote that "sometimes it is easier to ask people to give their lives than to give up their prejudices" *(Race Beat* 23). Perhaps he was referring to himself as well as to others.

Carter Jr. was not so dissimilar from Ethridge, Daniels, and McGill. He had won the Pulitzer Prize for "editorials that attacked bigotry across racial, economic, and religious lines." But Carter Jr. also "opposed federal intervention against lynching, poll taxes, and discrimination in hiring," believing that these practices would eventually end without interference. According to Roberts and Klibanoff, Carter Jr. "felt that lynching's evilness would become so self-evident that it would disappear, and he thought the poll tax and job discrimination were not the federal government's business" (39). Furthermore, he believed in voting rights for blacks, but only when their educational status matched that of whites (39). One wonders, of course, how he believed a corrupt educational system would ever provide the opportunity for blacks to gain the knowledge they would need to vote intelligently; one also wonders why he made no distinction among educated and uneducated whites or advocated for a test that would measure a white voter's knowledge of political processes.

Like Waldron, many media critics and historians who write about Carter Jr. and others argue that they are to be celebrated because they surpassed most of those around them in their farsightedness. According to Roberts and Klibanoff, some editors "underwent their own personal evolution on racial matters as they began assuming positions of importance in communities throughout the South" (24). Those editors include Carter Jr., McGill, and Smith. Roberts and Klibanoff write:

> While most of their colleagues would address the paramount issues of the day in calls for resistance, in faint whispers of support for civil rights, or in silence, these editors would write and speak with the proselytic power and majesty of the newly converted. While each had local issues to tackle editorially, they could be relied on to push for national unity, obeying federal law, and rising above regionalism. (24-25)

In addition to the fact that Carter Jr., Ethridge, Heiskell, and McGill were becoming more open to integration and more tolerant of difference, their interrelationships also are interesting. Illustrating how their lives intersected is best accomplished by providing brief biographies and references to their statements about the crises of the time. The primary focus for this study, of course, is on how their belief systems evolved and why they identified Smith as someone who needed and deserved their assistance.

Editors in this study were educated and traveled in a circle that included numerous well-known writers, politicians, educators, and other professionals. For example, Ralph McGill went to Vanderbilt in the 1920s and was influenced by the Fugitives, who are cited in the introduction and conclusion to *Burning Crosses and Activist Journalism*. Roberts and Klibanoff describe the literary figures and faculty members known as the Fugitives as those "who advocated the preservation of southern culture against the onslaught of modern industrialism, but who sought to shed old-fashioned artistic conventions. The group, which a decade later evolved into the Agrarian movement, was widely credited with launching the Southern Literary Renaissance" (29). The Fugitives include Donald Davidson, John Crowe Ransom, Allen Tate, Robert Penn Warren, and a collection of their work entitled *I'll Take My Stand* became a manifesto for the group.

The Fugitives influenced McGill and others by espousing a way of life that championed rural values, commitment to others, and love of one's homeland. Because they had read broadly and because many of them spent their careers in colleges and universities in the South, their philosophies elevated the study of the literature and culture of the South, and they achieved wide popularity throughout the United States. In *Away Down South: A History of Southern Identity,* James C. Cobb links the "Lost Cause" of the Southern sensibility to the Agrarians, Fugitives, New Critics, and Vanderbilt intellectuals. Believing in the "Lost Cause" and in the virtues of Southern life "meant defending secession and the southern war effort, extolling Confederate valor and virtue, and condemning the foul and vindictive deeds of the black-hearted Yankee oppressors" (101), Cobb writes.

Like the other editors profiled in this chapter, Carter Jr. would be blessed during his lifetime with the friendship and acquaintance of numerous people of letters, including Shelby Foote and Cleanth Brooks. As Waldron notes in her biography of Hodding Carter Jr., Cleanth Brooks, who would become a leading literary critic, lived in a boardinghouse at Tulane with Carter Jr., John Crowe Ranson and Donald Davidson had been Brooks's professors at Vanderbilt, and Brooks introduced Carter Jr. to the Fugitives and to regional studies. Later, Shelby Foote, who would become a prominent historian, worked for the *Delta Star* and then in the print shop of the *Delta Democrat-Times.* Foote's brother Horton would write numerous screenplays, including the award-winning script drawn from Harper Lee's novel *To Kill a Mockingbird.*

A publishing company called Levee Press brought together several editors and literary figures of note, although the endeavor was short-lived. Ben Wasson, who wrote for the *Delta Democrat-Times,* had roomed with William Faulkner at Ole Miss and worked as his literary agent. He, Carter Jr., and Kenneth Haxton, who ran a book department at a local department store, decided to establish a company that would print limited editions written by emerging Southern writers. Eudora Welty's *Music from Spain,* Faulkner's *Notes on a Horse Thief* (later part of *A Fable),* and other books were published before the Levee Press founders ended the operation.

Before the company folded, several twentieth-century literary giants collaborated with Carter Jr. and others in their venture. For example, Faulkner signed 900 copies of his book for Levee Press in Carter Jr.'s office at the *Delta Democrat-Times.* The book, *Notes on a Horse Thief,* was published at the same time Faulkner received the Nobel Prize. Other writers who were approached to contribute manuscripts to Levee Press include Carson McCullers, Flannery O'Connor, and Robert Penn Warren. "After trying and failing to get a manuscript from Tennessee Williams," Waldron writes, "the Levee Press ceased to exist" (193). Although the Williams manuscript was not essential to the enterprise, Carter Jr. and his colleagues were too busy with their full-time jobs to make a success of the press.

The interconnections between literary giants and prominent editors do not end here, although at least one of the associations was less than positive. One writer connected to Carter Jr. was Lillian Smith, who wrote a negative review of one of his books and a negative assessment of him in *Killers of the Dream.* However, Erskine Caldwell, who was editing a book series, admired Carter Jr. He asked him to write *Gulf Coast Country,* which he published in 1951.

As noted in "Hazel Brannon Smith and Editor Ira B. Harkey Jr.," Harkey's stylebook emphasized ways to make coverage of black and white citizens more equal. Concerns about courtesy titles, clarification of marital status, indication of social position in the community, and use of photographs of black residents existed throughout the print media. According to Roberts and Klibanoff, standards that for us would be obvious were revolutionary to Carter Jr., Ethridge, Harkey, Heiskell, McGill, and Smith. They write:

> Many newspapers didn't carry any news at all about Negroes; some printed only social snippets under such headlines as "Activities of Colored People." And some devoted a full page to Negro news, in editions circulated only in Negro neighborhoods; to make space for the page, editors would cut the financial news page that appeared in the editions that went to white readers. The papers didn't carry Negro wedding announcements or obituaries. Journalistic orthodoxy still demanded that the newspapers unfailingly refer to white women as "Miss" or "Mrs." but drop the title when referring to Negro women, no matter what their station in life. The practice, which had its origins in slavery and had changed little in the years since the Civil War, was not limited to newspapers, which both reflected and perpetuated the custom. (55)

That editors would eliminate the financial news section for black readers to allow for "Negro news" is especially interesting, given the fact that black business people made up a large portion of the population; in fact, it was against them that the White Citizens' Councils directed much of their harassment. Such discriminatory news practices continued, of course, in the 1960s and 1970s, when "women's news" involving social gatherings, family issues, and engagement announcements were considered the particular province of women. Politics, sports, and international news—frankly, everything considered hard news on the front pages of America's newspapers—were the domain of men. The editorial custom changed only slightly in the 1970s, when women's pages became part of the proliferating "lifestyle" sections.

The content of news is often determined by issues of class, gender, and race and ethnicity. In the 1940s and 1950s, newspaper editors debated whether "Negro" should have an uppercase "n." In 1946 the *New York Times* opted to discontinue reference to race unless it was important in a description of an alleged perpetrator of crime or in an explanation for a confrontation. In 1952, the *Columbus* (Georgia) *Ledger-Enquirer* surveyed 35 dailies in the Deep South and learned that half used courtesy titles for blacks or ran "regular columns or pages of black news" (6), writes Davies. The *Montgomery Advertiser* and the *Alabama Journal* published separate editions for black readers for more than 30 years, "finally discontinuing them in the 1960s because they were too costly to produce" (7). Even today, conversations occur among those who produce the *Associated Press Style-*

book, used in classrooms and print media organizations throughout the country. The phrase "colored" and the words "negro," "Negro," "black," and "Black" have undergone a complicated evolution, as have words such as "homosexual" and "gay" and "Miss," "Mrs.," and "Ms."

Like Carter Jr. and others, McGill, too, struggled with the appropriate use of language and what the linguistic changes signified about social progress. Like them, he was not initially an integrationist but believed in judicial equality. McGill's own words reinforce the conclusions Roberts, Klibanoff, and others draw about his initial failure to understand the complexities of the African American push for equal treatment. Sounding a great deal like Carter Jr. and Hazel Brannon Smith, McGill wrote, "There may be separation of the races and still equal justice before the law; equal opportunity to use one's skills and still not have to mix with other workers; equal opportunity for education, without mixing in schools" *(Race Beat* 39).

McGill was quick to remind readers and listeners that he was a Southerner to the core and quick to empathize with the fear Southerners felt as the African-American population grew and as they began to fight for equality in pivotal ways, including the right to vote. "I figure I am as Southern as cornbread, having lived, worked, studied and thought nowhere else," he said. "My immediate Confederate ancestors, and my Welsh ancestry, which causes me to weep over sad pictures, books and lost causes, are so much a part of me." He added that socially conservative Dixiecrats, who advocated strongly for states rights versus federal government intervention, "do not represent the South. They are a minority's minority. But they do represent many Southern fears" *(Race Beat* 41).

In spite of his difficulty embracing federally legislated integration, McGill understood that the South would suffer if it did not make substantive changes in social policy. In "One Day It Will Be Monday," published in April 1953, McGill warned his readers that the days of segregation were numbered and encouraged them to change with the times:

> Days come and go, and Monday is among them, and one of these Mondays the Supreme Court of the United States is going to hand down a ruling which may, although it is considered by some unlikely, outlaw the South's dual school system, wholly or in part.
> It is a subject which, because of its emotional content, usually is put aside with the remark, "Let's don't talk about it. If people wouldn't talk about these things, they would solve themselves."
> It is an old reaction, best illustrated by Gone With The Wind's Miss Scarlett O'Hara who, when confronted with a distasteful decision, pushed it away with the remark, "We'll talk about that tomorrow."
> But "tomorrow" has a ugly habit of coming around...So, somebody, especially those who have a duty so to do, ought to be talking about it calmly, and informatively. *(Race Beat* 48-49)

The shift in McGill's ideas was obvious by 1964, when he began to realize that the leadership of the South was too angry and perhaps too ignorant to support legislation that would move the region into the new decade.

He also decried the violence that had become part of the daily narrative of the South. "He had started out arguing that separate was okay as long as it was accompanied by equal and that the federal government should not regulate poll taxes and ban lynching because those were state prerogatives," write Roberts and Klibanoff. "But he had found that position less defensible in the face of the South's clear lack of interest in equality, its violence, and the toxic tone of so many of its demagogic leaders" *(Race Beat* 371).

In many ways, McGill attained the stature of Carter Jr. His columns had national syndication in 300 newspapers, he wrote for national magazines, he appeared on television, and he spoke in national forums. On May 4, 1964, McGill endorsed President Lyndon Johnson's civil rights bill. On August 6, 1965, Johnson followed up the earlier legislation by signing the Voting Rights Act into law, and McGill argued for law and order in his beloved South. According to Roberts and Klibanoff, "All the activity added up to a distinct mission: he wanted to show that there were two Souths, one of them wanting more opportunity and fairer play for Negroes" (372). A few years later, at a 1967 UCLA symposium on African Americans and the press, McGill said that 90 percent of the Southern press had "abdicated its responsibilities on the topic" of race and equal rights (Lyle 42).

It is easy to read about his support for Smith and his professional connections with Carter Jr. and others and forget that McGill changed his mind slowly and was affected by the cultural shifts around him as often as he imposed his own beliefs on the world outside his newspaper office. McGill's progressive attitudes on race issues evolved, and "that evolution had been accelerating as he watched the white South abandon all sense of justice and fair play in dealing with Negroes," write Roberts and Klibanoff. "But even so towering an editor as McGill had not always been free to say so" *(Race Beat* 62).

Like Carter Jr., Ethridge, and others who socialized with the well-known writers and philosophers of the day, McGill found solace in discussions with his fellow editors and with writers such as Carl Sandburg. Before Sandburg died in 1967, McGill and he gathered "for weekends of quiet talk and expansive debate, rocking in chairs and walking in the woods at Sandburg's antebellum home, set inside the 240-acre Connemara Farms in Flat Rock, North Carolina" *(Race Beat* 205).

In *The South and the Southerner* (1964), McGill quotes Carson McCullers, suggesting his own struggle to change and grow: "There's a guilt in us—a seeking for something we had...and lost" (Cobb 199). Whatever the cause of the guilt—whether it was linked to slavery and other crimes against humanity or tied to an individual's essential character—McGill continued his quest to understand himself and the region he loved.

Another of those who supported Smith and who committed himself to changing the social hierarchy of the South was John Netherland Heiskell. As early as 1927, he retaliated against a mob and the police who failed to deal severely with a white mob that lynched a black man and burned his body. The whites then dragged the black man's "charred remains" through

Little Rock. The headline in Heiskell's newspaper read "With Officers Making No Attempt at Restraint, Mob Burns Negro's Body and Creates Reign of Terror" *(Race Beat* 32).

Like his colleagues, Heiskell "favored the separation of the races in social matters but thought in terms of fair play and justice for all" (33), according to Roberts and Klibanoff. But the seed of fairness had been planted, and when it came time to join the Tri-Anniversary Committee and advocate for the editor of the *Lexington Advertiser,* Heiskell did not hesitate.

Fundraising and Hazel Brannon Smith

That Carter Jr., Ethridge, Heiskell, and McGill were fair and compassionate people interested in social change is relevant to their perception of their colleague Hazel Brannon Smith. Connected to one another ideologically, they were also connected to the literary, political, and philosophical giants of their day. They loved their homeland, and they enjoyed the free interplay of ideas. They were not threatened by energetic discussion of ideas, and they were men of letters. It is little wonder that they heard about Smith's plight and determined to help her.

In spite of the commitment and stature of the white male editors who worked on Hazel Brannon Smith's behalf, their fundraising efforts had limited success. This fact is due largely to the work of racist groups and of the campaign conducted by the rival newspaper, the *Holmes County Herald,* in Smith's community.

An article entitled "Hodding Carter to Head Drive for Holmes County Publisher" on page one of the November 9, 1961, issue is representative: "A group of out-of-state agitators, masquerading as do-gooders and moderates, have begun a fund-raising campaign to buy themselves a voice in Holmes County...It is now absolutely apparent that the integrationist and socialist elements who hate this country and state are determined to have an outlet for their views." The article then attacks Carter Jr., Heiskell, and McGill and concludes with the following diatribe: "The cold fact remains...that they are buying an outlet for idealistic babblings of their ilk. They will continue to pay only so long as their views are printed. The 'free press' they support is a press free only to print the ideas of how someone in New York, Chicago or Atlanta thinks we should live" (Wallace 126).

The *Holmes County Herald* did not stop there. It also sponsored a public meeting at Lexington City Hall November 20, 1961, to announce a circulation drive. At the meeting, *Herald* supporters again attacked the Tri-Anniversary Committee's efforts on Smith's behalf and "classified the action as a community problem concerning every citizen in Holmes County" (Wallace 127).

However, at that time, all was not yet lost. Although she was more than $100,000 in debt, Smith didn't know how to quit. After she won the Pulitzer Prize, she began speaking around the country in earnest, earning from $300 to $1,000 per speech. In addition, as noted earlier, the *Columbia Journalism Review* endorsed the "Hazel Brannon Smith Fund" to support her flagship newspaper, and black farmers, teachers, preachers, and business people of Holmes County came to Saints Junior College in Lexington for "Editor's Appreciation Day." Smith was given a box with an orchid and a check for $2,855.22. Smith later called the day "the most wonderful day of my life," according to Bernard L. Stein. The "Editor's Appreciation Day" organizers then formed a committee to offset the boycott against Smith by the White Citizens' Council, and in two years, the movement "made its support for Mrs. Smith explicit," Stein wrote. "Among the three objectives of a new selective buying campaign was a demand that the city, county and local businesses advertise in her papers" (n.p.).

Wallace and other media historians argue that although Smith's story inevitably would have a devastating finale, the efforts of her colleagues prolonged her time as editor and had profound impact on those throughout the nation who read her work:

> Had it not been for the support of their fellow journalists and civil rights advocates, the papers of P.D. East and Hazel Brannon Smith would have likely been unable to survive. The financial strain that resulted from these attacks brought their newspapers to the brink of closure, while Ira Harkey's circulation and advertising income dropped steadily in the months following the Ole Miss crisis. Yet, in the face of such challenges, civil rights advocates and journalists from across the country worked to provide the necessary support to keep these crusading papers in print. Contributions ranged from a single dollar to donations in the thousands, with wealthy East Coast philanthropists and struggling Mississippi African Americans uniting to protect these beacons of hope. Through their messages of justice and moderation, these papers had become invaluable symbols of the civil rights movement. As such, ensuring their survival became an integral front in the fight against segregation and injustice. (Wallace 120)

In an era during which newspaper readership is declining and newspaper editors are not necessarily part of the intellectual elite in a particular community, it is difficult to understand the impact of print media during the civil rights movement. The time the Tri-Anniversary Committee bought for Smith has immeasurable importance. In his article "In the South—When It Mattered to be an Editor," Dudley Clendinen, a former national correspondent for the *New York Times,* focuses on the power local newspaper editors possessed during the civil rights struggle:

> Across the South in neighborhoods like ours, literate whites were accustomed to looking to their newspapers' editorial pages to tell them what to think about things. They looked to the editorial pages for local, state and Southern perspective, and to news weeklies like *Time* and *U.S. News and World Report* to understand America and its place in the world...
> Romance about the past has been the South's addiction, but we should not wax romantic about the unclouded vision and unbiased sense of

social justice evidenced by the Southern editors who rose to the occasion. They weren't Solomons. They weren't detached. They weren't omniscient. And they weren't in charge. They didn't all believe in integration, not personally or immediately and certainly not at first, and they couldn't always see clearly all the ramifications of right and wrong in whatever piece of the issue was before them at the moment. They couldn't always write all of what they could see either, for fear of getting so far ahead of their readers that they would lose credibility. (14-15)

Clendinen is correct in his warning that we must not make any of these editors into a "home-made God," as Carson McCullers describes John Singer in *The Heart Is a Lonely Hunter*. They were made of flesh and blood, and their lives and careers depended upon their being alert and responding cautiously to the explosions around them: "The owners of small-town papers could write what they wanted to write. They owned the presses. But the ones with the moral courage to criticize the culture in which they lived and did business did so at the peril of their lives and livelihood. 'Every one of them that I knew was scared pissless while they were doing it,' said Hodding Carter III. 'It has always defined bravery for me'" (Clendinen 17).

The Pulitzer Committee, according to Clendinen, knew how much efforts by the small-town editors had cost them personally and professionally. Carter Jr. was honored in 1946 for editorials about race, religion, and economic issues in Mississippi. He was the first Southern editor in almost 20 years to be honored in this way, but 11 of the 15 awards for editorial writing from 1946 to 1971 went to other Southern editors, including Harkey and Smith.

Into a hostile and discriminatory landscape stepped Hazel Brannon Smith, a young and inexperienced graduate of the journalism program at the University of Alabama. In her twenties, excited about a new life in which she could develop her voice, she bought a rural newspaper and promoted her dream of producing fair and balanced local news stories that would serve her community. She understood how essential the journalistic enterprise was, both in changing attitudes and in providing support for the editors who were engaged in similar pursuits. "A lot of other little editors in a lot of other little spots is what helps make this country," Smith said. "It's either going to help protect that freedom that we have, or else it's going to let that freedom slip away by default" (Moritz, ed., 384). The road to the freedom she envisioned was long and rocky.

Smith had no idea when she walked into her newspaper office on her first day of work that Mississippi would become a cauldron of civil rights struggle. It is unlikely that she realized that the largest newspapers in the state, the *Jackson Clarion-Ledger* and *Jackson Daily News*, would undermine her efforts and incite white citizens of Mississippi to oppose the equal rights and personal safety of African Americans in her beloved state. Certainly, although the Jackson newspapers were poorly written and edited, they were powerful influences. Roberts and Klibanoff write that the *Jackson*

Clarion-Ledger and the *Jackson Daily News* "were journalistically the worst major-city newspapers in the South, not because the owners, top editors, and columnists were fervently segregationist—which they were—but because they allowed their zealotry to dictate the scope, depth, tone, and tilt of their coverage. The newspapers were vindictive, poorly written, and error-ridden" *(Race Beat* 82). It is precisely because the editors of the *Jackson Clarion-Ledger* and the *Jackson Daily News* produced error-ridden copy, supported the status quo, and still boasted circulations of 40,000 each that one cannot minimize the impact of Smith's tenacity and forthrightness as she stood her ground against the prominent newspapers and their editors.

Before reviewing Smith's contributions to Mississippi in "Racial Issues in Southern Literature and Journalism," it is important to remember that she published a newspaper for Medgar Evers and the African-American community. It was hardly the only newspaper springing up in the state that provided news by blacks for blacks, but by publishing the paper, Hazel Brannon Smith stepped boldly into a new age.

Momentous Changes in News Coverage

According to U.S. Census data from 2006, 61 percent of the residents of Mississippi were white and 36.3 percent were black. Mississippi is first in the nation with the percentage of blacks, and it leads the nation in the number of elected black officials (892), followed by Alabama (756) and Louisiana (705). At the time Cassandra Johnson conducted her research for the paper "Journey to Justice: The Evolution of Mississippi's Largest Newspaper from Oppressor to Crusader for Racial Equality," the *Jackson Clarion-Ledger's* newsroom was more than 35 percent black. The first black executive editor, Ronnie Agnew, was hired in 2001. At that time, the managing editor, assistant managing editor, metro editor, assistant metro editor, and features editor were black (26). In 2006, the slogan for the newspaper was "Real Mississippi," a reflection of the newspaper's focus on fair and balanced coverage.

Much has changed in Mississippi journalism since the Hedermans owned two of the top newspapers for more than six decades. While it devastated her and her supporters when Hazel Brannon Smith was eventually run out of business, she made a significant contribution and, in the end, her political and social views were vindicated.

Burning Crosses and Activist Journalism is a tribute to Smith and a record of the society in which she lived and worked. When her contributions are placed in context, it becomes clear that she faced daunting odds. "The white authorities of Mississippi had no intention of complying with the new law, the legislature, by concurrent resolution, declaring that the '1964 Civil Rights Act is unconstitutional and the citizens of this state should resist the enforcement of this Act by all lawful means,'" Whalen writes. "The Association of Citizens' Councils of Mississippi urged school boards to suspend operations rather than desegregate" (177). The editor of the *Hattiesburg American,* Andrews Harmon, told Mississippians to stand united against the Supreme Court's ruling: "If all of the people of Mississippi want to retain racial segregation in the public schools they can do it simply by standing together...No power on earth can compel more than a million people to do something that is against the law of God and nature" (Weill, "Mississippi's Daily Press" 27).

However, the Civil Rights Act was passed in 1964 and gradually enforced. Lyndon Johnson signed it into law, thereby granting equal access to public institutions and facilities for everyone. Carter III provided editorial support for the decision. The Voting Rights Act was signed into law in 1965. Evers, Martin Luther King Jr., and Robert Kennedy became martyrs for equality. Although they defied the law for years, Mississippi legislators and citizens began actively to desegregate schools in 1969.

The world was changing, and Hazel Brannon Smith was one of the reasons for those changes. Smith articulated her views before a national audience. A week after the disappearance of three civil rights workers in Neshoba County, Mississippi, Smith appeared alongside white and black civil rights leaders in a panel discussion for the American Newspaper Women's Club in Washington, D.C. "You don't have to have a sheet to belong to the Klan," she told the group. "It's as much a state of mind as anything else" (Moritz, ed., 385).

As noted earlier, Smith also advocated for leaders such as Medgar Evers, whom she knew and admired, and the admiration often was reciprocated. In part to support Smith's efforts, Evers founded the *Mississippi Free Press,* a weekly, in 1961. Editors of the *Mississippi Free Press* said that "when [black] leaders in Jackson decided that Mississippi Negroes should have a voice for truth, they consulted Hazel Brannon Smith. The *Free Press* slogan, 'The Truth Shall Make You Free,' describes the very soul of the great woman who suggested it" (Whalen 137).

As noted in "The Unlikely Heroism of Hazel Brannon Smith," in addition to the other major stories of the time, Smith covered Freedom Summer when, in June 1964, 600 to 1,000 volunteers—mostly white college students from the North—came to Mississippi to help blacks register to vote and to set up what Weill calls "black cultural awareness programs" ("Mississippi's Daily Press" 40). More than 2,000 students were involved in similar projects throughout the nation. "Although calculations vary regarding the violence in Mississippi during the Freedom Summer campaign, there were at least three summer workers killed, eighty beaten, thirty homes and thirty churches in the black community burned or bombed, and more than a thousand arrested" ("Mississippi's Daily Press" 40), said Weill. According to Waldron, crosses were burned in 64 of the 82 counties. In June, six Mississippi churches were burned. Between January and August, 30 blacks were murdered by whites.

Project Mississippi was a program covered by editors such as Carter Jr. Black leaders of the National Association for the Advancement of Colored People (NAACP), the Student Nonviolent Coordinating Committee (SNCC), the Congress of Racial Equality (CORE), and the Southern Christian Leadership Conference (SCLC) came together under the banner of the Council of Federated Organizations (COFO). Black and white volunteers came to Mississippi and Alabama in 1964 to work on voter registration and other issues important to the black community. "They were backed up by 140 paid workers from SNCC and CORE and a hundred clergymen and volunteer lawyers," according to Waldron. "The State of Mississippi prepared for the invasion, increasing the number of highway patrol personnel from 275 to 475" (309).

Chaos reigned following the influx of activists and the support by a few enlightened editors. Carter Jr. and Hazel Brannon Smith were on opposite sides of the fence when it came to their perspective on the youth workers. Smith welcomed them; Carter Jr. did not. Waldron writes:

> Hodding detested the young reformers from out of town. While conceding that some of them were idealists, he said they were "beatniks who thought the way to be a brother to the Negro was not to bathe; boys in beards, and dirty little girls in tight slacks with their hair down to their waists walking hand in hand with Negro boys down streets where this couldn't possibly do anything but antagonize the local white people and stir up violently angry reactions...He huffed and puffed when "the COFO boys and girls had a mixed dance in the Negro VFW Hall." It did not seem to him to be the "best way to register Negroes." Time was passing the old moderate by. (309-10)

Federal legislation, murder, civil rights workers, harassment of blacks who tried to vote, and other issues created a maelstrom of chaos and despair in the state Smith loved. She understood what can happen when a few good people do nothing, and she refused to be one of those people. She and the white male editors who tried to prevent her bankruptcy would have understood Flannery O'Connor's short story "The Displaced Person," and they would not have sympathized with the fictional characters who stood on the sidelines and watched a farm worker murdered.

The story of Hodding Carter Jr., Mark Ethridge, J.N. Heiskell, Ralph McGill, and Hazel Brannon Smith is about flawed human beings who—confronted with the vestiges of slavery and the plight of the poor and uneducated in Mississippi—gradually changed their minds about specific social issues but always argued for equality as they understood the word. We may argue that they changed their views slowly and that they did too little too late, but their sympathy for and commitment to one another is one of the most inspiring realities in a dark time in the American South.

Chapter 5.
Racial Issues in Southern
Literature and Journalism

As noted earlier in this study, Hazel Brannon Smith was not a hero, and she would have reacted negatively to being considered one. Although she was recognized for her contribution to equal rights and was honored with a Pulitzer Prize, she occasionally fell victim to prevailing social norms and racist attitudes. Smith was a human being who tried to live up to the tenets of her profession in a difficult and dangerous time. She was a person of courage who continued to believe in herself when familiar social, political, and religious supports were shifting beneath her.

Smith's story is an important one that reminds those in diverse disciplines of the value of emblematic narrative. Although perhaps reductive and oversimplified in the retelling, stories of Mississippi editors during the civil rights movement represent the ways in which flawed and common people can perform uncommon acts of courage and conviction and sacrifice.

The introduction and the first chapter in this study detail Smith's contributions, but it is worth summarizing them again here. Hazel Brannon Smith is known as a champion of civil rights and in 1964 was the first woman to be awarded a Pulitzer Prize for editorial writing. She owned four small Mississippi newspapers, the *Banner County Outlook*, the *Durant News*, the *Lexington Advertiser*, and the *Northside Reporter*. Her column "Through Hazel Eyes" began in 1936 and lasted throughout much of her ca-

reer; in it, Smith attacked social injustices and crusaded for balanced reporting.

Although Smith won much recognition, she eventually was driven out
of business. A reform journalist, Smith was called a "pariah" by local politicians and residents, had crosses burned on her lawn, and had a newspaper
office firebombed.

However, not everyone ostracized her, and during her career, Smith
amassed numerous honors and was an officer in or a member of important
professional organizations that include the Mississippi Press Women, the
International Society of Weekly Newspaper Editors, the Mississippi Press
Association, the National Federation of Press Women, the Mississippi
Council of Human Relations, and the U.S. Civil Rights Commission.

Smith also won the Elijah Parish Lovejoy Award for Courage in Journalism (1960), was named "Mississippi Woman of the Year" (1964), and
was named to Who's Who in America (1968-69). In addition, she won the
top editorial award from the National Federation of Press Women in 1946
and 1955 and was named "Woman of Conscience" by the National Council
of Women of the U.S. in 1964. In addition, Smith was featured in a made-
for-television movie ("A Passion for Justice") and a documentary ("An Independent Voice").

What would eventually lead to Smith's professional downfall was a
1953 editorial in which she denounces a local sheriff, Richard F. Byrd, as
unfit to occupy office. According to witnesses, Byrd had shot a young African-American man in the leg without provocation. After her editorial,
Byrd sued her for libel. An all-male, all-white jury found her guilty and
fined her $10,000, although the decision was overturned by the state su-
preme court. Because of this and other activist editorials, the White Citizens' Council pressured advertisers to boycott Smith, and the boycott lasted
more than a decade. In the 1970s, she was forced to sell two of her newspapers. Ultimately, she lost all four of them.

In spite of her powerful opponents, Smith was not without friends and
supporters. Several Southern editors were among those who banded together to try to protect Smith. Pulitzer Prize-winner Hodding Carter Jr.,
publisher of the *Delta Democrat-Times* in Greenville, Mississippi, formed a
committee in 1961 to help raise money to offset her losses in advertising. In
addition, the *Columbia Journalism Review* supported a fund to insure the
survival of her papers, and African-American supporters collected donations to help her remain in business.

Although much of *Burning Crosses and Activist Journalism* celebrates
Smith's contributions, her influence never matched that of editors such as
Hodding Carter Jr. In her biography of Carter Jr., Waldron writes:

> Although Hazel Smith was as brave as Hodding, her paper was not as
> good as his; she never covered local news as intensely as he. After the ra-
> cial controversy heated up, she was always on the edge of bankruptcy.
> Hodding and Betty tried to tell her that in order to fight the overpowering
> racism in Holmes County, she first had to make her paper profitable and

build a base of community support. Hodding did everything he could to help Smith: cosigned her notes at a Greenville bank, talked about her in speeches he made in the North, wrote articles about her, nominated her for awards, and finally implemented a campaign to raise money from northern liberals. These donors contributed to the Tri-County [sic] Fund, administered by Hodding, which paid for advertising space in the *Advertiser* that was used by national charity and civic organizations such as the Red Cross. Smith remained virtually friendless in Holmes County. (263)

Waldron provides no evidence that Smith covered local news less determinedly than did Carter Jr., but there is no doubt that she did not have his stature in the state. That he was her friend and supporter is a tribute to him and to his belief in the freedom of the press and in the values of the civil rights movement.

The efforts of Smith's newspaper colleagues were to no avail. Smith eventually went bankrupt in 1985 and in 1994 died penniless and suffering from cancer and memory loss in a Tennessee nursing home. But Hazel Brannon Smith's story doesn't end here. Robert and Jane Downs write of Smith in *Journalists of the United States:* "Smith has strongly supported the civil rights movement, a stand that has hurt advertising revenue, led to public harassment, acts of vandalism, and the firebombing of her editorial office in 1964, while she was attending the Democratic national convention. Her courage and determination, however, have remained steadfast, and she has received support and awards from many directions" (318). The 1964 Pulitzer Prize was awarded for the "whole volume of her work...including attacks on corruption" *(Good Housekeeping Woman's Almanac* 274), and its prestige will remain a part of her legacy.

The Old South Reconfigured

One of the reasons for Hazel Brannon Smith's professional demise is rooted in the fact that the Old South has always been a shadow over the New South. In Dudley Clendinen's "In the South—When It Mattered to Be an Editor," he writes about the postwar South and its "old caste law, still cloaked in its old myths and habits of mind" (12). In addressing the contributions by Hazel Brannon Smith, we must acknowledge the intellectual, social, and political underpinnings of the culture when she—full of energy and commitment to journalism—first looked at notices of newspapers for sale.

Three books, *The Burden of Southern History, I'll Take My Stand: The South and the Agrarian Tradition,* and *The Mind of the South,* and at least one American author, William Faulkner, must factor into any analysis of the Mississippi that Smith knew and loved. *The Burden of Southern History* is an attempt to deal with the divergent mythologies that characterize the nation and those that define the American South. *I'll Take My Stand,* mentioned in the introduction and in "White Civil Rights Editors and Hazel Brannon Smith" because of its authors and the agrarian movement they advocated, includes essays by several "unreconstructed" Southerners who cherished the best of Southern values, including a love of the land, a respect for the importance of family, high regard for the intellectual and the genteel, and a commitment to a system of manners that guide human interaction. Moving forward often suggests first moving back, and an exploration of what defined the South of Smith's time is essential here.

In *The Burden of Southern History,* C. Vann Woodward describes the chasm between the myths of America and the myths of the South. America, he argues, is defined by 1) economic abundance, 2) success and invincibility and 3) innocence (16-21). "In that most optimistic of centuries in the most optimistic part of the world, the South remained basically pessimistic in its social outlook and its moral philosophy" (21), he said.

Given the fact that two literary renascences occurred in the South, it would be foolish not to understand the reasons that Southern writers were both tortured and transported by the past. As Woodward addresses the contributions of Faulkner, Robert Penn Warren, Eudora Welty, Thomas Wolfe, and others, he argues that the nation has a great deal to learn from the South:

> After Faulkner, Wolfe, Warren, and Welty no literate Southerner could remain unaware of his heritage or doubt its enduring value. After this outpouring it would seem more difficult than ever to deny a Southern identity, to be "merely American." To deny it would be to deny our history. And it would also be to deny to America participation in a heritage and a dimension of historical experience that America very much needs, a heritage that is far more closely in line with the common lot of mankind than the national legends of opulence and success and innocence. The South once thought of itself as a "peculiar people," set apart by its eccentricities, but in many ways modern America better deserves that description. (25)

Like Woodward, James C. Cobb writes in *Away Down South: A History of Southern Identity* about the dichotomy between the North and the South:

> Not only was the North every*where* the South was not, but in its relative affluence and presumed racial enlightenment, it had long seemed to be every*thing* the impoverished and backward South was not as well. As we know, the vision of the North as the essence of the nation and of the South as its antithesis had surfaced in the early national era and matured in the heat of antebellum sectional conflict. If the defeated southern states had emerged from the Civil War as a relatively cohesive "South," the triumphant North had simply affirmed its credentials as "America." (215)

Not only is the North different from the South, but it is imminently superior, a bias that filtered into literature, journalism, and the popular culture and a bias that could do nothing but inflame the anger of Southerners.

Much of the two Southern renaissances (sometimes called "renascences") in literature can be attributed to the haunted South, a land in which white people came to understand that some of them had been complicit in slavery, one of the greatest crimes ever perpetrated against humanity. The poetry, novels, and short stories that emerged from the region are testament to the interest in and connection to the influence of the past. Unlike American mythology—in which the hero is always looking forward—and the legends of the American West—in which the frontier is the imagined answer to restlessness, poverty, and sadness—the South was a place characterized by both the achievements and horrors of its history. In *Intruder in the Dust*, Faulkner pays tribute to the ways in which the past is never the past: "It's all *now* you see. Yesterday won't be over until tomorrow and tomorrow began ten thousand years ago" (194). The past is understood to exist in the present. In *Requiem for a Nun*, Gavin Stevens says, "The past is never dead. It's not even past" (535).

The rich literary history of the South both informs and impacts daily journalism. Not only did educated Southern editors immerse themselves in the literature and culture of the time, but they understood that the South had been formed because of historical events they could describe but not alter.

The Civil War, which was about states rights as well as about preserving slavery and a rural economy, had been lost, but the rage that followed the humiliation—a rage exacerbated by Reconstruction and the influx of carpetbaggers and Northern businessmen interested in capitalizing on the devastation—continued. A generation of young men was gone. General William Tecumseh Sherman's "March to the Sea" cut a giant swath of carnage as his army burned and pillaged its way to the Atlantic Ocean, and although he spared Savannah in order to present the magnificent city to President Abraham Lincoln, other cities and towns of the South would not recover their former glory. As Woodward writes:

> It is not the period nor the subject that is the point but, in [Allen] Tate's words, the consciousness of the past in the present. Here, among many possible illustrations, one thinks of Katherine Anne Porter's Miranda in *Old Mortality*, seeking through the years of her youth to find and come to terms with her family's past and her own past and to relate them to the present. Or of Thomas Wolfe's Eugene Gant, "the haunter of himself, trying for a moment to recover what he had been part of...a stone, a leaf, an unfound door," and lyrically imploring, "Ghost, come back again." Or of Faulkner's Quentin Compson in *Absalom, Absalom!* groping through the convolutions of Colonel Sutpen's incredible legend for an answer to Shreve McCannon's questions in 1910. Or of Warren's Jack Burden in *All the King's Men* brooding endlessly over the faded letters and diaries of Cass Mastern for a lost meaning to the past and a key to the present in the 1930's. (35-36)

In Louis D. Rubin Jr.'s 1977 introduction to the 1930 classic *I'll Take My Stand*, Rubin underscores John Crowe Ransom's essay "Reconstructed but Unregenerate" in its description of America's economic and ecological predicament. His concern about the way in which the United States under-values and exploits natural resources is reinforced in contemporary popular culture. He is not a Southern apologist as much as a philosopher who seeks to learn from the history of his homeland, and he believes the nation has much to learn about itself and its values. He writes:

> In the 1970s we have learned to worry about such things. We begin to realize that our continent and our planet do not constitute an inexhaustible supply center of natural resources. We are concerned over the destruction of what is left of our wild places, in the name of Progress. We note the economic and social chaos and hardship that result from even temporary dislocations within an industrial system so huge that it can take no cognizance whatever of the needs of individuals, or even of the plight of towns, cities, even regions. We are disturbed at the appetite of our industrialized, electrified, mechanized consumer society, its willingness to use up a disproportionate share of the world's energy at an alarming rate. We begin to suspect that our vaunted material standard of living is being purchased at the cost of others, who now begin to show signs of impatience at their exploitation. And we have the uneasy feeling that there is something to the notion that wars may have played a greater role in our economic well-being than we like to think. What it all means we are not sure, but we begin to perceive that there is more to progress and improvement than had once seemed apparent. (xviii-xix)

Rubin separates the values of Southerners and the commitment of the South to the land and to its resources from the horrific crime perpetrated against blacks who were bought and sold like livestock and who accounted for much of the wealth the landed gentry enjoyed. He understands the ways in which the South has been stereotyped, ridiculed, and dismissed, and he has no interest in watching the region sink into further isolation. He writes:

> For there *was* a southern tradition worthy of preservation, and it had little or nothing to do with racial segregation, Protestant orthodoxy, or states' rights: it was that of the good society, the community of individuals, the security and definition that come when men cease to wage an unrelenting war with nature and enjoy their leisure and their human dignity. If never in the history of the South had that goal been fully realized, and however much it had been largely restricted to only a part of the population, it was not thereby rendered any the less desirable as a standard to be cherished. (xx-xxi)

One of the reasons for the torment and self-flagellation apparent in the literature of the modern South is that Southerners—whether they addressed the topic in public or not—knew there was something rotten at the core. The number of abolitionist groups had proliferated—dwarfing the number of similar groups in the North—because if people live daily with a crime against humanity, they will either learn to overlook it or they will be tortured by it. There is no doubt where William Faulkner, Carson McCullers, Flannery O'Connor, Eudora Welty, and other celebrated writers of modern literature weighed in on issues of equality, although they were in many cases as conflicted as Hazel Brannon Smith.

William Faulkner and Race Relations

The internal struggle to make peace with oneself is nowhere more pronounced than in the allegorical novel *Light in August.* Here, Faulkner creates a character named Joe Christmas, a man who believes he is part black but has no records to support or deny his feeling. His violent childhood and ill-fated adoption by the McEacherns are responsible for his becoming a man without purpose and without focus, a man who lives in the shadow of the shacks in the black section of town, a man who seeks God but who believes himself separated from God's mercy. Christmas is desperate for self-awareness and for a sense of worth before God:

> Christmas lit the cigarette and snapped the match toward the open door, watching the flame vanish in midair. Then he was listening for the light, trivial sound which the dead match would make when it struck the floor; and then it seemed to him that he heard it. Then it seemed to him, sitting on the cot in the dark room, that he was hearing myriad sounds of no greater volume—voices, murmurs, whispers: of trees, darkness, earth; people: his own voice; other voices evocative of names and times and places—which he had been conscious of all his life without knowing it, which were his life, thinking *God perhaps and me not knowing that too* He could see it like a printed sentence, fullborn and already dead *God loves me too* like the faded and weathered letters on a last year's billboard *God loves me too.* (105)

In the novel, Christmas runs—away from his past, away from white society, and away from himself. Running through town and into the "negro section" called Freedman Town, Christmas understands how lost and alone he is. Faulkner describes him by saying, "In the wide, empty, shadow-brooded street he looked like a phantom, a spirit, strayed out of its own world, and lost" (114). He writes about Christmas's panic as he leaves the town:

> Beneath it a narrow and rutted lane turned and mounted to the parallel street, out of the black hollow. He turned into it running and plunged up the sharp ascent, his heart hammering, and into the higher street. He stopped here, panting, glaring, his heart thudding as if it could not or would not yet believe that the air now was the cold hard air of white people. (115)

The community of Christian people, including the Rev. Gail Hightower, don't know what to make of Joe Christmas, the angry, taciturn product of his abusive past. "They have been calling him Nigger for years" (133), writes Faulkner, addressing the importance of knowing how our identities affect our destinies. Christmas may be black; he may not be. Faulkner writes, "And he says 'I aint a nigger' and the nigger says 'You are worse than that. You dont know what you are. And more than that, you wont never know. You'll live and you'll die and you wont never know...'" (384). It is the life lived in between that will destroy Joe Christmas and lead to his violent death. From his birth to his execution, he suffers in his confusion and rage: "They all want me to be captured, and then when I come up ready to say Here I am *Yes I would say Here I am I am tired I am tired of running of having to carry my life like it was a basket of eggs"* (337).

The confusion and dread Christmas experiences reflect the experience of a region that upheld white supremacy, that enslaved a race of people, and that was all but destroyed by what some Southerners referred to as the "War of Northern Aggression." In *Writing the South: Ideas of an American Region,* Richard Gray argues convincingly that one of the characteristics that defines the South is rooted as much in what its literature and other cultural forms omit as what they include. In a reference to the Agrarian polemic *I'll Take My Stand,* he writes: "It will perhaps be obvious what all this suggests: that *I'll Take My Stand* is not just Southern as a matter of historical accident but distinctively and determinedly so. It belongs first and last to a body of writing for which the constitutive absence, the invisible or at best marginal character, is and always has been the black" (145).

Gray is not alone when he describes another central theme in Southern literature and popular culture: an obsession with the past. What W. Fitzhugh Brundage calls the "contested history" (344) of the American South makes for "corrosive debates over the past" (338). For many Southern writers, the past so permeates the present that it is never really absent. As noted earlier, in *Requiem for a Nun,* Faulkner writes, "The past is never dead. It's not even past" (535), and in *Go Down, Moses,* one of the chapters is entitled "Was," but Faulkner suggests that contemporary events reflect what has been. Gray emphasizes what he understands to be the South's "habitual preoccupation with the past, its long romance with memory, and the evident rift, the growing discontinuity it was experiencing between its notions of the past and the present" (216). This preoccupation is one of the thematic elements that make Southern literature and culture essential to an understanding of the nation as a whole. The South "can hardly be called an idea that has outlived its time—not for everyone, at least, not entirely, not yet" (288), Gray writes.

The Convergence of Literature and Journalism

Faulkner's dark vision of race relations is underscored by the experiences of Southern newspaper editors such as Hodding Carter Jr., Ira B. Harkey Jr., and Hazel Brannon Smith. They lived in a beautiful land of dense forests, red clay, and plentiful lakes and rivers. But they also feared the corruption, cowardice, and ignorance of those who tyrannized African Americans in their communities, and they were themselves threatened and ostracized.

Southern writer Willie Morris, who wrote the text to accompany the photographs in *Faulkner's Mississippi,* is worth quoting in a study of the cultural and historical South. With great love for his homeland, Morris describes the Mississippi Delta, which factored prominently in writing by local newspaper editors and by Faulkner himself. He then writes about the conflicts and despair that lay beneath the surface in the state he loved:

> The 1954 Supreme Court decision on the integration of the schools introduced a new day fraught with violence and tension. For many whites it spelled doom; the savagery would worsen with time. At stake was the soul of the state, and meaningful dissent was all but impossible. The daily newspapers in Jackson, the capital city, were likely the most openly and virulently racist of any in America. Six months after the Supreme Court decision, the white citizens of Mississippi approved by a five-to-one margin a constitutional amendment tightening voting requirements; the amendment, in effect, made it impossible for blacks to register to vote. Soon after this, the voters approved by two-to-one another amendment authorizing the state legislature to abolish the entire public school system if this were deemed necessary to prevent integration, either locally or statewide. These were the result of the general hardening of opinion, as well as the lobbying of the White Citizens Council, composed largely of prominent professionals and businessmen...
>
> There was a resurgence of lynchings, all of them unsolved. A fourteen-year-old black boy visiting the Delta from Chicago was murdered for whistling at a white woman; the white men indicted for the crime were unanimously acquitted. Subsequently a State Sovereignty Commision, subsidized by official funds, established an extensive network of paid informers and set up secret files on hundreds of private citizens...In the entire state only three or four lawyers would publicly admit that Mississippi would sooner or later have to accept the Supreme Court decision. With rare notable exceptions, the white people of the state were entrusting their votes and support to anxious, marginal, visionless men, inconstant and cynical and unmanly men, who came exceptionally close to destroying Mississippi. This was the backdrop against which Faulkner would begin speaking his opposition to racial injustice in his state in the 1950s... Faulkner had also been talking with Hodding Carter, Jr., the intrepid editor of the Greenville *Delta Democrat-Times,* and the pair had agreed that Mississippi and two or three other Southern states would be the last holdouts against any modicum of change. (130, 134)

Certainly, Mississippi newspaper editors were familiar with the importance of local authors. In *The Mind of the South,* W.J. Cash jokes about the proliferation of Southern writers such as Faulkner: "The end of the decade saw Thomas Wolfe and William Faulkner tower into view almost simultaneously. The thirties opened with Erskine Caldwell's *Tobacco Road.* And thereafter the multiplication of Southern writers would go on at such a pace

until in 1939 the South actually produced more books of measurable importance than any other section of the country, until anybody who fired off a
gun in the region was practically certain to kill an author" (376).

Certain texts became essential to an understanding of the American
South, and they were prominent in discussions by educated Mississippians,
including reporters and editors. David Goldfield writes in *Southern Histories: Public, Personal, and Sacred* about the books he considers essential to
an understanding of Southern culture:

> As I tell my students, only slightly tongue-in-cheek, if they want to learn
> southern history, they need only three books as primers—Cash's *The Mind
> of the South,* William Faulkner's *Absalom, Absalom,* and the Bible. These
> are history books minus the historian. Southern history is more likely ex-
> plicated by those adept at touching the soul and the spirit. Cash wrote po-
> etry disguised as prose; Faulkner wrote about the human condition in the
> South beneath the mask of fiction; and the Bible is an inspiration to the
> spirit in the garb of religious history. (73-74)

In addition to writing "poetry disguised as prose," however, Cash also addresses the power of journalism as a profession and as an art form, suggesting how important it is for the South to keep its young editors who are capable of producing prose that will revitalize the region. He writes:

> Just as important was the fact that many of the smaller newspapers
> were now getting more liberal and intelligent editing. One of the happy re-
> sults of the depression, from the standpoint of the welfare of the South,
> was that it had gone a long way toward halting the old exodus to the North
> of talented young men with journalistic ambitions. The development of
> standardized daily journalism helped to that end, also. Unable to secure
> jobs in the East or Middle West, they were perforce driven into service at
> home, and carried their brains with them. They were far from free, even
> where they owned their papers, and had to proceed against the prevailing
> prejudices with great caution; but in the course of time they gradually en-
> larged their latitude. (374)

Having spent time as a journalist, Cash was particularly interested in
the ways in which Southern editors were amassing prestige and exerting
influence. Gene Roberts and Hank Klibanoff, also journalists, address
Cash's interest in the profession in *Race Beat:*

> Never since Horace Greeley and Charles Dana had editors loomed so
> large. Harry Ashmore, Ralph McGill, Gene Patterson, Lenoir Chambers,
> Pete McKnight, the two Hodding Carters, Mark Ethridge, Jonathan Dan-
> iels, Buford Boone, Hazel Brannon Smith, Ira Harkey, and others stepped
> into a vacuum created by southern politicians who did not want to be as-
> sociated with racial integration even when it was ordered by an authority
> as high as the Supreme Court of the United States. The national racial
> trauma might have been even more agonizing if the liberal and moderate
> editors had not assumed leadership and reached out to the rest of the na-

tion—even at the risk of angering their readers, defying governors and congressmen, and touching off advertising and circulation boycotts. If not for these editors, the gulf between the South and the rest of the nation might have grown wider and harder to bridge. (404-405)

The days when newspaper editors influence the political and social attitudes of their readers in a pronounced way are gone. This is not to say, of course, that newspaper readers have disappeared or that the editorial and op-ed pages are not essential to the structure and purpose of print media. However, newspaper readership continues to decline in the twenty-first century, and editors who cast big shadows and are influential enough to inspire threats by those who oppose their editorial platforms are rare. But the troubled South of the 1950s and 1960s was another place entirely, and the importance of Carter Jr., Harkey, and Smith cannot be exaggerated.

An Editor Ahead of Her Time

Hazel Brannon Smith was born into a world in which the educational system and every other public institution privileged a particular race of people just by virtue of their skin color. In the early 1900s, black children made up more than 50 percent of Mississippi public schools, "but black schools received less than twenty percent of the state's public school allocation" ("Mississippi's Daily Press" 23), Susan Weill writes. By 1950, black students made up nearly 60 percent of the public school population but received only 30 percent of public school funds, and, according to Weill, salaries for black teachers were approximately half of what white teachers were able to earn ("Mississippi's Daily Press" 23).

Smith could not make her peace with discrepancies such as these, and her internal conflict made it impossible for her to have the friends and the social life she had always dreamed would be hers. As Garrett Ray, a former community newspaper editor and professor, said, "It was this feeling for people—this need to be connected—that made social exile from her beloved community particularly painful...She referred to herself as a leper" (Whalen 183).

In other circles outside of her beloved South, Smith was, of course, celebrated. For example, at the 50th anniversary dinner of the Pulitzer Prize awards May 10, 1966, in New York, Sen. Robert Kennedy asked Smith if she would come with him to meet his mother. "I think it was, perhaps, the greatest compliment that anyone had ever paid me," she later wrote. "Mrs. Rose Kennedy is a beautiful and dear woman" (Whalen 215-16).

But at home, Smith was not only a "leper" and a "pariah," as she described herself. She was also a target of violence. In 1966, Smith ran a story entitled "KKK Would Kill Ed. Hazel Smith." Based on Associated Press stories, the rumors to which she referred indicated that Grand Giant Billy Buckles of Natchez, an officer in the Ku Klux Klan, had threatened her life.

Buckles had been quoted as saying that Klansmen from Jackson were asking KKK leaders for permission to "eliminate" Smith (Whalen 214).

From supporting the status quo and believing that the time was right for a woman editor in the South to questioning the social order and fearing for her life, Smith had made a 180-degree turn since she purchased a small newspaper called the *Durant News* in 1936. John A. Whalen writes in his biography of Smith that the transformation she underwent was nothing short of astonishing. In her intellectual and moral development, Smith became a symbol to the rest of the nation of what is possible. Whalen writes:

> From her adulation of Jefferson Davis and his career, as voiced back in 1937, to her realization that the Civil War was a tragic mistake; from her abhorrence of mixed racial marriages as a sin to the assertion that if people wanted to intermarry they should be allowed to do so; from her view of "socialistic" and "Communistic" meddling by the federal government in the lives of Americans to her embrace of the programs of President Johnson's "all-out-war" on poverty, Hazel had made an almost 100 percent about-face in her thinking from her early days at Durant and Lexington. (200-201)

Hodding Carter III, son of a man who championed Smith during her darkest days, said: "Hazel, who was a nice segregationist white woman, just decided that her Christianity, her moral and political beliefs, couldn't allow her to support what was being done. She made a lot of enemies because here she was, a little Alabama girl, just kicking butt in a place they weren't used to it" (Whalen 168).

Those who misjudged Hazel Brannon Smith and underestimated her were in for a long stalemate. She could stand strong against criticism and threats: "Since I was a little girl, I have been very independent. I reserve the right to do my own thinking, to act as a human being," she said. "I just can't keep quiet." And in an interview in 1966, she said, "You finally come to a point when you must decide whether you're for law and order or against it, and it's also been a matter of people being able to pressure the free press with its rights and responsibilities" (Moritz, ed., 386).

David R. Davies calls Mississippi's eventual acceptance of equal rights a "painfully slow accommodation" (14). The "accommodation" by individuals was no less slow, but in Smith's case, it would prove life-changing and would lead her to advocate for "the least of these," including the shooting victim Alfred Brown. Pulitzer Prize-winning editor Bernard L. Stein wrote an article entitled "This Female Crusading Scalawag" that deals with Brown's murder. Years after Hazel Brannon Smith's death, Stein visited her beloved town of Lexington and interviewed residents, especially African Americans, as he sought to retrace her steps and better understand her life. He writes compellingly about Smith's coverage of Brown's shooting:

> On a hot June night in 1963, Alfred Brown lay on the sidewalk in front of the honky-tonks on Yazoo Street in the small Mississippi farm town of Lexington, bleeding his life away. At a time when headlines and

telecasts blazed with stories of confrontations between Southern blacks and police, his death went unremarked, except by the tiny weeklies responsible for keeping the residents of rural Holmes County abreast of the news.

"Alfred Brown, negro, was killed in an altercation with Lexington police on Yazoo Street Saturday night," reported the Holmes County Herald in a terse three-paragraph story. "Patrolman W.R. McNeer shot Brown in the chest as he advanced on him with a knife, Police Chief George Musselwhite said."

Lexington's leading newspaper told the story quite differently from the account that appeared in the Holmes County Herald. "Alfred Brown, a Negro Naval veteran of World War II and father of five children, was shot to death in Lexington Saturday night," the Lexington Advertiser's story began.

The Advertiser's long and circumstantial account made it clear that the dead man, a mental patient who still wore the bracelet of the hospital from which he had just been released, was a victim of racist police. They pursued him down the street, accusing him of being drunk, shot him when he pulled out his pocket knife, then stood over him, guns drawn, to prevent his relatives and others who had gathered at the scene from going to his aid.

That the two stories appeared to arrive from different universes is no surprise. By 1963, the Advertiser's editor and publisher Hazel Brannon Smith had become notorious, driving the racist powers that be of the region to flights of apoplexy. As state Rep. Wilburn Hooker of Holmes County told the director of the State Sovereignty Commission, the state agency established to spy on civil rights organizations, she was "this female crusading scalawag domiciled in our midst." (n.p.)

In his article, Stein interviews black residents of Lexington, including James T. Wiley, who was the mayor of Durant in 2000. As a teenager, Wiley had worked part-time in Smith's print shop, and he later used his experience working for Smith to get a job at the *Chicago Defender.* His late brother Will Edward Wiley also worked with Smith. James T. Wiley told Stein that Smith's decision to oppose the sheriff caused her immediate injury: "That didn't make her too popular," he said. "From that time on, things went downhill with her. From that time forward, as well, you will search in vain for a defense of segregation in the pages of the Advertiser" (n.p.).

As noted earlier in this study, Smith also aroused suspicion by printing a newspaper for Medgar Evers, the *Mississippi Free Press,* which concerned the Mississippi Sovereignty Commission because of its purpose: It allowed civil rights activists to reach blacks in Mississippi. On December 15, 1961, the director of the commission and an investigator saw Smith and her husband talking to Medgar Evers and staff members of the *Free Press.* State Representative Wilburn Hooker and state Senator T.M. Williams, both from Holmes County, denounced her. In March 1961, according to Stein, a commission investigator said "everyone whom I talked to considered Hazel Smith, a white female, a trouble maker and integrationist" (n.p.) but also reassured white residents by saying that there was little civil rights activism in the county.

Smith supported African Americans as they sought to register to vote. According to the U.S. Commission on Civil Rights, there were 4,773 white adults in Holmes County, and 4,800 registered white voters when Smith was editor. Black adults numbered 8,757. Twenty were registered. When Hartman Turnbow and other black farmers went into Lexington April 9, 1963, to register at the courthouse, they probably suspected nothing good could come of it. Soon after, Turnbow's home was firebombed. His wife and 16-year-old daughter ran from the house. Night riders fired on them, but Turnbow fired back. According to Stein, Turnbow and four civil rights workers later were "charged with setting the fire themselves" (n.p.). Hazel Brannon Smith wrote three editorials in response, while the *Herald* "ignored the assault and later repeated the party line that the activists had faked the attack" (n.p.), Stein said.

Smith supported African Americans as a collective and as individuals. She remained close to the African Americans whom she hired, and she gratefully accepted financial and personal support during her most demanding years as editor:

> "The only business that she could get, at least when I was working there, was from the black community," said Willie B. Davis, a retired high school science teacher, who worked his way through school at the print shop and who was particularly close to Mrs. Smith. The jobs were substantial. They included the monthly Baptist Observer, which Mrs. Smith edited as well as printed. Mr. Davis remembered sweating to get out books for the black Baptist Convention, the job he was working on when the printing plant was bombed in 1967. Reflecting on her evolution from the days when she supported segregation, he attributed the change to her reliance on African Americans for work in the plant as white advertisers deserted her papers. Not only did the boycott give her an economic incentive to support the aspirations of black people, he said, but also it brought her into increasing contact with them and deepened her understanding. (Stein n.p.)

The only forces Hazel Brannon Smith could not surmount were bankruptcy, memory loss, and cancer. Eventually, after viewing the documentary about her life entitled "A Passion for Justice" in her nursing home, Smith died. The *New York Times* published her obituary, entitled "Hazel Brannon Smith, 80, Editor Who Crusaded for Civil Rights," on May 16, 1994. Published with a dateline signifying the location of the nursing home in which she lived, the obituary read:

> CLEVELAND, Tenn., May 15 (AP)—Hazel Brannon Smith, a Pulitzer Prize-winning editor in Mississippi known for her stance against racism, died on Saturday at the Royal Care Nursing Home here, where she had lived for several years. She was 80.

As publisher and editor of The Lexington (Miss.) Advertiser, Mrs. Smith was one of the few white Southern editors to speak out against white extremists during the 1950's and 1960's. In 1964, she became the first woman to win a Pulitzer for editorial writing, with the awards panel citing her "steadfast adherence to her editorial duty in the face of great pressure and opposition."

Last month, her career was the subject of an ABC movie, "A Passion for Justice."

Reared in Gadsden, Ala., Hazel Brannon moved to Mississippi in 1935, buying a weekly newspaper, The Durant News, with a $3,000 loan. She went on to buy three other Mississippi newspapers, including The Advertiser.

For 20 years, she prospered as a country editor, crusading against bootleg racketeering and becoming known for her broad-brimmed hats and her Cadillac convertible. While on an ocean cruise, she met her future husband, Walter B. Smith, the ship's purser, and brought him home to Lexington.

Then in 1954, when the local sheriff shot a young black man in the back, Mrs. Smith wrote in a front-page editorial in The Advertiser that the sheriff had violated "every concept of justice, decency and right."

As a result of her stands, Mrs. Smith's newspaper became the target of an economic boycott, and the segregationist White Citizens Council started an opposition paper. The boycott lasted 10 years, drained Mrs. Smith financially and eventually forced The Advertiser to close. But she continued to speak out against racism and bigotry.

One of her papers, The Northside Reporter in Jackson, was bombed in Mississippi's "Freedom Summer" of 1964 when hundreds of civil rights workers registered blacks to vote and segregationists terrorized the rights advocates.

Her husband died in 1983. Ailing in later years, Mrs. Smith first lived with relatives and then moved to Cleveland to be close to her nieces. (B8)

The testimonials did not end with the tribute in the *New York Times*. Garrett Ray, formerly a professor of journalism at Colorado State University, called Hazel Brannon Smith one of his heroes (Whalen 327). Richard Lee of the Department of Journalism and Mass Communication at South Dakota State University said Hazel Brannon Smith was the "bravest journalist I have ever known. No qualifiers. She wrote in a time and place when you could be killed for what you wrote. She wrote anyhow" (Whalen 328).

These descriptions of Smith reflect the changes in her beliefs and the changes she then made in her newspapers. They also reflect our desire to believe in someone who rages against insurmountable odds, supports the disenfranchised, and refuses to accept defeat. Unfortunately, the odds against Hazel Brannon Smith were, in fact, insurmountable, although she never pretended to be more important than those around her. Although she might not have appreciated being called a hero, many of her actions were nothing less than heroic.

Although those who seek heroes need for Hazel Brannon Smith to be more than she was, she was human. A native of Alabama, she championed the American South and believed in its social structure until she began to see the ways in which discrimination and inequality were eating away at the very heart of the region she loved. Long before she would abandon her segregationist views, Smith understood the importance of courageous people acting on behalf of others. In 1955, she said:

> Today we have too few people who will stand steadfast for truth and justice when they are being abused. Most of us are like the people in the crowd when they crucified Jesus—we don't have the guts to speak out. We need men who will live and practice Christianity, not just preach it— men who will not only stand up for what is right—but cry out against evil. We can fool men—but the man has not yet been born who can fool God. (Whalen 93)

Like Flannery O'Connor, Smith understood that the damage done by those who stand passively by is perhaps even more dangerous than the damage done by the dictators, demagogues, and bullies who initiate hatred and violence. Those who could have supported her were too often silent and afraid. Those who could have overturned a system of discrimination too often retreated in the vain hope that the world would somehow change without their activism.

However, in fear of the wrath of God and in commitment to others, Hazel Brannon Smith assumed her role as a public figure and as the conscience of her community. She lived a courageous life. Those who came to know about her after she died take comfort in the fact that she is one of many literary and journalistic giants who left their indelible mark on the past and the future of a state and a region and a nation.

Conclusion.
The Legacy of Civil Rights Journalism

In the introduction, I quoted from a short story by Flannery O'Connor entitled "The Displaced Person." In the allegorical tale about a "D.P." named
Guizac, there is an active agent of evil and there are those who stand by and
watch the murderer pull the brake on the tractor. O'Connor challenges us to
reconsider the cost of passivity, the danger to others that results from our
inaction. She suggests that such behavior has its own consequences: Perhaps one is not found guilty in a court of law, but in the case of her fictional
characters, some lose their jobs and one, Mrs. McIntyre, is bedridden and
unable to speak. Father Flynn sits by Mrs. McIntyre's side and reads to her
about Purgatory, the awkward space that awaits those who are not either
sufficiently evil or sufficiently good to enter hell or heaven in the afterlife.

Hazel Brannon Smith lived according to her conscience and was
wounded both by those who actively committed wrong and by those who
stood by and watched when citizens of Mississippi were injured. Her fellow
editor Ira B. Harkey Jr. believed that if "bigots" are allowed to silence those
who know that inequality is wrong, then not only do the prejudiced people
win, but the silent ones are equally culpable and cannot escape the results of
their cowardice.

O'Connor has been criticized for being overly didactic, but her statements about our responsibility to others are central to *Burning Crosses and
Activist Journalism*. Like Eudora Welty, O'Connor did not consider her role

to be that of an outspoken social critic; however, her belief system is no secret to those who read her novels and short stories. In *Unspoken Hunger,* Terry Tempest Williams questions whether she should devote herself to living on the page or in the world, to living as a writer or as an activist. O'Connor and Welty chose the former, but their work encourages readers to become the latter.

For O'Connor, pride remains our greatest sin, and those afflicted with it are often ignorant of their own inadequacies and failures and are hostile to others. In one of her most stark tales, "The Life You Save May Be Your Own," Mr. Shiflet is dismayed at the "rottenness of the world" that is "about to engulf him." Physically and spiritually handicapped, Mr. Shiflet lacks a moral center. After robbing a young woman, Mr. Shiflet abandons her and drives toward Mobile, Alabama, as a storm approaches. He raises his arm and lets it "fall again to his breast" as though in supplication: "'Oh Lord!' he prayed. 'Break forth and wash the slime from this earth!'" O'Connor continues:

> The turnip continued slowly to descend. After a few minutes there was a guffawing peal of thunder from behind and fantastic raindrops, like tin-can tops, crashed over the rear of Mr. Shiflet's car. Very quickly he stepped on the gas and with his stump sticking out the window he raced the galloping shower into Mobile. (62)

As he begs God to wash the rotten from the earth, he fails to understand the significance of the torrential rain hammering his car. Blinded by pride, he cannot perceive his own sin. O'Connor's message to the reader needs no explanation.

O'Connor often portrays the prideful among us as though she is listening in on their conversations. In "Good Country People," Mrs. Hopewell and Mrs. Freeman discuss a young Bible salesman. Mrs. Hopewell tells her companion, "He was so simple, but I guess the world would be better off if we were all that simple." The double entendre is lost on Mrs. Freeman. O'Connor writes: "Mrs. Freeman's gaze drove forward and just touched him before he disappeared under the hill. Then she returned her attention to the evil-smelling onion shoot she was lifting from the ground. 'Some can't be that simple,' she said. 'I know I never could'" (194-95).

In what may be the most famous line in O'Connor studies, the Misfit, a serial killer, shoots a grandmother in "A Good Man Is Hard to Find" and tells his accomplice, "She would of been a good woman, if it had been somebody there to shoot her every minute of her life" (22). If we were fully conscious in our daily lives and made decisions according to our moral compass, O'Connor seems to suggest, we might have a chance at being good people.

But although arrogance and the human tendency to live unconsciously are prominent in O'Connor's work, it is in "The Displaced Person" that issues of racism and the inability of the characters to support one another are most pronounced. Mrs. Shortley exhibits both personal and nationalistic pride as she sneeringly evaluates the immigrant family that has come to America and gained employment at the same farm where she and her husband work:

> She looked closer, squinting. The boy was in the center of the group, talking. He was supposed to speak the most English because he had learned some in Poland and so he was to listen to his father's Polish and say it in English and then listen to Mrs. McIntyre's English and say that in Polish. The priest had told Mrs. McIntyre his name was Rudolph and he was twelve and the girl's name was Sledgewig and she was nine. Sledgewig sounded to Mrs. Shortley like something you would name a bug, or vice versa, as if you named a boy Bollweevil. All of them's last name was something that only they themselves and the priest could pronounce. All she could make out of it was Gobblehook. She and Mrs. McIntyre had been calling them the Gobblehooks all week while they got ready for them.
>
> There had been a great deal to do to get ready for them because they didn't have anything of their own, not a stick of furniture or a sheet or a dish, and everything had had to be scraped together out of things that Mrs. McIntyre couldn't use any more herself. They had collected a piece of odd furniture here and a piece there and they had taken some flowered chicken feed sacks and made curtains for the windows, two red and one green, because they had not had enough of the red sacks to go around. Mrs. McIntyre said she was not made of money and she could not afford to buy curtains. "They can't talk," Mrs. Shortley said. "You reckon they'll know what colors even is?" and Mrs. McIntyre had said that after what those people had been through, they should be grateful for anything they could get. She said to think how lucky they were to escape from over there and come to a place like this.
>
> Mrs. Shortley recalled a newsreel she had seen once of a small room piled high with bodies of dead naked people all in a heap, their arms and legs tangled together, a head thrust in here, a head there, a foot, a knee, a part that should have been covered up sticking out, a hand raised clutching nothing. Before you could realize that it was real and take it into your head, the picture changed and a hollow-sounding voice was saying, "Time marches on!" This was the kind of thing that was happening every day in Europe where they had not advanced as in this country, and watching from her vantage point, Mrs. Shortley had the sudden intuition that the Gobblehooks, like rats with typhoid fleas, could have carried all those murderous ways over the water with them directly to this place. If they had come from where that kind of thing was done to them, who was to say they were not the kind that would also do it to others? The width and breadth of this question nearly shook her. Her stomach trembled as if there had been a slight quake in the heart of the mountain and automatically she moved down from her elevation and went forward to be introduced to them, as if she meant to find out at once what they were capable of. (198-200)

Flannery O'Connor is writing about Polish immigrants. Or is she? The superiority Mrs. Shortley assumes, the hatred of what is different, the manner in which her self-worth depends upon having people beneath her in the hierarchy are all ideas central to the status quo of the Deep South during the time Hazel Brannon Smith was editing her newspapers and during the time the White Citizens' Council was determined to drive her out of business. Whites swimming in a pool with black children, white children attending school with black children, and white people intermingling socially with black people were unthinkable. For whites, staying away from blacks was imperative because, like the Gobblehooks, African Americans were like "rats with typhoid fleas."

The illogical underpinnings of racism in the South are staggeringly primitive to those living in the twenty-first century, but the vestiges of racial hatred remain, as does suspicion of disenfranchised groups all across America. Furthermore, the hatred is especially illogical among those who consider themselves Christians, a realization that transformed Smith and was important to the social theories Ira B. Harkey Jr. espoused. The Roman Catholic writer Mary Flannery O'Connor was no stranger to Southern customs and Christian doctrine, as she made her way personally and professionally in the Protestant town of Milledgeville, Georgia. In "The Displaced Person," she makes it clear that the black servants, the Polish immigrants, and Jesus himself were displaced—"extra"—people. The introduction of the peacock, which was significant to O'Connor as a bird and as a symbol, becomes especially rich in "The Displaced Person":

> The peacock stopped just behind her, his tail—glittering green-gold and blue in the sunlight—lifted just enough so that it would not touch the ground. It flowed out on either side like a floating train and his head on the long blue reed-like neck was drawn back as if his attention were fixed in the distance on something no one else could see. (196-97)

The peacock figures prominently throughout the story, especially when Mrs. McIntyre and Father Flynn struggle and fail to communicate. Their radically different perceptions of the bird represent their radically different understanding of the Guizac family, although O'Connor may or may not be privileging the priest's opinions, since he is singularly unable to focus on Mrs. McIntyre and tailor his message to her needs. In any case, Mrs. McIntyre is stubbornly unable to understand any perspective but her own, and her racism and hatred of that which she fails to understand are pronounced. Like Mrs. Shortley, Mrs. McIntyre considers the beautiful, nearly celestial creature "nothing but a peachicken" (202). The following excerpt is essential to understanding the rift that existed as communities were confronted with the horrors of racial inequality in the post-Civil War South. The conversation focuses on the fate of Mr. Guizac, a hard worker whom Mrs. McIntyre fears:

> The priest, with his long bland face supported on one finger, had been talking for ten minutes about Purgatory while Mrs. McIntyre squinted furiously at him from an opposite chair. They were drinking ginger ale on her front porch and she had kept rattling the ice in her glass, rattling her beads, rattling her bracelet like an impatient pony jingling its harness. There is no moral obligation to keep him, she was saying under her breath,

there is absolutely no moral obligation. Suddenly she lurched up and her voice fell across his brogue like a drill into a mechanical saw. "Listen!" she said, "I'm not theological. I'm practical! I want to talk to you about something practical!"

"Arrrrrr," he groaned, grating to a halt.

She had put at least a finger of whisky in her own ginger ale so that she would be able to endure his full-length visit and she sat down awkwardly, finding the chair closer to her than she had expected. "Mr. Guizac is not satisfactory," she said.

The old man raised his eyebrows in mock wonder.

"He's extra," she said. "He doesn't fit in. I have to have somebody who fits in..."

The cock stopped suddenly and curving his neck backwards, he raised his tail and spread it with a shimmering timbrous noise. Tiers of small pregnant suns floated in a green-gold haze over his head. The priest stood transfixed, his jaw slack. Mrs. McIntyre wondered where she had seen such an idiotic old man. "Christ will come like that!" he said in a loud gay voice and wiped his hand over his mouth and stood there, gaping.

Mrs. McIntyre's face assumed a puritanical expression and she reddened. Christ in the conversation embarrassed her the way sex had her mother. "It is not my responsibility that Mr. Guizac has nowhere to go," she said. "I don't find myself responsible for all the extra people in the world."

The old man didn't seem to hear her. His attention was fixed on the cock who was taking minute steps backward, his head against the spread tail. "The Transfiguration," he murmured.

She had no idea what he was talking about. "Mr. Guizac didn't have to come here in the first place," she said, giving him a hard look.

The cock lowered his tail and began to pick grass.

"He didn't have to come in the first place," she repeated, emphasizing each word.

The old man smiled absently. "He came to redeem us," he said and blandly reached for her hand and shook it and said he must go. (237-40)

In spite of her inability to communicate, it is Mrs. McIntyre who lives, and it is Guizac who must die. Told that she should consider Jesus as a "Redeemer to mankind," Mrs. McIntyre says defiantly, "As far as I'm concerned, Christ was just another D.P." (243).

African Americans had sustained the economic structure of the agrarian South. Set free by legal mandate, they often comprised more than half of the population in the counties in which they resided, and whites feared retaliation and dreaded the impact of their votes, their demands, and the rights that would continue to follow their full emancipation. Integration was bigger than black schoolchildren sitting next to white children, bigger than blacks refusing to ride in the back of a bus, bigger than social intermingling.

Integration demanded Mrs. McIntyre's understanding that Mr. Guizac was her equal in every way and that because she had wealth and privilege, it was her responsibility to address his needs and help him to succeed. Furthermore, it was not enough to tolerate his advancement; she would be required to celebrate his successes and encourage his contributions to her community. Mrs. McIntyre—like many of the residents of Lexington, Mississippi—could not fathom such a notion. Mr. Guizac is murdered, Mrs. McIntyre collapses, and Father Flynn has the last word:

> A numbness developed in one of her legs and her hands and head began to jiggle and eventually she had to stay in bed all the time with only a colored woman to wait on her. Her eyesight grew steadily worse and she lost her voice altogether. Not many people remembered to come out to the country to see her except the old priest. He came regularly once a week with a bag of breadcrumbs and, after he had fed these to the peacock, he would come in and sit by the side of her bed and explain the doctrines of the Church. (251-52)

Unified by Courage and Hope

American writers such as O'Connor factor significantly in the story of Hazel Brannon Smith and other Mississippi editors. Certainly, the lives of writers and historians overlapped with those of journalists, and they were interested in many of the same issues. As noted in the introduction, William Faulkner played a dominant role as a national figure who commented often on race relations in his beloved state. In *First Person Rural,* Hodding Carter Jr. includes an essay entitled "Faulkner and His Folk." He also refers to historian Shelby Foote and writers Carson McCullers, Willie Morris, Flannery O'Connor, Robert Penn Warren, Lillian Smith, Eudora Welty, and Tennessee Williams. Ann Waldron notes that Carter Jr. also praised James W. Silver, a history professor at the University of Mississippi who had "befriended James Meredith when nobody else would speak to him" (313).

Faulkner was the most famous of the writers and historians who were drawn to the rich history and massive social problems of Mississippi. Carter Jr. writes of the reservoir of stellar Southern prose and poetry proudly and acknowledges the role that conflict played in the creation of art in the region. He says:

> Ours is a region of conflict. It is bound to produce writers as it does because it is a region in transition, a region that is subject to strange and often sudden change and that challenges.
> We, more than any other part of our nation, have subjected ourselves and have been subjected to constant examination and constant criticism. No other region in the United States has for as long a period been examined as closely by as many of its own people and so critically and often so blindly from the outside. That in itself has produced relations which help explain why Southerners write. We have the tools, we have the inspiration at hand, we have the challenge to write about this still disorderly region of ours. *(First Person* 69)

As one of the greatest novelists of the twentieth century and as someone who looked unflinchingly at the horrors of inequality among the races,

Faulkner was the focus of a lengthy section of Carter Jr.'s *First Person Rural*. The excerpt cited here reveals both Carter Jr.'s respect for Faulkner's legendary talent and his concerns about overstating issues and caricaturing people in the South. Again, Carter Jr.'s pride in and anxiety about his home are both positives and negatives. They provided him with the optimism he needed to continue his work in the civil rights era, but they also occasionally blinded him to the social devastation experienced by poor white and black citizens. Of several Mississippians who won the Pulitzer Prize, including Tennessee Williams, Carter Jr. writes:

> Four left Mississippi's soil. Only William Faulkner remained and he to withdraw, in spirit, for so long a time into the dark tarns of the world of the Sartorises and the Snopeses, of Popeye and Temple Drake, of Addie Bundren and Quentin Compson, or Lucas Beauchamp and the rest of this tortured, torturing, ineradicable legacies of man's inhumanities and man's endurance of them.
>
> But I am not here to talk of William Faulkner's self-created world, the imaginative dwelling place which has angered and bewildered and frightened many among those of his fellow Mississippians who have come upon it either through hearsay or by investigation of his printed word. These fellow citizens, and others in the South, took pride in him, or they did until he began speaking to us warningly in words we could all understand, about an ancient conflict that plagues our souls. The pride was awed and even resentful, but it was nonetheless real; for we rejoiced that Mississippi seemingly produces at least as many writers of books as readers of them, and that at the head of our authors was William Faulkner, whose writing, which we comprehended the least, commanded mankind's attention. (72)

Faulkner was not universally beloved among those who found his statements about race and ethnicity either too liberal or too restrained. As James C. Cobb writes, "The race issue would continue to confuse and bedevil Faulkner until his death in 1962, as he continued to take positions that seemed alternatively enlightened and reactionary" (189). In "Faulkner and the Southern White Moderate," Noel Polk responds to charges that Faulkner vacillated in his support for black Mississippians and that his novels and short stories reveal a writer who was ambivalent about equal rights. He compares Faulkner to Carter Jr. and other white Southerners who disagreed with what he calls "social amalgamation" but who encouraged "political and economic justice" (145). Polk writes:

> Was Faulkner a racist? If by "racism" one means a hatred or fear of Negroes, one can say, I think, clearly No; Faulkner seems never to have been any more intolerant of blacks than of whites, or any more fearful of their capacity for mischief; he seems, in fact, to have been equally intolerant of just about everybody. If, however, by "racism" one means a belief in the inferiority of Negroes, one could probably answer that question with a Yes, but only by citing his numerous invocations of historical, rather than biological and genetic, circumstances as being responsible for the

Negro's social and economic and cultural disadvantages. In this, too, he was fairly consonant with other moderate Southerners of his day. (145)

Certainly, Faulkner and other well-known white Southerners did not go far enough. With the exception of Harkey, even the editors whose lives are celebrated in this study did not fully embrace integration.

Hazel Brannon Smith, Ira B. Harkey Jr., and Hodding Carter Jr. are dead, yet historians continue to research their lives and contributions and to contextualize their beliefs and reprint their editorials. Obviously, those who value the stories of white civil rights journalists have a particular interest in them, but, in fact, those in other disciplines have created documentaries and collected their work as well. In spite of what would most assuredly be their dismay at being celebrated, Smith, Harkey, and Carter Jr. are symbols of people who stood for something that cost them dearly. In fact, Smith's crusade to be true to herself and her evolving value system cost her everything. Harkey created another career as an author and an academician. Carter Jr. lost his optimism in the face of health problems and an inability to continue as editor of his beloved *Delta Democrat-Times*.

For us, though, their stories reverberate and provide a glimpse into a time and place that was as exciting as it was terrifying. The Deep South profited from their contributions, their courage, and their chronicle of race relations in the 1950s and 1960s. We continue to profit from their stories and to be challenged by their tenacity and their humanity. If we are to learn anything from them, it is that they did not consider themselves to be heroes. They were simply human beings struggling mightily in the face of daunting odds. In many ways, they lost their individual wars, but, as Harkey said, they succeeded, too:

> I won the fight.
> I won, but I lost, too.
> When it was all over, after we had welcomed back the defecting advertisers and had increased circulation to 8500—fifteen percent more than it ever had been—I found I could not remain in Pascagoula, could not bear to exist in the vacuum of an ostracism that remained in force even after victory, could not function in a silence of total isolation as if I were underwater or in galactic space. I was a pariah. (2006, 18)

But in addition to relating the individual contributions made by Carter Jr., Harkey, Smith, and others, this study emphasizes the manner in which the editors supported one another. As white editors in Mississippi, they cared for one another, believed in one another, and cheered each other's successes. They won Pulitzer Prizes and through their speeches throughout the United States provided others with an understanding of their accomplishments and failures—and of the accomplishments and failures of their homeland. Undoubtedly, it is more important to consider the impact of their interrelatedness than it is to describe their final days. Nathaniel Hawthorne believed that it is through community that we are saved, through human interaction that we best know ourselves. Certainly, the lives of Carter Jr., Harkey, and Smith are testament to his belief.

In Waldron's biography of Hodding Carter Jr., she writes that Carter Jr. "was an example and an inspiration to newspaper men and women across the South who could look to Mississippi—of all places—and see a newspaper publisher who could be liberal and still alive" (xiii). Carter Jr. was not a liberal, in his own estimation or in the eyes of most of those who have studied his life and his commitment to social evolution; however, Waldron is correct that he was an inspiration to those around him, and his long-time friendship with Smith is one of his most important contributions: "While it is true that outside forces integrated the state against its will, those outside forces who brought victory would have had an even tougher time—and might not have succeeded—without Hodding Carter's solitary voice of reason" (xiii).

In one way, the description of his solitary voice is accurate: Carter Jr. was often alone in a sea of segregationists. In another way, it is not accurate: Carter Jr. was supported by Ira B. Harkey Jr., Hazel Brannon Smith, and others, and reciprocally, he supported them. *Burning Crosses and Activist Journalism* is a tribute to the collaboration of white civil rights editors and a reminder that standing together is often one of our greatest acts of defiance against insurmountable odds.

Supporting one another is also a tribute to the way in which human beings change and develop. When Carter Jr. was a student at Bowdoin, he "spoke with affection of his black nurse but thought that slaves should not have been freed and that the South should have won the Civil War" (Waldron 2). He also refused to speak to a black student at Bowdoin, Lincoln Johnson. He moved to another dorm to avoid living under the same roof with Johnson, and he refused to play on an intramural team on which Johnson played. Rather than being appalled by his beliefs and behavior, I would argue that the evolution of his personal philosophy is his greatest contribution to us. Carter Jr., like Hazel Brannon Smith, was one ruled by his prejudices, but he found a way out of the maelstrom of hatred and false superiority.

Eventually, the institutionalized racism in Mississippi gave way. By 1946, as Waldron writes, "segregationists in Mississippi knew they were beaten" (316). "The politics of Mississippi changed, and white Mississippians gave in and said, 'We've had it.' Bumper stickers that said 'Welcome to Mississippi, the Occupied State' appeared" (Waldron 316). Given the tone of the bumper stickers and the editorials from this time period, the capitulation obviously was not a happy one. In some ways, racism simply went underground. But in a less cynical interpretation, legal change preceded real and lasting cultural transformation. Undeniably, the work of white civil rights editors brought about change more quickly than it would have occurred without them.

However, it is impossible to conclude a study about the contributions of white civil rights editors on a positive note because to do so would suggest that their struggles were confined to a particular time and place and that society has progressed to a point where the crimes perpetrated against a race of people are unthinkable. Not only do crimes against those considered "other" continue—whether the crimes are against young gay men such as Matthew Shepard or against Muslims on the streets of New York City—but many Americans live with the residual pain of events that occurred during the 1950s and 1960s in the South and elsewhere. One of those people is Pulitzer Prize-winning author Alice Walker, who writes in "To My Young Husband" of the recurring loss she experiences whenever she remembers Martin Luther King Jr.: "How will anyone ever understand how much we loved him?...Even today I can barely bring myself to listen to his voice. At times I force myself to do so. And sure enough, after thinking that my heart will break one more unendurable time, he resolutely pulls me through the pain" (336-37).

In her article about Freedom Summer, Susan Weill makes it clear that Hazel Brannon Smith stood alone. She also argues that women editors were no more likely to support equality during the 1950s and 1960s in Mississippi than were their male counterparts. Weill writes:

> When the Civil Rights Act of 1964 was signed by President Johnson in July, Hazel Brannon Smith was the only woman editor or publisher of a Mississippi newspaper who encouraged her readers to give the legislation a chance. When Freedom Summer volunteers arrived in Mississippi to assist blacks with voter registration, she was the only woman editor or publisher of a Mississippi newspaper who openly supported them...She was the only woman editor, and one of the few Mississippi editors, who openly advocated change in the state's system of repressive white supremacy...
>
> Smith's position took a toll on her publishing business and personal life. Traditional Mississippi society tended to place white women on a "pedestal," and gender is probably all that stood between Smith and a lynch mob...
>
> The findings of this study also suggest a need for scepticism concerning the question of whether the women editors in 1964 offered a "different, more human perspective to the news," as a 1997 survey by the International Women's Media Foundation reported of women journalists three decades later. The findings suggest that unequivocally, they did not. The women of the Mississippi press covered the civil rights issues in the same manner as did the men—they rejected the concept. (557-58)

Uncomfortable with being called a crusading journalist, Hazel Brannon Smith simply wanted to produce ethical news stories and editorials and to support humane social policies. A *Time* magazine reporter in 1955 wrote in "The Last Word" that her column "Through Hazel Eyes" "had long sounded like the county's conscience" (n.p.). Certainly, she spoke for many who longed for a more compassionate world. The odds were more than daunting, and Smith—a moderate by today's standards—threatened the status quo and became a lightning rod for fear and racial hatred. In 1964, another *Time* magazine reporter described Hazel Brannon Smith in "Just Doing the Job":

"Mrs. Smith couldn't be more unpopular in Mississippi if she were an integrationist, which she isn't. But she is the next best thing" (n.p.).

Today, those who know about Hazel Brannon Smith consider her a heroic spokesperson for justice during the civil rights movement. Cited by Senator Al Gore and other well-known politicians and mentioned on numerous web sites, Smith will be remembered long after the Holmes County residents who opposed her are forgotten.

Garrett Ray provides the simplest and most accurate summary of Hazel Brannon Smith and her journalism career when he writes, "The gracious Deep South aristocrat showed a generation of small town editors the meaning of courage" (n.p.). Surely, given their respective impact, Hodding Carter Jr., Ira B. Harkey Jr., Smith, and the other white Southern editors celebrated in these pages should be remembered alongside William Faulkner, Flannery O'Connor, Eudora Welty and other significant figures in American arts and letters.

Works Cited

Baldwin, James. "Going to Meet the Man." *Short Stories of the Civil Rights Movement: An Anthology.* Ed. Margaret Earley Whitt. Athens: U of Georgia P, 2006. 258-74.

Banning, Stephen A. "Courageous Performance: Examining Standards of Courage Among Small Town Investigative Reporters in the 1950s and 1960s." *American Journalism* 17.2 (Spring 2000): 53-68.

Beasley, Maurine H. E-mail interview. 18 Oct. 2007.

Beasley, Maurine Hoffman, and Richard R. Harlow. *Voices of Change: Southern Pulitzer Winners.* Lanham, Md.: University Press of America, 1979.

Bennett, David L. "Ira B. Harkey, Jr., and the *Pascagoula Chronicle.*" *The Press and Race: Mississippi Journalists Confront the Movement.* Ed. David R. Davies. Jackson: Mississippi UP, 2001. 172-207.

Blount, Luke."Trail Blazer: The Story of Baylor's First African-American Professor." *The Baylor Line* 70.2 (Spring 2008): 80.

Bosisio, Matthew J. "Hazel Brannon Smith: Pursuing Truth at Her Peril." *American Journalism* 18.4 (Fall 2001): 69-83.

Brundage, W. Fitzhugh. *The Southern Past: A Clash of Race and Memory.* Cambridge: Belknap Press, 2005.

Carter, Ginger Rudeseal. "Hodding Carter, Jr., and the *Delta Democrat-Times.*" *The Press and Race: Mississippi Journalists Confront the Movement.* Jackson: Mississippi UP, 2001. 265-93.

Carter, Hodding Jr. *First Person Rural.* Garden City, N.Y.: Doubleday, 1963.

———. "Woman Editor's War on Bigots." *First Person Rural.* Garden City, N.Y.: Doubleday, 1963. 217-25.

Carter, Hodding III. "Comment on the Coverage of the Domestic Press." *The Black American and the Press.* Ed. Jack Lyle. Los Angeles: The Ward Ritchie Press, 1968. 38-41.

———. *The South Strikes Back.* Garden City, N.Y.: Doubleday, 1959.

Cash, W.J. *The Mind of the South.* 1941. New York: Vintage, 1991.

Clemens, Samuel. *The Adventures of Huckleberry Finn.* New York: Charles L. Webster and Co., 1885.

Clendinen, Dudley. "In the South—When It Mattered to Be an Editor." *Media Studies Journal* 9.1 (Winter 1995): 11-21.

Cobb, James C. *Away Down South: A History of Southern Identity.* New York: Oxford UP, 2005.

Davies, David R. "Introduction." *The Press and Race: Mississippi Journalists Confront the Movement.* Ed. David R. Davies. Jackson: Mississippi UP, 2001. 3-15.

Dewan, Shaila. "41 Years On, Guilty in Mississippi." *International Herald Tribune* 23 June 2005: n.p.

Downs, Robert B., and Jane B. Downs. *Journalists of the United States.* Jefferson, N.C.: McFarland and Co., 1991.

Faulkner, William. *Intruder in the Dust.* New York: Random House, 1948.

———. *Light in August.* 1932. New York: Modern Library, 2002.

———. *Requiem for a Nun.* In *William Faulkner: Novels 1942-1954.* New York: The Library of America, 1994. 471-664.

Fowler, Doreen, and Ann J. Abadie. *Faulkner and Race.* Jackson: Mississippi UP, 1987.

The Good Housekeeping Woman's Almanac. Ed. Barbara McDowell and Hana Umlauf. New York: Newspaper Enterprise Association, 1977.

Goldfield, David. *Southern Histories: Public, Personal, and Sacred.* Athens: U of Georgia P, 2003.

———. *Still Fighting the Civil War: The American South and Southern History.* Baton Rouge: Louisiana UP, 2002.

Gray, Richard. *Writing the South: Ideas of an American Region.* New York: Cambridge UP, 1986.

Harkey Jr., Ira B. *The Smell of Burning Crosses: An Autobiography of a Mississippi Newspaperman.* Jacksonville, Ill.: Harris-Wolfe and Co., 1967.

———. *The Smell of Burning Crosses: A White Integrationist Editor in Mississippi.* 1967. Bloomington, Ind.: Xlibris, 2006.

Harkey Jr., Ira B., and John Wilds. *Alton Ochsner: Surgeon of the South.* Baton Rouge: Louisiana State UP, 1990.

Harris, T. George. "The 11-Year Siege of Mississippi's Lady Editor." *Look* 29 (16 Nov. 1965): 121-22, 127-28.

"Hazel Brannon Smith, 80, Editor Who Crusaded for Civil Rights." *New York Times* 16 May 1994: B8.

"Hazel Brannon Smith, 80, Editor Who Crusaded for Civil Rights." *The New York Times Biographical Service* 25.5 (May 1994): 747.

Huie, William Bradford. *Three Lives for Mississippi.* 1965. Jackson: Mississippi UP, 2000.

I'll Take My Stand. The South and the Agrarian Tradition by Twelve Southerners. Ed. Louis D. Rubin Jr. 1930. Baton Rouge: Louisiana State UP, 1977.

Isaacs, Barbara, and Kevin Nance. "Other Lexingtons Offer Attractions for Travelers." *Lexington* (Ky.) *Herald-Leader* online (http: www.kentuckyconnect.com/heraldleadernews). 5 Aug. 1999.

Johnson, Cassandra. "Journey to Justice: The Evolution of Mississippi's Largest Newspaper from Oppressor to Crusader for Racial Equality." American Journalism Historians Association. Wichita, Kansas. 11-14 Oct. 2006.

"Just Doing the Job." *Time.* 15 May 1964. http://www.time.com/time/magazine/article/0,9171,871056,00.html. 7/17/08.

Katagiri, Yasuhiro. *The Mississippi State Sovereignty Commission: Civil Rights and States' Rights.* Jackson: Mississippi UP, 2001.

Kaul, A.J. "Hazel Brannon Smith." *Dictionary of Literary Biography: American Newspaper Publishers (1950-1990).* Ed. Perry J. Ashley. 127. Detroit: Gale Research, 1993. 291-301.

———. "Hazel Brannon Smith and the *Lexington Advertiser.*" *The Press and Race: Mississippi Journalists Confront the Movement.* Jackson: Mississippi UP, 2001. 232-62.

Kirby, Jack Temple. *Media-Made Dixie: The South in the American Imagination.* Athens: U of Georgia P, 1986.

"The Last Word." *Time.* 21 Nov. 1955. http://www.time.com/time/magazine/ article/0,9171,866658,00.html. 7/17/08.

Lewis, Anthony. *Make No Law: The Sullivan Case and the First Amendment.* New York: Vintage, 1992.

———. *Make No Law: The Sullivan Case and the First Amendment.* New York: Random House, 1991.

Lyle, Jack, ed. *The Black American and the Press.* Los Angeles: The Ward Ritchie Press, 1968.

McGill, Ralph. *The South and the Southerner.* Boston: Little and Brown, 1963.

McMillen, Neil R. *The Citizens' Council: Organized Resistance to the Second Reconstruction, 1954-1964.* Champaign-Urbana: U of Illinois P, 1971.

———. *Dark Journey: Black Mississippians in the Age of Jim Crow.* Champaign-Urbana: U of Illinois P, 1989.

"'Mississippi Burning' Trial Begins." CNN.com. http://www.cnn.com/2005/LAW/ 06/13/Mississippi.killings/index/html.

"Mississippi: Determined Lady." *Columbia Journalism Review* 2 (Fall 1963): 38-39.

Moritz, Charles, ed. "Hazel Brannon Smith." *Current Biography Yearbook.* New York: The H.W. Wilson Co., 1973. 384-86.

Morris, Willie, and William Eggleston. *Faulkner's Mississippi.* Birmingham, Ala.: Oxmoor House, 1990.

Newman, Mark. "Hazel Brannon Smith: Pulitzer Prize Winning Journalist." *Mississippi History Now.* Mississippi Historical Society. (http:www.ms.history.k12.ms.us/hazel-brannon-smith-pulitzer-prize-winning-journalist).

———. "Hazel Brannon Smith and Holmes County, Mississippi, 1936-1964: The Making of a Pulitzer Prize Winner." *Journal of Mississippi History* 54.1 (February 1992): 59-87.

Newton, Eric, ed. *Crusaders, Scoundrels, Journalists: The Newseum's Most Intriguing Newspeople.* New York: Times Books, 1999.

O'Connor, Flannery. "The Displaced Person." *A Good Man Is Hard to Find and Other Stories.* 1948. New York: Harvest, 1955. 196-252.

———. "A Good Man Is Hard to Find." *A Good Man Is Hard to Find and Other Stories.* 1948. New York: Harvest, 1955. 1-22.

———. "The Life You Save May Be Your Own." *A Good Man Is Hard to Find and Other Stories*. 1948. New York: Harvest, 1955. 47-62.

"A Passion for Justice: The Hazel Brannon Smith Story." 1994.

Polk, Noel. "Faulkner and the Southern White Moderate." *Faulkner and Race*. Ed. Doreen Fowler and Ann J. Abadie. Jackson: UP of Mississippi, 1987. 130-51.

Ray, Garrett. "Hazel Brannon Smith." *Grassroots Editor*. Winter 1987. http://www.mssu.edu/iswne/bios/Smith.htm. 7/17/08.

Riley, Sam G. *Biographical Dictionary of American Newspaper Columnists*. Westport, Conn.: Greenwood Press, 1995.

Roberts, Gene, and Hank Klibanoff. *The Race Beat: The Press, the Civil Rights Struggle, and the Awakening of a Nation*. New York: Alfred A. Knopf, 2006.

Rubin, Louis D., Jr. "Introduction." *I'll Take My Stand: The South and the Agrarian Tradition by Twelve Southerners*. 1930. Baton Rouge: Louisiana State UP, 1977. xi-xxxv.

Silver, James W. *Mississippi: The Closed Society*. New York: Harcourt, Brace and World, 1964.

Smith, Hazel Brannon. "Bombed, Burned, and Boycotted." 1984. http://www.aliciapatterson.org/APF0702/Smith/Smith.html. 9 Nov. 2007. 1984.

———. "Case Study of an American Community Newspaper Under Pressure." Assignment for Alicia Patterson Fellowship. Washington, D.C. 1983.

———. "Looking At The Old South Through Hazel Eyes." 1984. http://www.aliciapatterson.org/APF0702/Smith/Smith.html. 9 Nov. 2007.

Stein, Bernard L. "This Female Crusading Scalawag: Hazel Brannon Smith, Justice and Mississippi." http://www.freedomforum.org/publications/msj/courage.summer2000/y09.html. 9 Nov. 2007.

Taft, William H. *Encyclopedia of 20th Century Journalists*. New York: Garland, 1986.

Waldron, Ann. *Hodding Carter: The Reconstruction of a Racist*. Chapel Hill, N.C.: Algonquin Books of Chapel Hill, 1993.

Walker, Alice. "Advancing Luna—and Ida B. Wells." *Short Stories of the Civil Rights Movement: An Anthology*. Ed. Margaret Earley Whitt. Athens: U of Georgia P, 2006. 232-48.

———. "To My Young Husband." *Short Stories of the Civil Rights Movement: An Anthology*. Ed. Margaret Earley Whitt. Athens: U of Georgia P, 2006. 301-37.

Wallace, David James. "The Freedom of the Press in a Closed Society: Civil Rights Movement Journalism and Segregationist Pressure." Thesis. Colorado,

2006.

Weill, Susan. "Conserving Racial Segregation in 1954: *Brown v. Board of Education* and the Mississippi Daily Press." *American Journalism* 16.4 (Fall 1999): 77-99.

———. "Hazel and the 'Hacksaw': Freedom Summer Coverage by the Women of the Mississippi Press." *Journalism Studies* 2.4 (2000): 545-61.

———. *In a Madhouse's Din: Civil Rights Coverage by Mississippi's Daily Press, 1948-1968.* Westport, Conn.: Praeger, 2002.

———. "Mississippi's Daily Press in Three Crises." *The Press and Race: Mississippi Journalists Confront the Movement.* Ed. David R. Davies. Jackson: Mississippi UP, 2001. 17-53.

Welty, Eudora. "Where Is the Voice Coming From?" *Short Stories of the Civil Rights Movement: An Anthology.* Ed. Margaret Earley Whitt. Athens: U of Georgia P, 2006. 213-19.

Whalen, John A. *Maverick Among the Magnolias: The Hazel Brannon Smith Story.* Bloomington, Ind.: Xlibris, 2000.

Whitt, Jan. *Allegory and the Modern Southern Novel.* Macon, Ga.: Mercer UP, 1994.

———. "Burning Crosses and Activist Journalism: The Unlikely Heroism of Two Mississippi Editors." 9 (Summer/Fall 1998): 87-108.

Williams, Roger. "Newspapers in the South." *Columbia Journalism Review* 6 (Summer 1967): 26-35.

Woodward, C. Vann. *The Burden of Southern History.* 1960. Baton Rouge: Louisiana State UP, 1982.

Index

T

"A Time to Kill," 6-7, 11, 14-15
"Through Hazel Eyes," 31-33, 36, 38,
    113, 138
Tri-Anniversary Committee, 88-89, 95,
    105-107, 115

W

Walker, Alice, 7, 14, 138
Warren, Robert Penn, 101-102, 116-17,
    134
Welty, Eudora, ix, 12, 14, 102, 116,
    118, 129-30, 134, 139
White Citizens' Council, 1, 4-5, 11, 13,
    26, 28-29, 37, 42-46, 54, 56, 71-
    85, 88, 95-97, 99, 103, 127, 132
Williams, Tennessee, 102, 134-35
Wolfe, Thomas, 116-17, 121

About the Author

Jan Whitt is a professor in the School of Journalism and Mass Communication at the University of Colorado at Boulder.

Having begun her career as a newspaper reporter and editor in Texas, Whitt is the author of *Allegory and the Modern Southern Novel* (Macon, Ga.: Mercer UP, 1994), *Women in American Journalism: A New History* (Champaign-Urbana, Ill.: Illinois UP, 2008), and *Settling the Borderland: Other Voices in Literary Journalism* (Lanham, Md.: UP of America, 2008).

She edited the collection *Reflections in a Critical Eye: Essays on Carson McCullers* (Lanham, Md.: UP of America, 2007), which won a 2008 Eric Hoffer Book Award (culture category) and a 2007 *ForeWord Magazine* Book Award (women's issues category) and was a finalist in the anthology/collections category of the 2008 Colorado Book Awards.

The proposal for *Women in American Journalism* won the Mary Ann Yodelis Smith award for feminist scholarship (2005) from the Commission on the Status of Women, a group of scholars in the Association for Education in Journalism and Mass Communication. The book was one of six finalists for the 2009 Kappa Tau Alpha (Frank Luther Mott) Research Award and one of seven finalists for the 2008 *ForeWord Magazine* Book Awards (women's issues category).

Current projects include books about the television series "The West Wing" and about Terry Tempest Williams, author of *Refuge: An Unnatural*

History of Family and Place, Unspoken Hunger: Stories from the Field, and other works of nonfiction about the American West.

The author of more than 70 articles and book chapters, Whitt publishes in literary, media, and popular culture journals. Her articles appear in *American Journalism, Clues, Journal of the American Studies Association of Texas, Journal of Homosexuality, Journal of Lesbian Studies, Journal of Popular Film and Television, Journal of the West, Journalism Educator,* the *Maine Times, Popular Culture Review, Society of Environmental Journalists Journal, Southern Literary Journal, Southern Studies, Southwestern American Literature,* the *Southwestern Mass Communication Journal, Studies in Popular Culture,* and other publications.

She has published chapters in books that deal with a wide variety of topics, including the history of women's press clubs, women in local television, lesbian publications, Southern literature, detective fiction and film, women and newspapers, American literature, and American television.

Having received teaching and advising awards at Baylor University, the University of Denver, and the University of Colorado at Boulder, Whitt teaches undergraduate and graduate courses in American and British literature, literary journalism, media studies, popular culture, professional writing, and women's studies. Her research focuses on contemporary media, diversity issues in literature and media, literary journalism, and media history.

Whitt completed her B.A. in English and journalism (1977) and her M.A. in English (1980) at Baylor University and earned a Ph.D. in literature at the University of Denver (1985).

A volunteer with Golden Retriever Rescue of the Rockies, Whitt enjoys skiing; running; hiking with her retrievers, Mackenzie and Riley; traveling; and reading.